ARMAND LAUFFER
School of Social Works
University of Michigan

Social Planning at the Community Level

PRENTICE-HALL, INC.,
Englewood Cliffs, New Jersey 07632

Library of Congress Cataloging in Publication Data

LAUFFER, ARMAND.
   Social planning at the community level.

   (Prentice-Hall series in social work practice)
   Includes bibliographies and index.
   1. United States—Social policy. 2. Public
welfare—United States. 3. Community organization.
4. Social policy. I. Title.
HV95.L38   361'.973   77-26972
ISBN 0-13-817189-0

Prentice-Hall Series in Social Work Practice
Neil Gilbert and Harry Specht, Editors

Printed in the United States of America

10 9 8 7 6 5 4 3 2 1

PRENTICE-HALL INTERNATIONAL, INC., *London*
PRENTICE-HALL OF AUSTRALIA PTY. LIMITED, *Sydney*
PRENTICE-HALL OF CANADA, LTD., *Toronto*
PRENTICE-HALL OF INDIA PRIVATE LIMITED, *New Delhi*
PRENTICE-HALL OF JAPAN, INC., *Tokyo*
PRENTICE-HALL OF SOUTHEAST ASIA PTE. LTD., *Singapore*
WHITEHALL BOOKS LIMITED, *Wellington, New Zealand*

to my parents,
Gisele and Georges

Contents

6 *Overcoming Resistance to Change* 105

7 *Assessment and Evaluation* 117

8 *Assessment Tools* 133

9 *Getting Things Done Systematically* 163

Preface and
Acknowledgments

Social planners are a special breed of professionals in the human services. As problem solvers, they deal with those institutional imbalances that combine to distribute resources and opportunities inequitably. Advocating on behalf of those with special needs, they employ new methods to influence the direction of social change. At the local level, they work to modify and expand existing human services, to design new ones and to establish coordinating mechanisms to assure equitable distribution of those services.

About This Book

Throughout this book I have drawn heavily from the work of social planners in many communities and in many fields of practice. In search of practice principles, I have attempted to integrate their experiences with new knowledge generated by the social sciences.

Some readers will prefer to go through the book chapter by chapter. Others will go directly to those chapters of particular interest to them. A detailed table of contents outlines the major topics covered. Each of the book's five sections open with an introduction. Although each chapter may be read independently, the concepts referred to in one may be dealt with more fully in another. Most chapters are followed by annotated recommended readings and suggestions for further reading. Where appropriate, I have included exercises and other activities that may be of use to both the experienced planner and to the student.

Social Planning at the Community Level grew out of an earlier volume entitled, *Area Planning for the Aging,* one of several publications prepared by the staff of Project TAP (Training Area Planners), a leadership training program conducted by the Institute of Gerontology and the Continuing Education Program in the Human Services of the School of Social Work at the University of Michigan. Project TAP was supported by a grant from the Administration on Aging of the Department of Health, Education and Welfare in Washington. For this reason, many of the illustrations throughout the text are drawn from the experiences of planners in the field of aging. Others are drawn from the work of planners in the fields of child welfare and public assistance, health and public health, mental health, developmental disabilities, corrections, drug abuse, and education.

Many of the concepts discussed in Chapters 2 and 3 were developed by staff of the Community Organization Curriculum Development Project at Brandeis University. I am indebted to my former colleagues on that project: Arnold Gurin, Robert Pearlman, Wyatt Jones and Joan Levin Ecklein. Our collaboration led to two earlier works. Some of the illustrations of practice found in the present text were drawn from the interviews with local planners conducted by the Brandeis staff.

Acknowledgements

Few books are written by a single author. In addition to the Community Organization project staff, I am indebted to many people—to none perhaps as much as William Lawrence. As co-director of Project TAP, Bill gave me constant encouragement and support and helped me think through the major ideas and select the content that is included in this volume. I am also greatly indebted to Wayne Vasey, former co-director of the Institute of Gerontology, whose invaluable suggestions are incorporated throughout. Ellen Saalberg read the volume with the experienced eye of a seasoned editor who cares as much about the reader as about the manuscript itself. Edwina Andrews consulted on the references included in the text. Lynn Nybell was instrumental in the design of several of the exercises found in Parts I and II. The manuscript also includes the inputs of a number of secretaries—among them Vivian Green, Jim Irwin, Marcia Cameron, Janet Hanford, Charlotte Whitney, Carol Wyman and Selma Sussman —whose contributions went beyond typing to the provision of critical comments and helpful suggestions.

I owe a great deal to three former teachers and two colleagues. Robert Binstock provided me with a historical overview of planning for the aging. Roland Warren, Robert Morris, Harold Johnson and Eugene Litwak read the original draft of this manuscript. Roland Warren contributed to many of my insights on advocacy planning, social choice and citizen participation. Bob Morris added to my understanding of the way in which planners attempt to influence key decision-makers at the organizational and interorganizational cooperation and with linkages between service agencies and their client populations. Harold Johnson, currently Director of the Institute of Gerontology, suggested ways to reorganize the book, cautioned me about technical jargon, and set me straight on some of the political facts of life as seen by an experienced community planner.

More than any others, of course, I am indebted to the planners and administrators who speak throughout these pages. Many were interviewed specifically for this volume and are currently employed in Area Agencies on Aging or in other planning settings at the local level. Not all the people interviewed were planners by training or occupational identity; but all have performed planning tasks and have contributed significantly to the development and coordination of human services. Among them was Byron Gold, formerly Special Assistant to the Commissioner on Aging, whose efforts on behalf of this manuscript went beyond the call of duty.

I have been selective in my choice of quotes, attempting to include only those most relevant to the issues discussed, and interweaving them with other material. At times I chose to modify some of the comments or to disguise them so as to maintain anonymity and to improve readibility. In each instance, however, I have tried to remain true to the person speaking and to the circumstances within which his or her actions were taken.

The selection of materials, of course, reflects my own bias and my conviction that planning and coordinating are complex processes. Planners are often faced with agonizing choices. Their selection of goals and means are frequently made against the socio-political contexts of competing demands on one hand, and citizen apathy on the other. Work toward long-range objectives is too often interrupted by the need for immediate victories. "It seems," a planner remarked to me, "as if each victory makes the task even more formidable." Perhaps, but as professional planners know well, there is no backing off.

ARMAND LAUFFER

The day is short and the work is great. It is not your duty to complete the work but neither are you free to desist from it.

Perke Avot
(The sayings of the fathers)

Introduction to Social Planning

In all industrialized societies a complex of social welfare services and institutions has come into being to replace earlier sources of supply. Rapid social and technological changes have changed people's perceptions of their needs. As the family and the economy have proven inadequate to meet those needs, new institutions and services have developed piecemeal in response to political pressures. The result is what many observers have called a "patchwork quilt" rather than a system of services; a quilt with too many holes, that leaves too much uncovered.

The development of welfare services then, is a societal response to the consequence of unplanned change. But it is often an unplanned, ad hoc response. *Social planning is an attempted corrective to this unplanned aggregate of services and institutions* that are frequently insufficient, inefficient, ineffective, or unresponsive. Planning is a method of intervention—a rather systematic method of matching means to goals, of calculating actions to achieve objectives.

Planning may be attempted at both the societal and the local levels. In *societal level planning,* the goals of the state must be defined and ranked, the costs and benefits of partial and full accomplishment assessed, feasible strategies established, and programs instituted. *At the local or community level,* planning serves as a substitute for or supplement to societal planning. Unfortunately, it frequently fails when it attempts solutions to problems that are actually national or societal in scope. It has its best chance of success when

1

it focuses on the local consequences and manifestations of these problems and when it is programmatic rather than structural in its orientation.

Unfortunately, as critics of social planning at the community level often point out, programmatic changes are often little more effective than band-aid therapies. The criticism is valid, but it is not quite fair. Social planning in the United States has been largely locality or community based for historical reasons that are described in this volume. It articulates well with an underlying federalist political philosophy, one that seeks a balance of initiatives from the federal, the state, and from local governments as well as from private sources.

Nevertheless, the gains made at the local level are frequently only incremental in nature. Sometimes, in fact, gains in one sector are such that they create imbalances in other sectors, which in turn necessitate new and different responses. The result is a state of constant flux, a process of dynamic change. Nonetheless, because changes at the local level tend to generate rather small gains, some observers accuse the social planner of being timid. This I do not believe is the case.

I have seen and interviewed too many social planners who are willing to take major risks and who in fact are successful in generating changes that have significant impact on the populations they seek to serve. But their ability to influence the larger social system within which they operate is limited. Social planners at the community level are not free agents. They are almost all employed by human service organizations, many of them in the public sector. Their mandates, the things they are permitted to do and the ways in which they are permitted to do them, are limited by the organizations within which they are employed. And the organizations themselves must operate within given social and political environments.

Social planners at the community level tend to be oriented toward dealing with problems in the here and now. Some critics argue that they should be more concerned with the future. Planning, they point out, should be a way for us systematically to move from where we are to where we want to be. In fact, there exists a school of planners who consider themselves futurists. Their writing is provocative, insightful, and bold. In some instances they have had opportunities to engage in some major social experiments. In time, particularly as their instruments become refined, they can be expected to have increasing influence over the direction of social policies, particularly at the societal level.

It's my impression, however, that the analyses employed by the futurists are not yet applicable to planning at the community level. For this reason I have not included any discussion of futurism or future planning in this book. Nor, for that matter, have I discussed national, societal level planning except where it may impinge on planning at the local level. In making this decision, I realize that I have not been fully comprehensive in my treatment of social planning in the United States. Nevertheless I do think that many of the chapters in this book can be of use to the social planner or the student of planning whether at the state and national levels or at the community level. It is important, after all, for all of them to understand the activities and the constraints on those activities faced by community-based social planners.

The pages that follow I have had to restrain myself from allowing too many of my biases to intrude in the pages that follow. I have often been tempted to tell the reader what I think he or she should do when confronted by one or another of the many predicaments that planners face every day. In some instances I have succumbed to that temptation.

Frequently, however, I have chosen to allow social planners to speak directly to the reader. In preparation of this volume and of two other works, I have had occasion to interview several hundred planners, social agency administrators, and community organizers throughout the country. Their wisdom and their experiences are reflected throughout the book.

Social Planning, Social Problems, and Social Services at the Community Level

Chapter 1 gets the reader "down to cases." The early stages of three local planning projects are described in some detail by the planners involved. These planners do not always agree, nor do they complement each other in style or perspective. This is as it should be. Planners have differences of opinion. Social problems are specific to each local situation. For this reason, many services are best developed and coordinated at the local level. Services should address the needs of local people, be responsive to their interests and desires. No single approach is appropriate to all planners or to all communities. Many of the issues opened up by the planners quoted in this chapter are dealt with in greater detail elsewhere in the book.

The term "planner," incidentally, is used generically. It is intended to designate someone performing a social planning task, working in a planning agency, or performing a planning function—not merely someone whose occupational or organizational title is "planner."

A number of planning tools are briefly introduced in Chapter 2. These include social indicators; benefit/cost analysis; consumer and client analysis; PERT; program planning and budgeting systems; evaluative research; input-output analysis; Delphi conferences; simulation and gaming techniques; and others. Chapter 2 also includes a discussion of how ideology, knowledge, experience, and organizational base affect the planner's perspective and orientation.

The kinds of problems that social planners tend to deal with, and the service deficiencies they address, are discussed in Chapter 3. This chapter includes an inventory of potential services and service providers at the local level. It also presents an historical overview of the development of institutional services in this country, and the parallel development of social planning efforts as correctives to a system in which resources and opportunities are not equally distributed. Together these three chapters serve as a foundation for the remainder of the book.

Before proceeding, look over the inventory of "Opinions on Planning Issues" that follows. Without taking too much time, check whether you agree or disagree with each of the statements made. These were drawn from our interviews and reflect the opinions of several planners. Keep them in mind as you read Chapter 1. You may find yourself changing your mind on some issues after completing the chapter, and reinforcing your opinions on others. Incidentally, many instructors have found this a useful exercise to begin discussion at the start of a course. Social planners have also found it a useful exercise for a staff meeting. It can be used to clarify one's position and to find out where concensus exists and where it is absent.

OPINIONS ON PLANNING ISSUES

Yes	No	Position
		1. It is more important to have the right people making any decisions than to have any people making the right decisions.
		2. You cannot do any real planning without facts. Know what the problem is first. Get the facts. Facts lead you to problems and tell you what you can do about them.
		3. Successful citizens' task forces require prestigious people. You need people with clout, whether it comes from political influence, social standing, money, expertise, or some other distinguishing feature.
		4. In formulating a plan, it is critical that as many opinions and viewpoints as possible are taken into account. Opposing positions should be reconciled, if possible.
		5. Planning is self-defeating if it is elite in its orientation. Greater participation in decision making is more important than accomplishing any specific goal.
		6. Planners should concentrate their efforts on behalf of the most needy populations—the poor; disenfranchised minorities; and other deprived local groups.
		7. Service agencies should employ their own planners rather than depend on the efforts of a central planning staff.
		8. There are enough resources available in America to take care of all our social needs. What planners must do is locate these resources and orchestrate them effectively.
		9. In an era of accountability, planners should be more concerned with the evaluation of program efforts, effectiveness, and efficiency than with the development of new and untried programs.
		10. The best way to determine where to intervene and what to do, is first to inventory your own (or your agency's) capabilities and the resources at your disposal, then to focus on what you can do with what you have.

Getting Down to Cases

Introduction

UNDERLYING ASSUMPTIONS

Planning is a professional activity. It proceeds from the recognition and definition of a problem through the implementation of a plan or a course of action to deal with that problem. The problem may be defined in terms of a current day's fraction in a social system or as a gap between the present and a desired future state of affairs. It often involves building new working structures, formulating policies and strategies, and establishing monitoring, feedback, and evaluation procedures.

All planning efforts are based on several assumptions.* One fundamental assumption is that the aggregate of unguided individual and collective activities does not adequately distribute either resources or opportunities. Planners also assume that preferable conditions are possible and that these conditions may be brought about through thoughtful guidance and professional intervention.

Social planning efforts flow from the further assumption that human services and human opportunities are not adequately distributed or sufficiently

*I am indebted for this formulation to a former teacher and colleague, Roland Warren.

available, and that certain populations may be partially or totally deprived of access to them. At the *community level* in the United States, social planning has largely been an attempt to influence the ways in which services are developed and delivered, and to introduce order into what many observers feel is an uncoordinated or under-coordinated service system. At this level, social planning serves primarily as a corrective device for a complex social service system that is frequently piecemeal and uncoordinated. Students considering a career in planning as well as seasoned practitioners at the community level can learn much from the experiences of their colleagues. The illustrative cases we present throughout this book draw heavily on these experiences.

In the first of three cases presented in this chapter, a planner describes how he initiated a planning process extemporaneously—as he was being interviewed for a position on the Mayor's Human Resources Commission. He claims to be more concerned with *who* makes the decisions than with *what* decisions may be made in the planning process. This approach is challenged by the planner in the second illustration. Charged with the development of a health services plan in a five-county rural area, he tends to place heavier emphasis on the technical aspects of planning and a proper selection of intervention targets. A third case illustration describes the first few weeks of a new Community Mental Health board. Staff deliberations and staff assignments are described by the administrator of the agency.

The experienced practitioner may find the issues discussed and the perspectives expressed in these vignettes familiar. Other planners may find them provocative. The stuff of practice, after all, is based on getting down to cases.

Illustration I: A Planner Organizes a Constituency

PLANNING STARTS WITH THE JOB INTERVIEW

"I'm not neutral when it comes to representing my constituents. I'm as partisan as they come," the newly appointed Planning Director for a metropolitan area-wide council on aging explained. "When I was being interviewed for this position I made it clear that involvement of the aging would be the cornerstone of my approach. I insisted that any task force or policy board with whom I worked would have to be made up entirely of older people, rather than the usual fifty percent quota. My reasoning went something like this:

1. As the only staff member of the Mayor's Human Resources Commission concerned exclusively with planning for the aging, I was going to need additional help. Many older people have skills and knowledge that are in short supply. More important, they've got time and energy. If properly supervised, they can make a significant contribution.

2. I would need some organized representation of the aging to counter-balance other groups putting pressure on the HRC. I leveled with the Mayor, explaining that in the scramble for scarce resources, I was going to need the backing of a strong constituent base in order to compete effectively with other departments within the HRC. In my arguments, I subtly hinted that the Mayor himself might find the support of the elderly useful.

3. Putting older people on the Council of Aging's task forces and policy board might be the first step in increasing their representation on policy committees of service agencies. Under-representation of older people, I pointed out, amounted to a policy of fewer rather than more services to the elderly.

"The Mayor bought my arguments. In effect, I had established a set of policy guidelines before even being hired for the position. Once on the job, it made my first moves that much easier. I know that many planners begin by doing community surveys of one type or another, identifying problems and populations in need. They assume that once you have the facts you can make the right decisions. I make no such assumptions. I assume that the right decisions are going to be made by the right decision makers. As far as I am concerned, planning is a political process. The Mayor saw it the same way. That's why I got the position.

PHASE 1: GETTING KNOWN AND GETTING PEOPLE INVOLVED

"My first set of activities after starting the job was to make it known that I was there—and that older people were there, too. It may seem corny, but I began with developing an old-fashioned directory of community services for the aging. To help me compile the directory, I approached three organized groups of older people: the Downtown Retired Businessmen's Association; the AARP,* which was made up mostly of retired teachers; and the West Side Golden Age Center. I had several things in mind. I wanted these people, who are relatively articulate and well-educated, to learn how agencies operated; to get a feel for what the whole system of services was like.

"I also wanted agency people to get to know them, to become aware that many not highly visible older people needed their services and that some older people might be helpful in expanding their agency's services. To get my volunteers started on their data gathering, I involved the HRC's Director of Information and Referral and a member of its research staff.

"To tell the truth, I really didn't need their technical expertise, but I wanted them involved so that they too would begin to focus on the needs of

*American Association of Retired Persons.

the elderly. Together, we identified the various agencies and organizations that my volunteers would visit and designed a schedule of questions. The three of us then jointly trained the volunteers. We trained them to write

1. a brief description of the service or services that each organization provided to the general population (if any) and those services explicitly for the aging (if any)
2. the eligibility critera (if any) in terms of need, residence, income, ethnic background, and so on; the procedures for applying for service plus appeals procedures (if any)
3. Special provisions (if any) for emergency situations
4. A list, by name, of other service providers with whom the agency regularly cooperated
5. A list, by name, of other agencies in the community that provided similar services

"You wouldn't believe how many agency people were unable or unwilling to answer many of these questions. Nevertheless, we compiled their responses as they came in. As you can imagine, we identified an enormous number of gaps, overlaps, service deficiencies, and the like. Before printing up our directory, we gave each agency a chance to review what had been written, to add or delete, and to include comments about new services or procedures in the planning stages. This last idea was a 'coup' suggested by one of my volunteers. 'You've got to give people a chance to save face,' he told me. 'If you point out somebody's shortcomings, you might as well give them a chance to explain how they are planning to correct them.' Not everyone included such plans, but even that was instructive.

A TV SHOW FOR THE RETIRED

"While the survey was in progress, I arranged with the local cable TV station to do a weekly show on the city's retired people and the social services available to them. One of our retired school principals became the moderator. He was well-liked in the community, and had all the wit and charm you can imagine. I played a behind-the-scenes role, working with an advisory committee of other older people on the selection of program content, how it would be presented, and so on. There were three parts to the show. Each week we interviewed an agency administrator. At first we picked only the best agencies: the ones that had good, well delivered services for older people. We wanted to highlight these services. Then we began to pick service agencies which had a variety of deficiencies. Instead of just probing at the deficiencies, we invited a panel of older people to make suggestions on how services might be improved. The idea was to get people talking, thinking, and acting.

"By the third week, we were getting a tremendous amount of fan mail, mostly from older people who had additional questions they wanted answered, and from others who had strong opinions about what was being said on the show. Some letters came from younger people who wanted to know how to handle problems with parents or older relatives. Some even came from professionals and from agency people. That's when we decided to add a third part to the program. We began taking a limited number of telephone calls at the studio and asking our agency guest and our panelists to respond to them.

GERI-ACTION REPORTER

"We still couldn't handle all the phone calls and letters we were getting. It was obvious that we needed something in the nature of an action line or an ombudsman. After only two or three months, the show was so well established that it didn't take very much to get a small grant from a local family foundation to hire a *Geri-Action* reporter. Together with a group of volunteers recruited from various organizations, this person began following up on the kinds of problems people were having, and reporting them on the show. I guess you could say they'd come to take on a social brokerage function, much like the brokerage performed in the earlier days of Mobilization For Youth in New York. With one exception. When somebody from *Geri-Action* approaches an agency, he gets action. Not too many agencies are willing to risk bad publicity on our show. We had an ombudsman who reported successes and failures on the air!

"All this wasn't accomplished without opposition. A lot of people would have been happy to see us off the air. We got our share of pressure. But we also had an increasingly large number of supporters, including the Mayor, who knows votes when he sees them.

"Since many of the problems the *Geri-Action* reporter was dealing with were similar, we published a supplement to our community directory called *Know Your Rights.* It told the reader how to find out what services an agency performs, how to get past an unfriendly or evasive intake worker, the responsibility certain agencies like nursing homes have to provide rehabilitation and other services, and other tips. We took as our model the kind of consumer-oriented guides published by the insurance commissioner in the State of Pennsylvania.

PHASE 2: TASK FORCES

"After six months we were ready to enter into our second phase of action: setting up a number of task forces to deal with specific problems of the elderly. So many people were waking up to the problems of the elderly in our community that the idea of a task force would have evolved without any pushing or preparation on my part. But I laid the groundwork for these task forces carefully. By this time, I knew pretty well what was foremost in the minds of the aging and the elderly, at least those who had been involved in developing the two manuals. From their point of view, the major issues were: (1) transportation; (2) community-based alternatives to institutionalization; (3) recreation and leisure time activities; and (4) a more responsive health care system.

"My groundwork covered the established agencies as well. I didn't want to risk any backlash and wanted to uncover hidden pockets of resistance. I spent a lot of time meeting with agency heads, both within government and in the voluntary sector. I pointed out that these task forces were an inevitable consequence of community interest in aging, and of the increasing militance of the aging themselves. I told them it would be good to consider participating on one of the task forces. I tried to feel each person out on his potential to contribute meaningfully, to inhibit or throw a monkeywrench in the works, or to grow and change through participation on a task force. I made sure that they were aware of the fact that new funds would soon be available (perhaps to their agencies) from state and federal sources for services to the aging.

"Based on my interviews with agency people and my acquaintance with many of the older people in the community, I drew up a list of suggested members for each task force and submitted it to the Mayor. I had one or two paragraphs of comments on each person. I tried to balance the task forces in a way so we could nullify or co-opt the opposition. I tried to make sure that people who had different racial, ethnic, neighborhood, or professional backgrounds were involved. But I made sure there were enough prestige people as well. You can either confer prestige on a committee by putting prestigious people on it, or you can confer prestige on participants by putting them on a committee. I tried to do a little of both in selecting people for the task forces. We wanted 12 people for each task force. I gave the Mayor a list of 16 recommendations so he could make the choices based on what his own political and social antennae suggested.

"In addition to four task forces, the Mayor appointed a new Commission on Aging to which the task forces were to report. The Commission developed out of the old council, which had been a voluntary association of interested people with no clout, but as an official agency with the Mayor's backing, it has some political muscle of its own. As I had suggested in my employment interview, it is made up entirely of senior citizens. Based on each task force recommendation, the Commission is to draw up a set of priorities for the next one, two, and three years. These priorities will become the bases for an area-wide plan. Two of the task forces are already under way. A third and fourth are to begin next week. In two days, I have my first meeting with the Commission."

At the end of the planner's first year on the job, the impact of his approach was clearly visible. The *Geri-Action* reporter was popular and well-established. Despite its reporting activities, *Geri-Action* volunteers actually did most of their work behind the scenes. This included giving case-by-case assistance and "brokering" relationships between agencies and their clients when necessary; helping agency personnel develop a new understanding of the client's point of view; case finding and referral; and gathering data on previously unidentified populations or unrecognized problems. The volunteers for *Geri-Action* recruited more participants from among their friends, and from among the organizations to which they belonged. Soon thereafter, a training program for volunteers was set up. Many of the original volunteers who had compiled data for inclusion in the two guides were now assigned to voluntary tasks within those agencies. Others had become the core staff of newly formed volunteer programs that permitted the expansion of meals on wheels, visiting homemaker, and friendly visitor services.

The city-wide task forces had themselves spawned other task forces. "Mini-task forces" dealing with similar issues were developed in three urban neighborhoods and four suburban communities. More were in the developmental stages. Each of these mini-task forces fed additional information to its metropolitan parent group. Each involved local senior citizens, agency representatives, and other interested residents. Two of the area's larger agencies—the Community Mental Health Center and the Model Cities agency—established their own task forces on the needs of senior citizens.

The end of that first year saw the planner engaged in consolidating many of these activities into a single structure: a metropolitan Information and Referral Service for the elderly, with satellite centers. The Service would be responsible for

1. continuing to gather data on community services for older adults
2. publishing the data periodically in updated guides
3. providing telephone information about resources and making informal referrals to the service agencies as well as to organized self-help groups
4. providing case advocacy and social brokerage where necessary during the follow-up stage in order to determine whether the service had been obtained or the clients still wanted it
5. providing outreach and case-finding services
6. engaging in advocacy for the development of new service programs through public reporting in the *Geri-Action* reporter
7. coordinating all efforts in community education, especially in local churches, schools, and community centers

8. preparing statistical reports on services provided and coordinating exchange processes between agencies.

There was some question about whether the Information and Referral Service should be integrated into the HRC's Information and Referral Service or whether it should remain separate and quasi-independent. The planner wanted an independent structure. He was certain that the Mayor would approve, but equally certain that others on the Human Resources Commission would not. He weighed their arguments and his need to have effective working relationships with them, with his conviction that specially designated services for the aging would reach a larger segment of his target population. This approach differs from that employed by the planners in Illustration II.

Illustration II: A Planner Applies Rationality

PERFECTIBILITY, NOT PERFECTION

"When I left the state agency to take over this five-county area planning operation, I was convinced of two things," said the director of a newly formed Health Planning Agency. "First, all health services have to be part of a network, a systemic structure which, although not perfect, is perfectible. Second, by proper management, any structure can be made more rationally effective and efficient; that is, we can make it more responsive to changes in the environment and to new and emerging needs.

"I don't agree with what you might call the agricultural-extension/community development model, which assumes that by bringing the right people of good will together, you can build an appropriate array of services. I know it serves as a model for some mental health and Title XX social services planning, but it doesn't fit the medical professions or the health field very well. As far as I am concerned, neither good will nor face-to-face meetings are enough when resources are scarce and expertise is almost nonexistent. Needed resources include money and credit, the proper facilities, manpower, and a fair amount of social standing and political influence behind your project or program. These don't just come to you by accident. You have to build, develop, and recruit these resources.

"Expertise is another thing. In part, it comes from experience. But it also comes from garnering the right technology and applying it when appropriate. That means knowing what to do and when to do it, and having some systematic approach for getting where you want to go. You can't turn professional decisions entirely over to a lay public, especially when you deal with such technical services as those provided by physicians and other professionals in the health field.

"You can't call what you do planning unless you are being rational about what you do. This requires *formulating the overall objectives* of the service systems a planner wants to develop or perfect. The planner must know who is to receive the services, what they are composed of, how they are to articulate with each other, and how extensive they are to be—that is, the planner must be able to specify the objectives in quantifiable terms. Increasing health or the quality of life is a nonobjective, pious hope. Increasing the numbers of children who receive early and periodic health screening and diagnosis, or adding a special bus service for the handicapped to get them where they can purchase food, get a hot meal, or get medical treatment, are quantifiable objectives.

"The second step is to list all the alternative means for accomplishing each of the objectives selected. Obviously there must be more than one way for people to be fed a balanced diet or be transported into town. There is no sense in getting all wrapped up in a single way of doing things. Rational choice requires alternatives.

"The next step is to select those objectives which seem to be most reachable; by that, I mean feasible. You use those means which optimize goal accomplishment. Optimizing means compromising. Remember, I said that the system is perfectible, but it will never be perfect. Optimizing requires a compromise between your objectives, the resources you have available or can get your hands on, and the technical capability of the people who will be providing the services. You might have the money for a new hospital wing and have as your goal outpatient treatment and preventative medicine for all the elderly in your region. But it does you no good unless you have personnel with the technical capability of providing the specified services. Being rational is being realistic.

"Finally you get to designing a functional organization or structure that would best facilitate the accomplishment of your objectives by the means selected. Here is where experience and knowledge of other people's successes and failures come in.

"Too many planners start by building a structure—task forces, committees, councils, action groups, and so on. The trouble with these groups is that they take on lives of their own. There is no sense in forming an action group unless it actually takes purposeful action. Too many planners view participation as an end in itself. I have no quarrel with participatory democracy, but it should be viewed as a means toward achieving a planning objective, not as the end. When you let yourself fall in the structure-participation trap, you lose all chance of controlling the planning process toward the accomplishment of your planning objectives. Planners should be task-oriented, not process-oriented.

"That doesn't mean you don't involve people. Obviously, the planner can't do it all alone. The planner's job is to see that the goal is met. The planner can help both the health service providers and the potential clients, because he has access to knowledge—plus experience and expertise. Health providers, for example, need to know that there are people out there who need services, what those people are like, how they feel about specific services, and what their principal needs and interests are. Consumers must become aware of what kinds of services health agencies provide, how these benefits can help them, and how to obtain them. Planning requires some careful analysis of what is *possible* as well as what is desirable. This means that the planner must be thoroughly familiar with actual or potential consumers of services—and actual or potential providers as well.

"There are too many obstacles between potential consumers and potential providers of service—barriers such as lack of money or other resources, insufficient knowledge and information, inappropriate technology, biases and prejudices. I mean the biases inherent in the medical professions as well as the bias and ignorance or just plain misinformation of the consumer. One of the first things a planner has to do is to assess the nature and extent of these obstacles. This will help him select those objectives which seem most reasonable and most reachable. Some obstacles may be just too deeply embedded. Sometime it's easier to go around a mountain than through it or over it."

CONTRASTS IN STYLE AND PERSPECTIVE

The two planners quoted in Illustrations I and II differ in both style and perspective. Their differences influence the actions they take and the objectives they seek.

The first planner's strategy is clear from the outset. He makes his perspective known as he is being interviewed for the position. His subsequent planning style is consistent throughout. He views himself as a partisan on behalf of the aging, playing out this role with them and through them. He recognizes early that he will require their help in providing needed manpower and in counterbalancing the pressures of other organized groups in the community.

Unlike the planner in the second illustration, he emphasizes the need to involve the elderly and to build a formal structure of relationships at the outset of the planning process. As he puts it, "The right decisions depend on the right decisionmakers."

This contrasts sharply with the techniques of the second planner, who is less concerned with who is involved than what is accomplished. In fact, the health planner speaks with some disdain about the "agricultural-extension/

community development" model in which people of good will are brought together in anticipation that they will make the right decisions about the right issues. Implicit in the second planner's perspective is a view of planning as a rational-technical activity in which relevant others are involved only when their involvement will lead to goal accomplishment. The reader might question: "Whose goals?"

The planner's emphasis on rationality in planning is reflected in four steps:

1. formulation of overall objectives
2. listing of alternative means for accomplishing those objectives
3. selection of the optimal objectives, and finally
4. design of a structure to accomplish those objectives.

This is not to suggest that the first planner is irrational or unsystematic. He too was clear about what he wanted and how he went about getting it. The second planner, however, viewed the planner's role in decisionmaking and in policy determination as much more central, based heavily on technical knowledge and expertise. Many planners show increasing evidence of technical expertise, much of it based on cumulative knowledge of past efforts toward planned social change.

Whatever their persuasion, planners are not free agents. The range of their activities and their choices are severely limited by the structures within which they function. The limits of their mandates are not always clear at the start and must be tested in practice itself. This is illustrated in the next vignette, which describes the activities of the staff of a newly formed community mental health board.

Illustration III: A Community Mental Health Board is Organized

THE STAFF MEETS FOR THE FIRST TIME

"It's going well," the director thought to herself. It was her first opportunity to bring her core staff together. At first she'd been a bit nervous about this meeting. It wasn't her first experience in administration. Until last month, she had been director of a family service agency and a member of the State Commission on Mental Hygiene. She knew from firsthand experience how uneven and fragmented mental health services were. That's why she welcomed the challenge of developing a mental health program for this semi-rural area of the state. Her new appointment came at a time when custodial mental health programs were declining in importance and heavy emphasis was being placed on community based services. Her agency was a creature of the State Department of Mental Hygiene. A federal grant made it possible to get a full complement of staff to demonstrate a new approach to resource mobilization. She was anxious to start mobilizing resources and expanding services.

In most cases, even basic services didn't exist. In others, services were inaccessible because of location or narrow eligibility requirements. At the meeting, she had just finished describing some of her experiences. She made the point to her new staff that their prime order of business was to build a comprehensive system of services for all the residents in the area, to make sure that the services were delivered properly, and that they be available to those in the greatest need. Her staff members were responding well, and she was sitting back, half listening to her own thoughts and half listening to the others.

"Let's face it," argued the associate director for planning, "while our work may be aimed at bettering the plight of individuals, our targets are not the consumers of services as individuals. We're not out to change them. We're out to change government agencies, citizens' groups, voluntary agencies, and everybody involved in the development and provision of services." Other members of the staff agreed. In no time, they were brainstorming enthusiastically about the kinds of accomplishments they hoped for. "Hang on there," she heard herself saying. "The results of our efforts are likely to take years. You can't change the structure of services in a community overnight. Some of us may not even be around to see the end products of our efforts."

"That's right." The woman she'd hired on a half-time basis to handle research and evaluation was speaking. She'd been teaching sociology for several years in the nearby community college, and was anxious to apply her skills and put her knowledge to practical use. "It may mean that evaluation would be on *how* we do things rather than on *what* we achieve." "No," disagreed the planner, "it's what we accomplish on behalf of the people in our area that counts. If we're going to be effective, we've got to have *impact* on the lives of people. And that impact depends on the services we can develop and deliver."

"You may both be right," the director interjected, trying to bring them together. "For all the talk about changing the structures of communities, and effecting new patterns in service delivery, the truth is that we've got to work on a day-by-day basis on specific projects. We've got to make sure that those projects are successful, and their impact has to be evaluated. But to make sure they're successful, we've also got to evaluate the way in which we operate, because it's the cumulative impact of these projects that will make the difference."

"Let's not forget that we're really limited in what we can do," added the comptroller, a man with several years' experience in public administration who would be acting as "grants manager" in the new agency. "First of all, we're limited by our mandate. The state agency only expects us to do certain things. And we'll have to get to know what those things are and test the limits of our mandate fast enough. Second, different people may expect different things of us, meaning that rather than doing more, we may wind up doing less but trying to do that less better.

"Third, we're really new at mental health planning. We don't know that much. But that should not be too hard to overcome. There are local people who know what's likely to work and what's not. There may be lots of opposition to and lots of encouragement in favor of any one of our projects. We'll need to get expert opinion and to involve the people that count."

"True enough," the director agreed. "We're not the only ones around here with any expertise or with ideas of what needs to be done. I think that we can pretty well expect that we're going to be rather limited in the prerogatives we can count on and the conditions we can effect in our planning and service area."

WHAT DIRECTION TO TAKE

For a first staff meeting, it wasn't bad. Later, in thinking over what had been said, the director realized that several basic questions had been raised.

Should the agency focus on process, on building relationships, on community development? Or should the emphasis be on concrete, measurable results, here and now?

To what extent would she and her staff hope to change long-standing institutional arrangements? Were these changes essential to providing more, better, and more accessible services to the population needing mental health services in the five-county catchment area*?

What kinds of services? To which populations? How were decisions to be made? Was the Community Mental Health board to function as an advocate for certain populations, for example, ex-mental patients, minority groups, children who are the victims of abuse, the aging, or should these groups be helped to advocate on their own behalf?

Was a long-range comprehensive plan necessary? Would it be best to concentrate on small progressive accomplishments?

Who could be counted on to support the CMH board's efforts? Who might be in opposition? Who else could be appealed to?

In the weeks to come, the staff would have successfully to lay claim to a mandate that would specify their goals, activities, and procedures. They

*The term "catchment area" is found in the mental health literature. It refers to a geographic locality in which populations at risk—those actually or potentially needing mental health services—may be found, and for which a Community Mental Health agency has responsibility.

would have to build relationships to a variety of constituencies—community influentials, government officials, agency administrators, funders, and of course area residents. They would have to build a resource base which would include money and credit, political influence, social standing, knowledge and expertise, legitimacy, and other resources. They would have to establish a pattern of resource allocation and test the limits of their advocacy functions.

As time progressed, they would have to specify the targets of their intervention efforts—populations, organizations, and decision centers. They would have to build, manage, and in a sense "orchestrate" a range of external relationships in order to facilitate accomplishment of their goals. There would be hoped-for successes, not a few failures, and not an inconsequential number of unanticipated consequences to their efforts. There would be many detours, many painful decisions, some disappointments, but in the end, she felt certain, there would be some measurable changes and these changes would make a difference to the residents in the area.

A CRASH EDUCATIONAL PROGRAM

Because all staff members were new to their jobs, they concluded the meeting with a decision to spend the next two weeks finding out everything they could about local mental health and services. The director drew up a simplified PERT* chart with all staff members' responsibilities specifically spelled out. Two staff members would look at the service system with the goal of identifying deficiencies and possible abuses. The other two would locate available data on the population at risk in the area and interview representatives of that population as well as seek expert opinion on their needs, wants, and interests. This would not be a systematic or scientific study. It was simply a way of "getting our feet wet," to get some ideas of "what it's all about," and to make some initial contacts that might be useful in later stages of the planning process. Each team was to record its impressions and to list a series of questions that might be important in later stages of the agency's operations. "Look for who might support or block any future efforts on our part," suggested the director.

The assistant director for planning and the comptroller began by developing a list of the actual and potential programs, services, and facilities that might fit into a system of mental health services. They divided their list and went individually to as many agencies as they could. Where possible, they interviewed the administrator and one or more line or supervisory staff people. At first it seemed as if there was a sufficient array of available services: income through Social Security and public welfare; recreation; health care; the tradi-

*Program Evaluation Review Technique, a way of scheduling events and activities. PERT will be discussed in greater detail in Chapter 9.

tional mental health services; some educational and cultural programs. But it soon became apparent to both investigators that things were not as they first seemed. Enormous gaps in services existed. State mandated services for ex-mental patients and the retarded were just not available. There was almost no home support or job training services. Some of the more traditional counseling and crisis services were administered poorly. Others were just inaccessible. Not too many people seemed to care. Agency people complained of insufficient resources to absorb ex-mental patients. Few saw the relationship of their services to the special needs of minority populations, especially transient minorities like migrant workers.

But lack of resources was not the only problem. Sometimes service providers did not understand the real needs of these populations, or were unwilling to change established practices to accommodate newly identified needs or long neglected ones. As one of the two staff members later wrote in his report: "It's not so much a lack of good will, it's a rigidity based on habit and lack of imagination, and an absence of leadership that we face." Together, they compiled the following inventory of what they termed "institutional abuses":

> In almost every agency, there was a reluctance to meet real emergencies. Really tough problems were ignored or referred elsewhere. In some cases, clients fell between the cracks, referred from one agency to another. They had nowhere to go.
> There were frequent delays everywhere, from being accepted for counseling services to being admitted to a state mental hospital, to receiving financial assistance. This was especially true for minority groups and for those who live in the area's "worst" neighborhoods and communities.
> Price schedules were frequently unfair, unrelated to the cost of service or care. This was especially true in the health field. What a client paid might depend on how he was financed or whom he saw. In many of the private or voluntary agencies, policies were inconsistent. As a client, what "you got" often depended on who handled your case.
> Rehabilitative knowledge and techniques were only minimally used.
> Clients were almost never represented on policy boards or committees. Board members were generally chosen for characteristics quite apart from their potential client status.
> Accountability mechanisms, if they functioned at all, almost never took into consideration special needs of the mentally ill or the developmentally disabled. This was especially so in those agencies that had been established for generic services, such as hospitals or recreation departments.
> There was an almost total absence of legal representation of the mentally

or emotionally disabled in conservatorships, guardianships, consumer
frauds, mental commitment, or entitlement to benefits due under innu-
merable local, state, and federal laws. Of the minority groups in the
area, only blacks were consciously sought out. No one considered the
large transient Chicano population.

Agencies' personnel were reluctant to work with friends or relatives of
the mentally or emotionally disabled, perceiving their involvement as
intrusion on professional prerogatives and a possible challenge to
professional competencies.

Partially dependent persons often became totally dependent by the very
nature of the service system (or lack of services). For some older
people, for example, there were no choices between the nearly total
dependence characteristic of the geriatric ward of a mental hospital or
a nursing home and the total independence required by community
living. There were almost no supportive services (homemaker, home
nutrition, home handyman, shopping and transportation help) that
would make it possible for many of the elderly and other former
patients to maintain themselves in the community.

There were no well-articulated public information programs that might
refer people to appropriate services, specify the range of alternatives
or choices available to them, and inform clients of their rights and
benefits.

Not surprisingly, their two colleagues who were charged with examination of the characteristics and needs of specific populations came up with a
complementary inventory. To get their information, they used a combination
of sources: (a) the 1970 census; (b) a study done two years earlier by the local
Health and Welfare Council; (c) a recent state survey conducted by the State
Department of Mental Hygiene; (d) three "users' studies" conducted by service agencies (the Department of Public Health, the Municipal Recreation
Department, and a family service agency); and (e) a battery of interviews with
knowledgeable people, staff of the service agencies, university people, and local
people who had once been recipients of mental health services. Here is what
they found:

There was no central place for people to obtain up-to-date and helpful
information about health-related, mental health, or social welfare and
recreation services.

Knowledge about services, even the availability of good and appropriate
services, was no guarantee that such services would be used. It takes
a good deal of courage (in addition to overcoming physical or tranpor-
tation handicaps) to ask for help.

Many people requesting help (income supplements, legal services, em-

ployment counseling and job placement, help in finding housing), were
often put off. They were told that their real problems lay in some other
service need (which the agency might be willing to provide if the
applicant recognized his real need), or that no services were available,
when in some cases such services might have been available elsewhere.

The fragmentation and lack of coordination of services tended to reinforce the bewilderment and the isolation of many formerly institutionalized people still in need of mental health services.

About seven or eight of every hundred older persons required some home
care services. Of these, fewer than one out of ten received them. Some
seemed to have no alternative but to enter a nursing home. Hospital-
ized elderly, following surgery or other treatment, could not be released into the community because of the absence of after-care or
personal care services. There was no continuity of care. The strains on
the elderly and their families were enormous.

Many of the area's youth showed evidence of anomie and alienation.
Joblessness was high. Alcoholism and alcohol abuse were at epidemic
proportions, although the use of hard drugs seemed negligible.

MINORITY POPULATIONS

The CMH board's assistant director for research and evaluation was
particularly interested in the problems and characteristics of the minority
populations. She found that one out of four or five whites fell below the official
poverty index, but one out of every two blacks and two out of every three
Mexican-Americans were poor. Four out of five Negro women and an even
larger proportion of Mexican-American women heads of households fell below
the poverty line. Life expectancy for whites was 71, for blacks 61, and for
Mexican-Americans 57. For this reason, few Chicanos ever qualified for Medicare, most of them never reaching the age of 62 or 65.

Further, language barriers and the difficulties in dealing with bureaucratic structures kept the Spanish-speaking population almost completely isolated from the community's service system. For many Mexican-Americans,
malnutrition was a way of life. They lacked not only the means with which
to purchase food, but basic information about proper eating habits. "No
wonder they die earlier," she mused.

Her documentation showed that all the poor, regardless of their ethnic
or racial background, faced appalling environmental conditions. Many lived
in isolation as individuals or as ethnic groups. The conditions of their housing
were shocking. In some rural neighborhoods, one out of three minority
households were without toilets directly on the premises. Dwellings were in
disrepair. "I interviewed one couple," she reported to her colleagues, "who
would talk to me only in their dimly lit hallway. After I'd gained their confi-

dence, I found out that they had burned out all their light bulbs, that they were afraid to let a stranger in their apartment, and that because of their infirmities, they were unable to replace the burned out bulbs."

The poor were stuck where they were. They had nowhere to go. They were fixed in time and place, having neither the means nor the experience required to find their way to services outside the neighborhood. Public transportation was expensive, sporadic, and inconvenient. There were no benches by bus stops, no physical aids to mount or dismount from buses. Those living in the center of the largest city in the area, or in its housing project, were frequently afraid to step out of their apartments or to wait too long (even in the daylight) on the street for a bus.

Their social lives were limited to their neighborhoods, and frequently the next house or apartment. Yet a wall of fear and alienation kept many of them isolated even from this proximate world. This was especially true for the elderly, many of whom had almost no contacts with their neighbors, had lost their friends through death, disease, or urban renewal. Contact with grown children was rare because of geographic or social distance. For many, the world seemed more and more constricted as the years went by. "It's as if the life space for older persons decreases as their past lengthens. The present becomes increasingly meaningless as the future diminishes. Whatever they may have achieved seems relegated to memory. I know it sounds corny, but it's a bitter harvest," she concluded in her report to the staff.

THE LAY SERVICE SYSTEM

The assistant director for planning had his own minority report. "Throughout these two weeks," he wrote, "I had the nagging but persistent feeling that we might be looking at the wrong service system. Most people with emotional problems don't go to professionals with their problems—and it may not be just because professional care-givers are not available, responsive, or accessible. Most people's problems are handled well enough in a more natural, informal, friendship or kinship-based helping system.

"Professionalized services are required when that system doesn't work, when friends and families can no longer provide for a person in need, and when physical or social distances become so great as to impede the effectiveness of this personal, face-to-face helping system. Perhaps," he concluded, "we should try to understand the lay service system so as to beef it up, reducing the load on the professional system."

THE STAFF MEETS AGAIN

"I'm really impressed by the work we've done," the director said at the next staff meeting. "I think you're all to be congratulated. We could take almost any of the problems you've identified and begin working on them. I was most impressed by the fact that these problems are almost defined operationally; that is, we could specify some operational objectives, some planning goals, directly from your descriptions of the problems. I like this notion of looking at the 'lay service' system. I never looked at things in quite that way.

"Our problem, of course," she went on, "is that we have no way of weighing one set of objectives against another. We have no ordered system or priorities, nor any mechanism for developing one at present. We've had two weeks without pressure. Now the luxury is over. The State Department of Mental Hygiene wants a detailed plan that specifies our priorities within three months. The state office wants us to take responsibility for funding all local mental health services right away. We've got to move quickly into establishing priorities and move ahead with the tasks of funding, program development, and service coordination.

"The plum in the pie is that we don't even know how much authority we have. Procedures for administering the new mental health regulations haven't been fully worked out yet at the state level, and I can't even tell for sure how much clout the State Department of Mental Hygiene has with these other service systems, or how much of that clout they'll transfer to us at the catchment area level. These are things we just won't know until we get into the business of setting priorities, making decisions about allocations, and building up constituent support. Being the first to demonstrate what can be done is exciting, but it won't be easy."

"There's something else, too," the planner thought to himself. "We've got two inventories of problems, but no way to integrate them. Somehow we'll have to categorize the issues so that we can act on them." He made some notes on a pad of paper, deciding to share them with the rest of the staff when he'd had a chance to think his notes through a little better. The notes read as follows:

Problems in the Service Delivery System	Problems in the Populations to Be Served
1. Lack of accountability to consumers	1. Lack of knowledge about services
2. Inaccessibility to some populations	2. Discomfort with agencies
3. Ineffectiveness, wrong helping technologies	3. No way of getting to the service providers
4. Inefficiency and lack of coordination	4. Nonexistent connections between
5. Unresponsiveness	5. professional and lay service providers

He had taken the first step in problem definition; grouping and conceptualizing observations in such a manner as to make it possible to determine which ones to deal with.

From Cases To Concepts

Although they may differ in style and perspective, the planners whose work we have just described are all professionals. Their activities are informed by a commitment to service; knowledge and expertise based on eclectic experience and an available technology; and a rational, disciplined approach to the solving of problems. This approach involves knowing their own areas or communities, systematically identifying the needs and conditions of the populations in need of services, becoming familiar with the range of formal and informal services available to them, and assessing the pockets of support and opposition to needed changes.

Planners must decide *whom* they want to help, *how,* and *when.* But planners are not free agents. Their decisions are most probably limited by the organizations that employ them, their advisory councils, and/or the settings in which they work. Nonetheless, they have a wide range of choices. These choices are often of strategic importance. Should they focus more heavily on organizing population groups to take action on their own behalf, as in the first illustration? Should they focus more directly on influencing the institutionalized service providers to change their programs, policies, and methods of resource allocation? Or should they direct their efforts at promoting interorganizational exchange, coordination, and service integration?

There are no simple answers to these questions. Nor are there single solutions to complex social problems. Throughout this volume, many planners will explicate answers they have found satisfactory, solutions that may strike a responsive chord with some readers but be unacceptable to others. There is no single way to plan, nor is there a single, universal strategy for fulfillment of the mandate implied by a piece of legislation or an act of an interested citizen's group that may establish a planning agency.

SUPPLEMENTARY QUESTIONS AND ACTIVITIES

1. Check those items you agreed or disagreed with on the inventory of opinions on planning issues that preceded this chapter. Reexamine each item on the basis of the perspectives on practice described in Chapter 1. Have you changed your opinion?

2. Review the three perspectives outlined in Illustrations I, II, and III. To what extent are they complementary? To what extent are they contradictory? Which of these planners would you identify as social brokers, coordinators, activists, facilitators, advocates? What do these terms mean to you? What other descriptive phrases might you add?

3. The planners in the first two illustrations do not describe explicitly their concern with minority populations or with the needs of the poor. Do you find that these concerns are implicit in their work, or that they are not expressed sufficiently? To what extent could or should the first planner have involved minorities in the TV show? On the task forces he organized? Would the construction of a well-developed area plan have helped him focus on these issues early in the game?

4. Which planner's style is the closest to yours? Why? How would you differ with that planner? Commit your thoughts to writing (no more than 2 or 3 pages). What questions do you have about:

   social planning at the community level
   planning approaches and styles
   the utility of one approach as against another?

5. Go back over the three illustrations and identify the planning principles that each planner seems to be following. You should be able to locate at least 40 to 50 practice principles. Write them all down. With which ones do you agree? With which ones do you disagree?

2

Planners,
Planning Settings,
and Planning Choices

Social Planning at the Community Level

PLANNING, ORGANIZING, AND COORDINATING

Most social planning activities in the United States are directed toward creating changes in the ways human services are conceived, developed, and delivered. In general, social planners concern themselves with modification, elimination, or creation of policies, programs, or resources for human services.

PLANNING SETTINGS

Professional social planners are found in many settings. They work in federal and state agencies, often assuming major roles in the development of legislation, the evaluation of social programs, the creation of designs or models for service delivery, and in the development of advisory committees and policy boards related to the development of human service programs.

At the sub-state and community levels, they may be employed by agencies under governmental or voluntary auspices. Frequently, they are engaged in sectorial planning activities aimed at specific service sectors or populations. These planners may be involved in efforts aimed at making corrections in the judicial system, in health care and delivery, in mental health, or in youth services. Others may be employed by direct service agencies; still others by organized consumer groups and voluntary associations; and some by organizations established primarily for the purposes of planning and coordination.

Planners employed by *direct service agencies* generally perform four tasks. They may

1. mobilize support for the agency's ideology, program, or financial needs
2. guide the process of interorganizational exchange of such resources as personnel, specialized expertise, facilities, funds, and influence
3. plan area services or programs
4. direct agency efforts at changing community resources and programs outside the direct jurisdiction of the agency itself but necessary to the welfare of its clients and constituents

Most direct service agencies tend to concern themselves primarily with the first two functions. They have neither the methods nor the staff and other resources necessary to engage in planning efforts on behalf of any other than their immediate clientele. Many agencies have clientele in common, however. This may require the assignment of planning and coordinating functions to such governmental organizations as urban renewal authorities, city planning commissions, state and regional health, mental health, and retardation planning councils, manpower planning councils, or commissions on human rights.

In the private sector, such organizations as drug abuse councils, councils on aging, and associations of family agencies frequently assume planning functions on behalf of a number of service agencies. Because these public or voluntary bodies tend to focus their planning efforts on one sector of the population (the aging, delinquent youth, the unemployed, those in need of public housing or health care services), they are called *sectorial planning agencies.*

Planning also takes place at the *inter-sectorial* or comprehensive level. The proliferation of sectorial planning bodies and service agencies, each aiming its efforts at a specific population, poses the problem of coordination and the need for more comprehensive approaches. Accordingly, a number of coordinating, allocating, or inter-sectorial planning bodies have developed. At the local level these include welfare councils, sectarian federations, Community Action Agencies, Area Agencies on Aging, Model Cities boards, Community Mental Health boards, and Human Resources Commissions.

Although attempts at *comprehensive planning* beyond the local level are still in their infancy, the council on government (COG) movement which has taken hold in many parts of the country, especially in the South, and other forms of intergovernmental planning commissions suggest that a new growth in inter-sectorial planning at the sub-state level may not be far away.

Where the planner sits in each of these types of agencies is no less important than the type of agency it may be. In a comprehensive planning agency such as a COG, the social planner may have little clout if he or she works in a unit that is isolated or apart from the physical and fiscal planning units. On the other hand, being lodged in either one of these units may reduce the planner's autonomy and visibility. In a direct service agency, the planner may also feel alienated, because his or her insights about the need for basic changes arc met with indifference or resistance by those charged with the provision of services. Management may be much more attuned to the messages it receives from the agency's service units than from its planners.

Several alternatives are possible. The planner might be lodged in the office of the executive director. This has the advantage of increasing the planner's access to principal decision makers and to implied authority, but the disadvantage of removing planning from service delivery, further isolating the planner from ongoing agency operations. Perhaps the most obvious answer is to locate the planner somewhere between management and operations, or with a foot in both worlds, according him or her both authority and responsibility for program development and implementation. This can be accomplished by giving managers some planning responsibility or by giving planners some management responsibility. Sometimes this is accomplished by getting departments within a large agency such as a department of social services or a mental hospital to assign staff to a planning team. Thus, representatives of middle management become "hostages" of the planning department. A process of cooptation has been set into motion. Managers can hardly kill a plan they have been party to designing.

Locating a planner in a service unit does much the same thing. It permits the planner to see a problem from the service provider's or manager's point of view. Giving the planner some responsibility for implementation may enhance his or her understanding of the implications of one course of action over another. But it may also result in something called "tunnel vision," in which the perspective of the whole organization's interests and missions is lost in favor of the particular unit's perspective.

The Planner's Personal Attributes

The breadth and scope of the planner's mandate depends on the authority of his or her employing organization and where the planner is lodged in that organization. What planners do is dependent on their position within an employing organization and the responsibilities assigned to the planner by that organization. Nevertheless, a number of degrees of freedom do exist. Every planner approaches the job with his or her own characteristics. These personal attributes include

1. a personal ideology or set of value commitments
2. the planner's characteristic way of looking at a problem
3. knowledge, skill, and previous experience
4. the planner's personality and personal credibility

IDEOLOGY

Ideology can be a significant factor in the way each planner examines issues and selects problems to attack. Some planners are oriented toward a search for unity and consensus. They tend to avoid controversy, selecting those issues around which significant factions in the community can agree. They argue that the interests of consumer populations can be best served by bringing providers and others together to work on problems of common concern. These planners tend to function as catalysts and as enablers, directing their energies toward reduction of competition, toward enhancing the exchange process between agencies or between agencies and their clientele, encouraging compromise where necessary. They may assume advocate positions on behalf of a particular population although they express their advocacy more in terms of concern with integration of client populations and service providers than with redistribution of power or authority.

Other planners start from a different perspective. They view themselves as representing the specialized or vested interest of a particular population. They may be less concerned with the common values of the affected groups than with accomplishment of specific objectives. They perceive themselves as partisan advocates and tend to be more tough-minded in attempting to achieve predetermined ends. They frequently employ concepts such as power and political influence, and are not reluctant to use either. They do not shy away from conflict and social action strategies.

Some planners argue for a grass roots approach to planning in which the consumer is consistently and centrally involved. Others argue for a hierarchical structure, in which experts initiate change on behalf of those to be served.

Important as their ideological perspectives may be, however, it should be noted that most effective planners are hard-nosed pragmatists. Although commitment to social values must be ever present, they tend to select means and ends in relation to local realities rather than any ideological considerations. At various times, and in relation to the exigencies of practice, the same planner may function as an integrative advocate or as a redistributive advocate, as an enabler and catalyst, or as a technical expert.

The planner's characteristic manner of looking at problems may be as influential as his or her ideological perspective. The questions one planner seeks to answer may be different from those addressed by another. One may begin by saying, "These are the skills I possess (for example, negotiations skill, or skill in the use of cost/benefit analysis or conducting surveys), and these are the resources at my disposal (so many dollars, so much time, knowledge, or political influence)." One might then ask, "Which of the problems that I observe are amenable to change within the constraints of my skill and with the resources I have at my disposal?" The starting point for this planner is often the tool he or she knows how to use. The planner chooses the planning problems in relationship to his or her capabilities.

Planners who have invested long years gaining expertise in the application of certain kinds of planning tools such as management by objectives (MBO), evaluative research, or PERT, are sometimes accused of being "operationalists." Taken to the extreme, this position may suffer from what philosopher of science Abraham Kaplan calls "the law of the instrument." Give a small boy a hammer, and he may find that everything in sight needs pounding. Unfortunately, he may have only a single hammer with which to pound. Some operationalists are not necessarily technical experts, but will use any process or approach with which they are familiar and comfortable as the basis from which and with which to do planning.

The director of a welfare council, for example, claims that "We spent the past 11 years perfecting the structure of committees, task forces, and policy boards Before taking on any new projects, I carefully calculate what the structure is capable of accomplishing within a reasonable amount of time. I then figure out which goals are feasible, and prime up the structure to accomplish them." Effective though it may be, narrow adherence to this one approach can restrict the planner's vision to an unnecessarily narrow range of alternatives.

Another group of planners may begin by seeking information on what needs repairing; only later will they assess their capabilities for performing the necessary corrections. This second group puts implicit faith in the utilization of data and theory in the formulation of goals. "How much can I possibly find out before taking action?" is the question they most frequently ask. The gathering of relevant information and the analysis of facts become the guiding criteria for their actions. Having gathered their data, they then gauge the distance between some normative ideal of what should be and the observed and measured conditions that exist. There is a tendency, however, for these planners to state their planning objectives in utopian terms, shaping objectives that are so distant or so general that they are rarely reached. In trying to maximize their goals, they may never reach them.

There is also the danger that planners who spend too much time in gathering and analyzing data may be immobilized when it comes to taking action. One may never know enough to make the absolutely correct decision. "My boss is a data jockey," complains a manpower planner from a large midwestern city. "He wants to know everything before making a decision, but you just can't ever fully anticipate the unanticipated. By the time he's satisfied that we've studied an issue or problem enough, the dimensions of the problem have changed on us, and our work is largely wasted."

For a third category of planners, the meaning of current situations and observed social problems lies in their implications. The question they most frequently ask is, "What difference does it make if this is so, and what difference would it make if it were altered in this manner or that?" Planners of this persuasion tend to be less selective about ends and more apt to see the interconnectedness of ends and means. They aim toward satisficing,* and let their actions be dictated by interpretations of what is and what is not feasible. Their critics often berate them for being too ready to settle for what is satisfactory rather than what is optimal—for winning specific victories but losing the larger battles that require a more long-range set of objectives.

For each of these three types of planners, the starting point is different. The first is limited by narrowness of vision; the second by expansiveness of vision and over-reliance on data; the third by willingness to accept what may be merely satisfactory. Note also that each of these approaches may be affected by pressure from any number of groups. Whatever the approach taken, solving a particular problem or set of problems requires considerable knowledge and skill.

KNOWLEDGE AND SKILL

A planner's knowledge and skill are based on personal characteristics and experience. Although skill in the performance of interactional activities need not preclude analytic competence, one planner may be particularly skillful in involving others in decision making, in negotiating and bargaining, or in the diagnosis of complex social phenomena. Another may have more technical expertise in the use of a variety of analytic tools, such as those used in operational analysis, projections, program evaluation, or cost accounting.

The planner may have gained expert knowledge while working on previous planning assignments, from his or her administrative work in other settings, or from previous professional and voluntary experience in work with specific populations. In general, those with prior work experience in a planning

---

*Finding a compromise between the planner's goals, the technology available to accomplish those goals, and the available resources.

or administrative situation, and with some familiarity with the social welfare and related service fields, will find their experience easily transferable to new work situations.

Most planners would agree that a good theoretic or practical grasp of organizational operations, of community political and decision-making structures, and of the needs, interests, and characteristics of the population to be served are essential to effective planning. Planners unfortunately may find their background experiences inadequate to their new tasks. This is perhaps inevitable. The practice of social planning is still quite new.

CREDIBILITY

Because of the public's unfamiliarity with this new field, the issue of the planner's credibility takes on special importance. The social planner may be regarded with mistrust by many persons, with a degree of incredulity by others, and with thinly disguised fear by service providers who are aware of their own deficits. Conversely, the planner and his or her agency may be welcomed enthusiastically—and uncritically—so that too much may be expected of them. Under either set of circumstances, it is important for the planner to establish his or her credentials, to make clear what planning can accomplish and what it cannot, and to gain a reputation for honesty and dependability.

The way in which these credentials are established will vary from one constituent group to another. "When I meet with other government officials or service agency administrators," reports a planner from a newly established employment agency, I establish my identity through formal credentials. I interpret the functions of my agency and let them know what my responsibilities are. They can't care who I am personally, but they do care who I represent. It's only later that they care about me—when we are working on something together, or when they know I'm after something and that I won't stop until I get it.

"It's different when I meet with representatives of self-help groups in the community," she continues. "They don't want to know your position in the bureaucracy. They want to know what you stand for, who you are as a person. With low-income people in particular, I've found, formal credentials don't mean a thing. Credentials even get in the way!" This may also be the case in work with minority populations whose increased militance and self-awareness often result in a mistrust of formal credentials. "It's easier for a minority group member to achieve acceptance from his own group," complains a planner in the Southwest. That may be true, but credentials need not exist in advance to achieve credibility. In the long run, credibility is bound in achievement, relationships, and trust. It is often tied to the planner's personality and ability to relate purposefully to others with similar or complementary concerns.

Planning Tools

For some planners, credentials may seem less important than their competence in utilizing certain planning tools, or their knowledge about the *availability* of these tools and *skill in orchestrating their use* by technical experts. Others will be only vaguely aware of the existence of these tools. Still others will feel uneasy in applying the tools themselves, but will depend heavily on consultants and experts for their application.

A sample inventory of tools that may be useful in social planning are mentioned in the following paragraph. None of these tools is useful in all situations. Some are still so primitive as to have only marginal utility. Most of them will be discussed at great length elsewhere in this volume where practitioners who have made extensive use of these tools describe the projects in which they utilized a specific technique. Social planners need not become experts in all or even most of these tools. They should, however, be familiar with how and when they are used, and should be comfortable in requesting the aid of consultants and technical experts when necessary.

Some of the most commonly used tools are social indicative program budgeting, benefit/cost analysis, management by objectives (MBO), and electronic data processing and retrieval processes. Recently planners have found Delphi and other projective techniques, simulations and model building, and consumer analysis of particular utility. Many planners use scheduling techniques to both plan and monitor complex sets of activities and events. They use Gantt Charts, Sched-U-Graphs, the critical path method, or PERT. Those familiar with economics have begun to use input-output analysis. Most planners are conversant with, if not expert in, using a variety of program evaluation methods.

Although these tools are of great potential benefit, some cautionary statements must be made. Most are still in their developmental stages, and some are quite primitive. Others were designed for one purpose and may have been transformed for another with insufficient consideration of the consequences. The Program Planning and Budgeting System (PPBS), for example, was designed with procurements for the Defense Department in mind. It did not transfer well to the Department of Health, Education and Welfare in the Johnson-McNamara years.

The application of some of these tools to delicate social problems is sometimes akin to using a tomahawk to cut a diamond. The tool may just not be refined enough. Both planner and planning student are encouraged to master more than one tool and to understand the utility of several others. But he or she is admonished not to succumb to Kaplan's "love of the instrument."

Choice in Planning

One should not assume that the availability of planning tools makes planning a fully rational process, or that a fully integrated technology for making planning choices exists. To the contrary, no adequate technology has yet been found to fully calculate the impact or the benefit of one course of action over another. Some observers argue that the very notion of "rational choice" is a contradiction in terms. Choices, they point out, represent preferences, and preferences are selected in a process of political tradeoffs. Planners are never free of the responsibility of making their own choices and of clarifying them.

Like the planning staff whose early activities were described in the third case illustration in Chapter 1, all planners must decide what kind of information is important, which problems to be concerned with, and which issues take precedence over others. They must determine the extent to which consumers, providers, and other participants will be involved in any significant decision-making process. And they must also choose between competing standards by which to evaluate the appropriateness, accessibility, and availability of services. At times, they must choose between assumptions about how the community may best be served: through a joint decision-making process, or through encouraging segmental and individual growth and enterprise.

Although almost all planners may begin by assuming that the aggregate activity of individual enterprise does not satisfactorily distribute resources and rewards to those populations with whom they are concerned, they must still decide whether to aim at coordination of efforts and concerting of resources, or whether to encourage greater competition, innovation, and experimentation.

The social planner at the community level is frequently caught between a desire to promote social and institutional change, and his or her dependency on external financing and on agreement by the providers of services. The most elaborate or well thought-out strategy will be worthless if no one is willing to finance it or if no service providers can be enlisted.

"You can't press the agencies too hard," explains one planner, "or the agencies will fight you tooth and nail. Some would just as soon go out of business rather than do something that they perceive as detrimental to their interests. Most of them can find other sources of funding anyway." For this reason, the planner may choose not to attempt to influence service agencies directly. Planners do after all have many other constituencies as well. It might be perfectly appropriate to redefine a particular agency as a target for intervention rather than as a constituent, and to use one's relationship to other agencies to pressure the target agency to change its programs or services.

Because the consumer of agency services is the one who is ultimately affected by the success or failure of the planner's efforts, and because the planner's success is often dependent on the support those efforts generate, some planners argue that their task is to clarify choices, not make them. This is a somewhat specious argument. Just as there is no value-free social science, there is certainly no value-free social planning. The very choice of which problems to address, then the choices involved in presenting the alternatives, and finally the determination of a decision-making group and its duties make the planner a central figure in the decisional process. Refusal to recognize this responsibility is no more than a refusal to accept the responsibility.

Perhaps the planner's most significant choices will come in involving others in the decision-making process. Who should be represented? To what extent can the consumers of services be represented? To what extent do individuals truly represent collective interests?

Sometimes the planner does not seem to have very many choices or options. A crisis or impending crisis, criticism from one side or another, a shift in available resources, or pressure from input/output constituencies may propel the planner into action before the options are fully clear. Then, too, a planner rarely has sufficient information upon which to base decisions; it seems there is never adequate time to communicate with others prior to making a decision. The pluralistic nature of the local community's social and political systems, with their emphasis on agency and program autonomy, may constrain the planner's actions. On the other hand, that very pluralism may open the opportunity for a planner to cut a vector across competing interests and positions.

Planning, then, is a complex process. Despite the availability of certain planning tools, planning may be much more art than technology. Despite the constraints of the planner's mandate and of those groups supplying funding or lending their auspices, the planner does have a range of choices before him. Those choices will be influenced by one's own knowledge and expertise, one's ideological perspective, and one's ability to sift out essentials from what may be an inadequate information base, with never enough time to examine all possibilities and all alternatives.

Perhaps even more important, choices will undoubtedly be influenced by resources available for particular projects. Planners never have sufficient resources under their control to accomplish all that they or their constituents might wish. Specifically, now and in the foreseeable future, sources of funds from federal and state sources are likely to fall short of needs. Social planners at the community level may have to make critical choices between two courses of action: (1) to work within the constraints of their own limited resources; or (2) to use their limited resources as a leverage on the larger system. In the first instance, the planner might be concerned with providing technical assistance to agencies applying for public funds. In the second case, he or she might be using the allocated funds to stimulate, induce, coerce, and cajole.

Whatever the constraints, a *choice within limits* will always be the planner's prerogative. No choice will ever be fully satisfactory. One individual may make one set of choices based on the systematic evaluation of need and feasibility; another may make a different set of choices based on similar data, but a different set of values. Because planning does not aim at perfection, choices are not expected to be perfect. They must, however, aim at an optimal solution to a troublesome situation or circumstance.

Planners must learn to live with their choices, imperfect as they will be. Many planners' choices have been documented throughout this volume. The reader may not agree with every choice or with each planner's rationale— indeed many reflect contradictory ideological perspectives, different experiences, divergent ways of looking at and defining problems. That planners act differently and choose differently is no weakness; it is proof that they attempt to respond to the situation in which they find themselves, making judgments that are often sound, often creative. Although error is inevitable, there is no escape from the necessity of selecting from among alternative possibilities. Nor is there any escape from the imperative to pursue such alternatives persistently and vigorously.

Review

The manner in which a planner approaches a task will be affected by the personal attributes he brings to it. A personal ideological position will affect the extent to which the planner seeks consumer involvement and will influence any listing of objectives. A planner's characteristic manner of looking at problems will determine the kinds of questions he or she raises. Some planners will be influenced by their own skills and by the resources they have at their disposal. Others will put greater faith in the utilization of data and theory in understanding problems and in formulating goals. Others will ask, like the pragmatist: "What difference does it make if this is so, and what difference would it make if it were altered in this manner or that?"

A planner's skill is based on knowledge and experience, and on the way both are utilized in interrelationships with others. A planner's effectiveness is often determined by the reputation he or she garners among those with whom or on whose behalf planning is done.

Planners have found a variety of tools of increasing utility in the planning process. These include social indicators; consumer and client analysis; benefit/ cost analysis; program planning and budgeting systems; evaluative research and impact analysis; PERT; input/output analysis; Delphi conferences; simulation and gaming techniques; and MBO. While planners need not develop expertise with each of these tools, familiarity with them or an ability to make use of consultants with expertise in one or another of the tools may be a significant factor in success.

1. Have you ever worked in a direct service agency, in a planning and coordinating body, in a sectional planning agency, or for an organized consumer group? If so, think back. What kinds of planning tasks were performed within that agency? By whom? What were the planners' mandate(s)? What constraints did the setting put on the planner(s)? If no one performed a planning role, who might have? What should that person have done? How would you characterize the settings in which the three planners quoted in the previous chapter worked: service, sectorial or inter-sectorial, public or private, sectarian or nonsectarian?

2. Look over the statements on personal attributes discussed in this chapter. Are you committed to a strong ideological posture or position? State it succinctly in one or two paragraphs. Does this position restrict or open up the range of planning strategies available to you? How does this position compare with any of those expressed by the three planners quoted in Chapter 1?

3. How do you look at problems? Which of the following ways of phrasing practice problems most clearly parallels your own approach?
   (a) "These are the skills I possess and the resources at my disposal: which of the problems before me are amenable to change within the constraints of my skill and with the resources I have at my disposal?"
   (b) "What information do I have? How much more do I need to know before I can make an intelligent decision about the actions I must take?"
   (c) "There are many alternatives open to me. What differences does it make if I do this or that? For whom?"
   Are there pitfalls in your approach? How might you correct for these?

Recommended Readings

ECKLEIN, JOAN LEVIN, and ARMAND A. LAUFFER. *Community Organizers and Social Planners, Part II.* New York: John Wiley and Sons, 1972.
Through case examples and textual material, this book depicts a variety of issues and projects handled by professionals involved in community organization and social planning. Part II, *Social Planners,* begins with a conceptual overview of planning, planners, and planning settings. The overview is followed by case and

illustrative materials depicting social planners at work in a variety of settings (e.g., welfare councils and direct service agencies).

GILBERT, NEIL, and HARRY SPECHT. *Dimensions of Social Welfare Policy.* Englewood Cliffs, N.J.: Prentice-Hall, Inc., 1974.
The authors develop a general framework for analyzing social welfare policy and explore some of the alternatives, values, and issues involved in making policy choices. Chapter 8 raises the question, "Who should be involved in planning?" The major issue here, according to the authors, is the degree to which planning decisions are influenced by the planner vis-à-vis other groups. The planner is not viewed as an "independent operator," and the social context is thus considered a major factor in determining the planner's role.

GILBERT, NEIL, and HARRY SPECHT. *Planning for Social Welfare Issues, Models and Tasks.* Englewood Cliffs, N.J.: Prentice-Hall, Inc., 1977.
This is the latest of a number of anthologies dealing with social planning and community organizing. Gilbert and Specht go beyond some of the earlier readers by including a number of papers dealing with analytic tools. Their juxtaposition of analytic and trend models of practice complements the stance taken in this text and in the works of Ecklein-Lauffer and Perlman-Gurin. Other suggested readers include those by Cox, Horton, and Kramer and Specht.

DEMONE, HAROLD W. "The Limits of Rationality in Planning." *Community Mental Health Journal,* Winter, 1965, pp. 375–382.
This article begins with a discussion of the central features of rational planning and the concept of rational choice. The author suggests that too great a reliance on rationality can be misleading and unrealistic. Nonrational factors such as the political constraints of the system in which the planner operates, the value judgments inherent in goal setting, and the limits of information are considered highly influential in the planning process. The author calls for flexibility in planning, and suggests that it may be necessary to accept incremental planning to achieve goals over a period of time.

Suggestions for Further Reading

APTHORPE, RAYMOND (Ed.). *People Planning and Development Studies: Some Reflections on Social Planning.* London: Frank Cass, Ltd., 1970.
COX, FRED, et al. (Eds.). *Strategies in Community Organization, A Reader.* Itasca, Ill.: F. Peacock Publishing Co., 1973 edition.
DAVIDOFF, PAUL, and THOMAS A. REINER. "A Choice Theory of Planning." *Journal of the American Institute of Planners,* May 1962.
FRIEDEN, BERNARD J., and ROBERT MORRIS (Eds.). *Urban Planning and Social Policy.* New York: Basic Books, 1968.
GANS, HERBERT J. *People and Plans: Essays on Urban Problems and Solutions.* New York: Basic Books, 1968.
HAYWARD, J. and M. WATSON (Eds.). *Planning, Politics and Public Policy.* Cambridge: Cambridge University Press, 1975.
HORTON, GERALD T. (Ed.). *Readings in Human Services Planning.* Atlanta, Ga.: The Research Group, 1975.

KAHN, ALFRED J. *Theory and Practice of Social Planning.* New York: Russell Sage Foundation, 1969.

KRAMER, RALPH, and HARRY SPECHT (Eds.). *Readings in Community Organization Practice.* Englewood Cliffs, N.J.: Prentice-Hall, Inc., 1973 edition.

MAYER, ROBERT *Social Planning and Social Change.* Englewood Cliffs, N.J.: Prentice-Hall, Inc., 1972.

MORRIS, ROBERT, and ROBERT H. BINSTOCK. *Feasible Planning for Social Change.* New York: Columbia University Press, 1965.

PERLMAN, ROBERT, and ARNOLD GURIN. *Community Organization and Social Planning.* New York: John Wiley and Council on Social Work Education, 1972. See especially chaps. 3, 4, 8 and 9.

STEIN, BRUNO, and S. M. MILLER (Eds.). *Incentives and Planning in Social Policy.* Chicago: Aldine Press, 1973.

3

Planning
and the Human Services
System

Social planning is relatively new to the spectrum of human services in the United States. The term itself was hardly used prior to the major social policy reforms of the New Deal in the mid-1930s. It did not acquire a technical connotation until planning concepts and techniques developed for wartime use were redesigned to deal with social problems after World War II. This may seem startling when one considers the enormous complex of services that exist under public, voluntary, and private auspices and the fact that human services now make up almost half of the United States' Gross National Product. Yet on reflection, it is not really surprising.

Services as Responses to Market Demands, New Knowledge, and New Perceptions

Historically, social and other human services in this country emerged as individual and institutional responses to the specific problems of particular persons in need. Americans have traditionally thought of themselves as independent people, capable of self-help. Help from friends, neighbors, relatives, and other "natural" helpers is generally sought and accepted prior to seeking outside help. It was only when self-help and aid through the natural helping system was inadequate that new institutional responses became necessary. In part, these institutional responses are the product of market demands coupled with scientific discoveries and the growth of technical competence. In part they are societal correctives to the inadequacies of market mechanisms which do not always distribute resources and services equitably or to those in the greatest need. Over the years, consensus on the meanings of "equitable distribution" and "greatest need" have changed to include new populations and new services.

The result is a complex of care-givers and care-giving institutions that developed piece by piece without much central guidance or planning. Professional care-givers such as physicians, lawyers, recreation personnel, social workers, educators, and others perform specific functions for which they have been trained and frequently licensed. Their services are generally offered through some formal organization such as a social services agency, recreation department, hospital or clinic, nursing home, physician's or psychiatrist's office, church, or community center.

Although many people continue to pay fees for services received, increasingly care is paid for through private or governmental insurance programs, through categorical programs supported by local, state, or federal tax money, or through voluntary giving under the aegis of a nonsectarian fund-raising body such as the United Fund. Tax dollars, more than any other, have become the major source for the development, delivery, and coordination of human services.

In many communities, a range of services is offered through departments of public welfare, mental health and community mental health, public health, employment security, education, and others. Many services are funded or coordinated through United Funds and Welfare Councils. Other services may be under the jurisdiction of area-wide human resource commissions, councils on government, housing authorities, public transportation departments, libraries, or school districts. Still other services are provided under a wide variety of religious or sectarian auspices.

The formal welfare structure is complemented by an informal, quasi-institutionalized structure. Bridging professional care giving with lay services, it is composed of a network of civic organizations, service groups, fraternal associations, church groups, social action groups, and others. Some fraternal organizations are primarily member-oriented, whereas groups such as the Rotary, Kiwanis, and Optimist clubs are concerned with the provision of services to needy populations. Other organizations, including the Junior League and the Chamber of Commerce, are primarily oriented toward civic service.

There are also many philanthropic foundations in the United States—corporations legally chartered for the purpose of channeling private wealth into general welfare. More than 100 community trusts are in existence nationwide. Established to promote the development of new and experimental ventures in community welfare, they frequently devote their resources to specific service objectives or particular populations such as the aging, migrant workers, and residents of deprived neighborhoods.

The complex of public, private, and voluntary services is often so confusing to the inexperienced planner as to make its components difficult to identify and to categorize. Many observers point out that rather than make up a system of services, they in fact make up a "non-system" of fragmented and uncoordinated services. To understand the causes of current fragmentation in the human services and to better understand the requirements of social planning at the community level, an historic overview may be helpful.

Growth of Institutionalized Services: An Historical Overview

THE FIRST TWO DECADES OF THE CENTURY

Contemporary forms of social welfare in the United States had their beginnings in the "progressive era" which spanned the first two decades of this century. Increasing urbanization and industrialization, accompanied by significant shifts in the location of wealth, contributed to intensification of existing social inequities and brought previously unrecognized social problems to light. Until the turn of the century, for example, standards for safety or sanitation in factory workshops had been virtually nonexistent. Employers were not considered liable for workers' injuries. Wages and hours were unregulated. Retirement income was entirely a matter of individual fortune. There was minimal government interest in the health and housing conditions of the working population, and no concern at all for those people who were unwilling or unable to work. Poverty, and the problems of the impoverished, seemed permanent and insoluble. Moreover, many felt that poverty was the problem of the poor, not of the society which in its apparent openness had permitted so many to move from rags to riches.

Nevertheless, these two decades witnessed rapid change in social perspective and philosophy. The science of sociology, with its new interpretations of social issues and social problems was gaining prominence. Professional social work had begun to challenge the existing order and the regressive notions of "social Darwinism." The Darwinist gospel that helping the poor was merely a way of perpetuating the unfit was further challenged by the new "social gospel" proclaimed in Protestant and Catholic churches and in Jewish synagogues. Reformists, with support of newly established labor unions, were moving to ameliorate the effects of exploitative capitalism through social welfare legislation.

The Charity Organization Societies and settlement house movement came into their own, representing a successful combination of the reforming zeal of the social worker and the philanthropic spirit of a number of well-to-do individuals. The New York COS initiated the nation's first social welfare publication. It was followed by many others. Foundations devoted to health, education, social welfare, and scientific research were established by wealthy individuals and by giant industrial corporations. Included among these were the Carnegie, Rockefeller, Rosenwald, and Russell Sage Foundations, and the Commonwealth Fund.

This was also the period in which a number of national service agencies were established. These included the Boy Scouts, Girl Scouts, Camp Fire Girls, and Boys Clubs. The United States Department of Agriculture inaugurated the 4-H Clubs. Public parks, playgrounds, recreation programs, and libraries grew at a prodigious rate, many of them financed by public funds.

New needs identified during the First World War spawned the growth of the American Red Cross and the National Recreation Association and created some of the earliest federal relief programs. Supplementary voluntary relief projects were organized by the American Jewish Joint Distribution Committee, the Friends, and other organizations under religious or ethnic group auspices.

State and local health departments, public health dispensaries, and general hospitals were established as the basic care-givers of the indigent ill. They were followed by special hospitals and sanitariums, convalescent and rest homes, child welfare offices, social hygiene and sex education clinics, and a limited number of state programs for the rehabilitation of the disabled. In 1920, the first Vocational Rehabilitation Bill was introduced in Congress and enacted into law. It provided for matching federal and state funds to develop service to the vocationally and physically disabled. Juvenile courts sprang up in cities throughout the country. Mental institutions began their transformation from insane asylums to hospitals and outpatient clinics for the mentally ill.

The B'nai Brith Anti-Defamation League, the American Jewish Committee, the American Civil Liberties Union, the National Association for the Advancement of Colored People, and the National Urban League were established, marking the beginnings of national voluntary efforts in the field of civil liberties and intergroup relations. There were few improvements, however, in the administration of state or local public relief programs, nor any significant movement to improve the lot of the aging. These improvements were not to come until the 1930s.

THE 1920s

The twenties marked a decade of prosperity in which many of the innovations of the progressive era were more fully institutionalized and consolidated. Prosperity sparked a large increase in philanthropic giving. Community chests evolved, later to become United Funds and Welfare Councils. Programs for the aging first gained widespread public support as statewide programs of old age assistance. They moved eastward from their origins in Alaska, through Montana, Nevada, Wisconsin, Colorado, and Kentucky. Championed by the American Federation of Labor, by the Fraternal Order of Eagles, and by other groups, Old Age Assistance was an early attempt to end total reliance on institutional care (hospitals and homes for the indigent) by providing sufficient funds to maintain financially dependent older people in their homes. The foundations of the Townsend movement were laid in southern California. In 1929, several of the larger midwestern cities began utilization of welfare departments to provide relief to the unemployed, including the unemployed older worker. New York State adopted a welfare law which emphasized home relief in preference to institutional care for the needy. But despite all these advances, most Americans still felt that to be dependent was to be morally defective.

THE 1930s AND THE 1940s

The Great Depression dispelled this and many other notions. Few people any longer opposed the use of local, state, and federal funds for relief. The notion that human needs were solely an individual, family, voluntary, or local responsibility was disabused once and for all. New Deal "alphabet soup" programs promulgated the concept of government responsibility for the consequences of economic disjunction, dislocation, and inequality.

Under Federal Emergency Relief (FERA), dollars were given directly to recipients through cash benefits or grocery orders rather than through social agencies. The Civilian Conservation Corps (CCC) and the National Youth Administration (NYA) established special programs for unemployed youth. The Public Works Administration (PWA) and the Civil Works Administration (CWA) provided employment opportunities for more than four million adult and older adult workers, many of whom were recruited from relief rolls. The Home Owners Loan Corporation (HOLC), established in 1933, was given authority to buy and to rewrite mortages so that destitute homeowners could pay their taxes, make necessary repairs, or arrange more convenient payments.

The Social Security Act was passed in 1935, and together with its subsequent amendments established the government's responsibility for social insurance, unemployment insurance, and old age and survivors' benefits. It provided for a grants-in-aid program to the states, providing funding for such categorical services as Old Age Assistance. The Works Progress Administration (WPA), also established in 1935, provided work relief during periods of recession, when private enterprise could not absorb slacks in the economy.

These government programs had a major impact on voluntary social welfare agencies. The notion that individual self-help and reliance on mutual aid groups or quasi-institutional services was the primary line of offense against social inequities and personal misfortune was permanently discarded. Voluntary social welfare and health agencies were no longer considered the basic back-up in times of trouble. Government had assumed an essential role in guaranteeing the welfare of its citizens.

Many of these programs were championed and promoted by the Townsend movement. This was the first significant organization of older people pressing for legislative changes which would take account of their interests. It combined elements of self-help with political action and partisan advocacy. Active chapters were established in small and large communities throughout the United States.

During the Second World War, Americans witnessed the consolidation of many programs. Immediately after the war, the federal government plunged into a variety of international relief programs, many of them through the United Nations. Parallel developments were expanded under voluntary auspices, through such organizations as the American Jewish Joint Distribution Committee, the American Friends Service Committee, CARE, the American Red Cross, and others. Involvement in these efforts, combined with a rediscovery of poverty in America during the late' 50s, led to a rapid expansion of social services.

THE 1950s

The fifties were witness to the growth of many new concerns. Preventive programs were aimed at combating juvenile delinquency. New forms of medical care and organization, coupled with a rapid expansion of medical care facilities, were financed in part by federal monies. Government-supported slum clearance and housing programs were established to benefit both low-income and moderate-income families. A progressively larger share of the federal dollar was being applied to social insurance and social welfare programs. It was increasingly clear that the services provided by voluntary associations were no longer adequate for the magnitude of the social problems occasioned by the economic and social dislocations of the thirties and forties. In some cases, however, agencies received federal funds through purchase-of-service agreements and other contractual arrangements. The distinctions between voluntary and public programs were becoming blurred.

Growth in the range and scope of welfare programs spurred equally rapid growth of coordinating councils and federations. Community organization was now accepted as a professional specialization within social work. Other professions also began to consider community organization and planning as professional specialties on a par with direct service methods. Relationships between community organization, community development, social reform, city and regional planning, health planning, and other similar fields were explored. New knowledge from the social sciences and the collective experience of practitioners from a number of professions contributed to the refinement of planning methods and the identification of commonalities.

These advances lulled Americans into a feeling that most social problems could and would be solved through good will, applied technology, and a little patience. Despite the disquiet engendered by the Cold War, the majority of white Americans felt reasonably secure. Employment was high. Confidence that the nation's problems were well in hand was pervasive. But the mood of complacency was not to last long.

The Explosion of the Sixties

A RUDE AWAKENING—POVERTY AMID AFFLUENCE

Americans were rudely awakened during the sixties by the discovery that poverty had not disappeared with the growth of affluence; that racism and discrimination had not disappeared with the passage of fair employment and civil rights legislation. The war in Southeast Asia shattered for many the belief that America could solve the problems of democracy or poverty abroad. The civil rights movement, the growth of black power, the awakening of other ethnic and ideological minorities, and the advent of street confrontations shattered America's collective belief that the country was well on the way to the resolution of domestic problems. Poverty was defined by the Department of Health, Education, and Welfare as an income of less than $3,000 per year for a non-farm family of four. According to the Census Bureau, almost 40 million people lived in poverty.

The sixties witnessed an explosion in legislation dealing with civil rights, tax reform, and anti-poverty projects. New structures were established at the federal and local levels to "solve" urban problems. These developments were accompanied by equally far-reaching legal decisions. Court rulings explicated the rights of individuals to equal opportunities in education and employment, privacy and freedom from harassment (protecting the constitutional rights of welfare recipients), free speech and assembly, and protective services.

CHALLENGES TO SOCIAL WELFARE AND SOCIAL WORK

Social work as a profession, social workers as providers of professional services, and social welfare as an institution found themselves at once praised and vilified. They were criticized both for doing too much and for doing too little. Critics of government spending claimed federal officials were intruding at the local level. Organized consumer groups and advocates of direct action at the local level challenged the same agencies and some federal officials for being too far removed from the local level—and unresponsive to the real needs of the poor. Established programs were altered, frequently on the insistence of organized client and citizen groups. Individual therapy and treatment became less dominant as social workers and allied professionals assumed a central role in the development of new programs aimed at prevention. Social problems became increasingly defined as structural in nature, rather than rooted in the defective individual. Despite its occasional recurrence, social Darwinism was laid firmly, if not finally, to rest.

THE NEW LEGISLATION

While many of the programs of the sixties enhanced the material and social well-being of the aging, perhaps none had such far-reaching significance as Medicare and Medicaid. Both these programs confirmed the principles that citizens had a right to certain services and that society had an obligation to provide them. Medicare, signed into law in 1965, provided medical assistance to the aging, and Medicaid assured additional benefits to needy persons of all ages. Vocational rehabilitation services were expanded. New programs for the mentally retarded and physically handicapped were established.

The Mental Retardation Facilities Act and the Community Mental Health Centers Construction Act of 1963 were subsequently amended to provide funds for staff and program development as well as for construction of facilities. Community mental health as a philosophy and as a structure for service delivery superseded other forms of mental health services. Emphasis was placed on the structural variables affecting mental health. Large numbers of mental patients, including many elderly previously defined as senile, were returned to the community. Although provisions were far from adequate, their return was supported in some communities by a quickly patched together network of new halfway houses, home-based facilities, and supportive services.

Many programs of the sixties promised more than they produced. Programs were frequently oversold in order to assure passage of legislation. The pace of change was too rapid for some Americans; for others it seemed an incredibly slow and inadequate response to the needs of the socially, culturally, and economically disenfranchised.

Despite some hostility toward those welfare programs that sometimes seemed to promote crisis rather than resolve problems, there emerged a greater understanding that many poor people simply had no alternative but to go on welfare. They either could not find jobs or were forced to take very low paying jobs. This led to an emphasis on job training and job placement as major weapons in the War on Poverty. This commitment was carried into the early 1970s and reinforced in the late 1970s.

THE WAR ON POVERTY

The Economic Opportunity Act of 1964, an omnibus piece of legislation, was designed to eliminate the paradox of poverty in the midst of plenty. It spawned a number of new programs and reinstituted many of the measures that had been created by the New Deal but permitted to lapse during World War II. Among those programs with New deal antecedents were the Job Corps and Job Training Centers. By providing client populations with "new careers," in the human services, they were given the particular flavor of the 1960s.

A major innovation in the Act was the creation of Volunteers in Service to America (VISTA), called the domestic peace corps. Later VISTA, together with the Peace Corps, Foster Grandparents Program, Senior Aides, and other volunteer programs, became a part of ACTION, an umbrella agency organized to coordinate and to further the provision of services by volunteers in every community where they were needed.

Perhaps the most innovative and controversial idea contained in the Economic Opportunity Act related to urban and rural community action. Indebted conceptually to the Ford Foundation's Gray Areas Slum Redevelopment Programs of the 1950s, and to New York City's Mobilization for Youth (MFY), the Act mandated the Office of Economic Opportunity to establish Community Action Agencies (CAA) and to develop Community Action Programs in local communities. The agencies were encouraged to maximize, to the extent feasible, the participation of the poor in the provision of services and in the development of service priorities and agency policies.

One of the results of this provision was the development of "new careers" for the poor. Opportunities were to be provided for poor people to enter the world of work as providers of semi-professional services to their neighbors and peers. New careerists were also expected to establish communication linkages between professional care-givers and the recipients of services. In many cases, they represented the interests of the poor in staff deliberations and in the development of service strategies. Other representatives of the poor were included on the boards of anti-poverty agencies or organized with staff help into neighborhood associations and councils for self-help and social action purposes.

Today's concepts of "advocacy" were tempered in the fires of social action during this period. Many community action programs saw community involvement, client control, and citizen participation both as their goals and as the means by which their goals could be accomplished.

FEDERAL-LOCAL RELATIONS

Most of the early programs of the War on Poverty were created in such a way as to provide direct contact between the federal government and local communities. Federal contracts were often awarded to local agencies, frequently bypassing state machinery as well as local units of government. This did not last long. By the end of the 1960s, control began to swing back toward more conventional lines of authority. However, the shift back to traditional bases of control did not result in a total shift away from neighborhood or local control.

Although the Model Cities program, for example, was made directly responsible to local political authorities, it continued to have citizen input through local advisory boards composed of residents of the affected neighborhoods. The underlying idea of the Model Cities legislation was to assure neighborhood rehabilitation through planning and coordination of education and health and recreation facilities as well as housing. Planning was not be be conducted by some centralized authority far removed from those affected by the planning process. Planning, to the contrary, was to have considerable input from residents of the neighborhoods designated for Model Cities grants through their participation on boards and councils.

From the 1960s Through the 1970s

CONSOLIDATION

If the 1960s was the decade of explosive new ideas and burgeoning new programs, the 1970s can already be characterized as a decade of continued growth with an emphasis on accountability, consolidation, and coordination. Federal priorities emphasize the need to build on the base of already existing programs and to consolidate the gains made in the 1960s. Unworkable programs or those which engendered controversy have been eliminated or deemphasized. Efforts have been made to eliminate duplication and waste wherever possible—too often, critics claim, at the expense of needy populations. Nevertheless, there is renewed emphasis on plugging the holes, on filling the gaps where services do not exist.

Probably the most significant change in current federal policy in the 1970s is the conviction that it is not possible to tailor programs at the federal level to meet local needs. This conviction, often described as the "new federalism," is intended to shift the balance to locally initiated, sponsored, and controlled services coupled with an emphasis on local, area-wide, state, and regional planning.

STATE AND LOCAL PLANNING

One of the best examples of state, local, and regional planning is found in Title XX of the 1975 Amendments to the Social Security Act which calls for the development of state plans for the provision of services to children, their families, and others served by public welfare. It requires local inputs into the planning process. In many states these have been provided through public hearings and open meetings, and the establishment of citizens' advisory groups and commissions with representatives of both public and private agencies at the local level. Local inputs are reflected in a state plan that must set priorities for service objectives during the coming year. The plan defines both the service priorities of the public welfare agency and the range of services to be provided by its sub-state units, as well as those to be provided by others through purchase of service agreements.

Another example is found in Area Agencies on Aging, which are funded under Title III of the 1973 amendments to the Older Americans Act. Mandated by state government but founded in large part through federal tax dollars, area agencies are responsible for planning and coordinating services at the local level for the aging. Each area agency is responsible for developing an annual plan which must conform to the state's overall priorities of services to the aging. Since many area agencies are lodged administratively in local (city, county, or regional) units of general-purpose government, they must be responsive to many political forces.

The transfer of authority to local political bodies for decisions regarding the allocation of funds to human service programs was perhaps best exemplified by the Revenue Sharing Act. General revenue sharing permits localities to determine how tax "refunds" are to be used locally. Special revenue sharing limits decision-making powers to specific sectors such as health, education, housing, and employment. Although critics of revenue sharing feel that the decisions made at the local level have often been to the detriment of those most in need, others applaud the shift in both authority and accountability to the locality.

ACCOUNTABILITY

Discussions of accountability are often laden with emotion. Proponents charge that without stringent accountability measures, service providers and planners have oversold programs that had little resemblance to their prior objectives, that were costly, or that had little impact on those served. Early opponents of the federal government's new emphasis on accountability charged that it was simply a slogan to cut the budget, slash programs, and generally deprive those in greatest need yet with the greatest vulnerability. Both positions miss the mark.

Accountability is a process comprised of a series of elements including problem identification and goal formulation, and which raises questions about quality of service, efficiency, and effectiveness in ameliorating specific social problems and their impact on selected populations.

State and federal auditing procedures, combined with new budgeting approaches and management techniques—although frequently awkward and prematurely applied—may foster a tightened accounting of how public funds are spent. Procedures for revenue sharing and for program initiation and development at the local level may increase citizen control over funds. Emerging federal policies for the seventies also emphasize the need to establish better coordinating mechanisms among federal, state, and local agencies. Together, all these policies and procedures are intended to assure that services can and will be provided in the manner promised, and that social problems and their adverse impacts may be effectively reduced at the lowest social cost.

It is certainly too early to pass judgment on these new emphases, or to state affirmatively that they will indeed characterize all of the seventies. Ultimately, perhaps, the success of the programs initiated during the sixties will depend on the results of these processes during the seventies.

Social planning at the local and sub-state level is itself an outgrowth of trial-and-error experimentation in the 1960s. Planners have emerged from their trial by fire with a stronger perception of what they can accomplish and how their accomplishments are to be managed. They enter the late seventies and early eighties with a knowledge base born of cumulative experience, social science research, and newer and more powerful technologies.

CHANGES IN PROGRAMS

The 1970s witnessed the separation of services from income maintenance through public welfare and an increasing use of "purchase of service agreements," in which public agencies contract for the provision of services to their clients by voluntary and private care-givers. Health services expanded rapidly and at enormous cost to the national treasury. Medicare benefits were extended. Medicaid (health benefits for those defined as medically indigent) was expanded through the operationalization of Early and Periodic Screening and through Diagnosis and Treatment of all children under 21 whose families are considered medically indigent. These were later called into question with the proposal of new legislation to thoroughly overhaul the health service delivery system.

Health Maintenance Organizations providing prepaid nonemergency health care received federal support. Retraining and other employment programs were expanded. Perhaps no change will have greater impact than the introduction of new "sunset laws" and zero-based budgeting.

Sunset legislation is designed to rid the government of self-perpetuating bureaus and programs that have outlived their original purposes or current usefulness. It requires that new programs and services be established for a limited period of time only, generally not to exceed five years. At that time, if a program is to continue, new legislation to that effect is to be introduced.

Zero-based budgeting begins with the assumption that each year's budget for a program or service begins at zero. Previously, most government programs began the budgeting process by assuming that they would begin with the previous year's budget, and then make adjustments for inflation, for expansion, or for reduction as needed.

Implications for Social Planning

The implications for social planning at the local level are enormous. Planning is increasingly seen as a corrective to the inadequacies of the market to distribute services equitably. Social planners are employed in a variety of settings (1) to address the needs and interests of specific populations; (2) to correct the deficiencies in services to those populations; and (3) for the creation of changes in interorganizational relationships leading to more effective and efficient service delivery.

Planners work toward the expansion or reduction of resources to individuals and service providers, toward changes in service priorities and policies, and toward better integration and coordination of services. They often involve both the providers and consumers of services in the planning and priority-setting processes. They work closely with units of general-purpose government and with the managers of categorical programs and bureaus. They often perform technical tasks related to the assessment of need, to accounting of costs and benefits of alternative programs and approaches, and to the evaluation of social programs.

Review

While most people tend to look to themselves when they face problems, they may also require the assistance of friends, neighbors, relatives, and other lay care-givers, and of institutionalized or quasi-institutionalized service providers.

The twentieth century has witnessed a phenomenal growth of institutionalized providers of service. During the first two decades of this century, the gospel of social Darwinism was displaced by the arguments of social reformers and social workers, and by new knowledge gleaned from the young science of sociology. National service agencies were established. Voluntary services offered at the local level became increasingly professionalized.

The 1920s witnessed a growth in philanthropic giving, paralleled by growth in government services to the needy. The first Vocational Rehabilitation Act was passed. Statewide programs of old age assistance were established in many parts of the country to reduce reliance on institutionalized care for the indigent elderly. The Townsend movement laid the base for future efforts at political organization of older Americans.

It was not until the 1930s and 1940s, however, that the foundations for today's social services were laid. The "alphabet soup" programs that followed the Great Depression served as patterns for many of the social programs of the 1950s and anti-poverty measures of the sixties. During the thirties, the federal government's responsibility for social insurance, unemployment insurance, and old age assistance was firmly established. Public programs had clearly supplanted voluntary efforts to deal with major social problems. The 1950s witnessed a rapid growth in preventive programs and in the development of coordinating councils and federations.

The mid-1960s saw an enormous flurry of legislation and legal judgments affecting the social welfare of all Americans. Poverty amid affluence was rediscovered and the Economic Opportunity Act of 1964 spawned a number of new programs relating to job training, placement, and development; expansion of volunteer efforts and new career opportunities in the human services; housing programs; and community action programs. The participation of clients and citizens' groups in the direct provision of services and in the making of policies for their provision was built into law. New mental health and vocational rehabilitation laws established new care-giving systems. Medicare and Medicaid established public responsibility for the health care of older Americans and needy persons of all ages.

Authority for planning was increasingly delegated to the local, regional, and state levels. Social planners were employed in a variety of settings to perform tasks aimed at correcting for the inadequacies of market mechanisms so as more equitably to distribute services and resources. The efforts of some planners have been directed at improving the conditions of specific populations and have thus provided us with valuable insights into how to correct those conditions. Others focus more directly on the service delivery system itself, both the providers of services and the network of relationships that exists among them.

SUPPLEMENTARY QUESTIONS AND ACTIVITIES

1. Select a human services organization with which you are familiar. During the 1970s, to what extent have its services been affected by: (a) changes in federal or state laws and regulations; (b) changes in perceptions of needs or populations in need; (c) new knowledge and new technical expertise?

2. How well do you know the service delivery system in your community? Can you identify the major providers of service to those populations that concern you the most? You may find the following exercise helpful in identifying these services. It includes a sample program resource matrix and instructions.

SAMPLE PROGRAM RESOURCE MATRIX FOR SERVICES TO CHILDREN AND FAMILIES

	Health	Court and Legal	Social Services and Mental Health	Income Maintenance	Education	Recreation	Church and Civic Assoc.
DIRECT SERVICES	Medicaid EPSDT General hospital Public health nursing Family physicians (private) Developmental Disabilities Center Well Baby Clinic	Legal aid Private attorneys Law clinics Friend of the court Probate court Circuit court court Juvenile court Detention home Probation services Correctional facility for juveniles	CMH Center Child Guidance Clinic Crisis Center Substance Abuse Center Suicide prevention Big Brothers Marriage and family counseling agencies Employment Protective services Run-Away Kids Foster care Adoptions After-care Child Care Center	Public welfare Social Security SSI Retirement programs Food Stamps Church or ethnic group income supports Foster care grants and group homes	Public schools Special services in the schools Parochial and private schools Community colleges Adult and community education Learning Disabilities Center Tutorial program Supplementary tutorial programs of college students	Public recreation Y's and community centers Boy Scouts, Girl Scouts, Campfire Girls, etc. Junior Achievement Boys Club, Girls Club 4-H	Churches Church youth programs Civic groups, like Kiwanis
FACILITATING SERVICES	Transportation for the disabled in formation with regional systems	Informal network of counselors	IER system escort service				

The Program Resource Matrix enables the planner to make an inventory of all the services available in a given geographic area. Our sample matrix includes services to children and their families.

In looking at the sample matrix, note that the headings of the vertical columns designate seven broad areas of service: health; court and legal; social services and mental health; income maintenance; education; recreation; church and civic associations. You may prefer to group services (program resources) under a larger or smaller number of categories in designing your own matrix. The sample matrix also has two lateral categories. *Direct services,* as the designation implies, provide direct benefits to the recipient. *Facilitating services* offer a *means* toward getting direct services.

Direct services are available to the general public by dint of right or need and are generally under public auspices. They are aimed at providing children and adults with a minimally acceptable quality of life. Some of these services are aimed specifically at children needing placement, parents who may have to place a child, or the foster and adoptive parents who take on the major responsibility of post-placement care of the child. You may be more familiar with these. But these services are only partially successful if not coordinated with other direct services, and many such services are of no value without facilitating services.

Facilitating services do not have any intrinsic value in themselves. They do, however, make it possible for people to make fuller use of direct services. Thus, child care and transportation services enable people to make use of job training or health services. Without facilitating services, other program resources may be either inaccessible or unavailable.

Please note that our matrix is far from complete—it is intended only to be suggestive. Some of the direct and facilitating services listed may not be available in your community. Perhaps there are others not listed. After you've looked at the sample, follow the instructions for building your own matrix.

EXERCISE: BUILDING YOUR OWN MATRIX *

1. Look over the sample matrix. Are you comfortable with the categories that head each column? Would you break some into more specific categories? Consolidate others? Add categories?

*This exercise may be conducted individually or in small groups. When conducted within an agency setting, the program resources or service agencies you select should be drawn from among those actually or potentially available in your community or service area. If the exercise is conducted in a classroom setting, students may have to select one community or to construct an imaginary one if they are to work in small groups. The exercise is drawn from a training guide for planners in the field of aging designed by William Lawrence, Lynn Nybell, Richard Bridgewatt, and others.

PROGRAM RESCURCE MATRIX

D:RECT
SERVICES

FACILI-
TATING
SERVICES

61

Make up your own program resource matrix for any population or service sector of interest to you. You do not have to limit yourself to children's or family services. Begin by selecting the categories that make the most sense to you. Use the blank form or enlarge your matrix on a piece of newsprint.

2. *Now fill in the matrix with what already exists.* Using a *black* pen or marker, write in all the program resources that exist in your community. You may find some of the services found on the sample matrix suggestive, but you may not like where they are located. You might consider "Employment" services as direct whereas someone else might perceive them as facilitating. It all depends on where you are working and how you perceive the client's problem.

3. Having specified what is, add what might be. Using a *red* pen or marker, *add services that are not now found in your community, but which you think should be there.*

4. Go back over your matrix of "What is" (the one written in black) and *underline those you feel need considerable modification to properly serve the population you have selected* in red.

5. Finally, in one or two paragraphs, given your reasons for designating services as direct or facilitating. If you've chosen to use different program categories than suggested on the sample matrix, indicate why you have done so in a paragraph or two.

Recommended Readings

TERRELL, PAUL. "Competing for Revenue Sharing: The Roles of Local Human Service Agencies." *Urban Affairs Quarterly,* 1976, *12* (2), 171–196.
Advocates of focused welfare spending often argue that the "new federalism" and revenue sharing prevent the advancement of social welfare efforts. Terrell argues the opposite case. In order to assess the impact of general revenue sharing on local social welfare, Terrell has conducted a survey of social service agencies in California. He concludes that revenue sharing and the new federalism hold "a potential for new human services funding and new service planning and delivery arrangements." According to the author, general revenue sharing has helped to bridge the gap between city and county operations, and helped to focus attention on the need for fair and systematic ways of funding, operating, and evaluating social programs.

WHEELER, GERALD R. "New Federalism and the Cities: A Double Cross." *Social work,* *19* (3), 659–664.
In this article, the author examines the effect that the "new federalism" of the '70s has had on five American cities, and concludes that urban citizens—especially the poor—have been "double crossed." The author points out that, prior to the

initiation of the general revenue sharing idea, most local and state authorities expected that current levels of grants-in-aid would be maintained. Since the implementation of revenue sharing, however, categorical aid for social welfare programs has been decreased substantially. The author contends that, although GRS was not originally designed to replace categorical aid, it has been used "as a vanguard to dismantle existing grant-in-aid programs."

SMITH, RUSSEL, and DOROTHY ZIETZ. *American Social Welfare Institutions.* New York: John Wiley and Sons, 1970.
Smith and Zietz cover the development of American social welfare institutions and the social work profession from the days of the Elizabethan Poor Laws to the Great Society era. Their book examines the history and origins of social welfare and some of the political, religious, legal, and economic forces which have shaped the field. A good, concise overview of welfare institutions.

GIL, DAVID *Unravelling Social Policy.* Cambridge: Schenkman Books, 1973.
This is a gem of a book, short and to the point, in which the author examines the development of social programs and policies on methodological, philosophical, political, and theoretical levels. He develops a model for policy analysis that is readily applicable to planning issues and problems.

GINZBERG, ELI, and ROBERT S. SOLOW. *The Great Society.* New York: Basic Books, 1974.
In *The Great Society,* twelve experts from a variety of social science fields take a close look at some of the major government programs and policies of the sixties. Included in this coverage are the Office of Economic Opportunity, Medicaid, and the Model Cities program. The book serves to highlight some of the major successes and failures of social welfare in the '60s.

KAHN, ALFRED. "Public-voluntary Collaboration." *The Social Welfare Forum.* New York: Columbia University Press, 1976, p. 47.
In the era of Title XX, the basis for voluntary public agency collaboration in the social services has changed. In this article, Kahn explores some of the reasons behind and the implications of these changes. He argues for an expanded personal social services system that can meet the "requirements of the family with a working mother, or of the aged who could continue living in a normal community environment if assured adequate social services and social care facilities." Success in this, the author suggests, will require collaboration between the public and voluntary sectors, with the latter performing the special functions of diversity, advocacy, and monitoring.

Suggestions for Further Reading

BINSTOCK, ROBERT. *Planning: Background and Issues.* Washington, D.C: White House Conference on Aging, 1971.
BOOTH, PHILIP. *Social Security in America.* Ann Arbor, Mich.: University of Michigan, School of Social Work, May, 1973.
BUTTRICK, SHIRLEY M. "Affirmative Action and Job Security: Policy Dilemmas." *The Social Welfare Forum.* New York: Columbia University Press, 1976, pp. 116–125.

CHAMBERS, CLARKE. "Social Service and Social Reform: A History Essay." *Social Service Review,* March, 1963.

CLOWARD, RICHARD, and FRANCES PIVEN. *The Politics of Turmoil: Poverty, Race and the Urban Crisis.* New York: Vintage Press, 1975.

COHEN, NATHAN. *Social Work in the American Tradition.* New York: Holt, Rinehart and Winston, 1958.

COUGHLIN, BERNARD J., S. J. "Interrelationships of Governmental and Voluntary Welfare Services." *Social Welfare Forum.* New York: Columbia University Press, 1966, p. 97.

Encyclopedia of Social Work. New York: National Association of Social Work, 1965, 1970, 1975.

FELDMAN, ALBERT G. (Ed.). *Delivering and Administration of Services for the Elderly.* Sacramento: California Commission on Aging, 1970.

FRIEDEN, BERNARD J., and MARSHALL KAPLAN. *The Politics of Neglect: Urban Aid from Model Cities to Revenue Sharing.* Cambridge, Mass.: MIT Press, 1975.

GALBRAITH, JOHN KENNETH. *The Affluent Society.* Boston, Mass.: Houghton Mifflin Co., 1969.

GILBERT, NEIL, and HARRY SPECHT. *Dimensions of Social Welfare Policy.* Englewood Cliffs, N.J.: Prentice-Hall, Inc., 1974.

GINSBURG, HELEN. *Poverty, Economics and Society.* New York: Little, Brown and Co., 1972.

GORDON, DAVID M. *Problems in Political Economy: An Urban Perspective.* Lexington, Mass.: D. C. Heath & Co., 1971.

GORDON, MARGARET S. *The Economics of Welfare Policies.* New York: Columbia University Press, 1963.

GROSSER, CHARLES F. "Community Development Programs Serving the Urban Poor." *Social Work,* July, 1965.

HARRINGTON, MICHAEL. *The Accidental Century.* New York: Macmillan, 1965.

KAHN, ALFRED. *Social Policy and Social Services.* New York: Random House, 1973.

LAMPMAN, ROBERT J. *Ends and Means of Reducing Income Poverty.* New York: Markham Publishing Co., 1971.

LEVITAN, S. A. *The Great Society's Poor Law, A New Approach to Poverty.* Baltimore, Md.: The Johns Hopkins Press, 1969.

LOWI, T. *The End of Liberalism.* New York: W. W. Norton Co., 1969.

LUBOV, ROY. *The Progressives in the Slums.* Pittsburgh: University of Pittsburgh Press, 1962.

LUBOV, ROY. *The Professional Altruist.* Cambridge, Mass.: Harvard University Press, 1965.

MAGILL, R. S. "Federalism, Grants-in-Aid, and Social Welfare Policy." *Social Casework,* 1976, *57,* 625–636.

MARRIS, PETER, and MARTIN REIN. *Dilemmas of Social Reform.* New York: Atherton Press, 1967.

MENCHER, SAMUEL. *Poor Law to Poverty Program.* Pittsburgh: University of Pittsburgh Press, 1967.

MIDDLEMAN, RUTH R., and GALE GOLDBERG. *Social Service Delivery: A Structural Approach to Social Work Practice.* New York: Columbia University Press, 1974.

MOYNIHAN, DANIEL P. *Maximum Feasible Misunderstanding.* New York: Free Press, 1969.

MOYNIHAN, DANIEL P. *The Politics of a Guaranteed Income.* New York: Random House, 1973.

PECHMAN, JOSEPH A., HENRY J. AARON, and MICHAEL K. TAUSSIG. *Social Security: Perspectives for Reform.* Washington, D.C.: The Brookings Institute, 1968.

PERLMAN, ROBERT, and ARNOLD GURIN. *Community Organization and Social Planning.* New York: John Wiley and Sons, 1972.

PLOTNICK, ROBERT D. "Progress Against Poverty?", *The Social Welfare Forum.* New York: Columbia University Press, 1967, pp. 105–115.

ROMANSHYN, JOHN M. *Social Welfare.* New York: Random House, 1971.

SMITH, RUSSEL, and DOROTHY ZIETZ. *American Social Welfare Institutions.* New York: John Wiley and Sons, 1970.

STEINER, GILBERT Y. *Social Insecurity.* Chicago: Rand McNally, 1966.

STEINER, GILBERT. *The State of Welfare.* Washington, D.C.: The Brookings Institute, 1972.

TERRELL, P. *Planning, Participation, the Purchase of Service: The Social Impact of General Revenue Sharing in Seven Communities.* Los Angeles: Univ. of So. California Regional Research Institute in Social Welfare, 1975.

TRATTNER, WALTER I. *From Poor Law to Welfare State.* New York: Free Press of Glencoe, 1974, esp. pp. 248–266.

TRECKER, HARLEIGH B. (Ed.). *Goals for Social Welfare: 1973–1993.* New York: Association Press, 1973.

WHEELER, GERALD. "New Federalism and the Cities: A Double Cross," *Social Work,* 1974, *19* (6), 659–664.

WILENSKY, HAROLD. *The Welfare State and Equality.* Berkeley, Calif.: University of California Press, 1975.

WILENSKY, HAROLD, and CHARLES N. LEDLAUX. *Industrial Society and Social Welfare.* New York: Russell Sage Foundation, 1958.

ZALD, MAYER (Ed.). *Organizing for Community Welfare.* Chicago: Quadrangle Books, 1967.

II

Systems and Social Planning

Social planning is a systematic effort at systematic intervention. That says a lot in a few words. It implies that planners draw heavily on systems concepts and systems theories, primarily as they evolved in the disciplines of sociology and economics. In Part II the reader is introduced to a number of systems concepts, many of which are expanded in subsequent chapters of the book.

In Chapter 4, planning is described as a systematic process, beginning with problem definition and moving in ordered fashion through the development of a planning system or structure of relationships, goal and strategy development, program or plan implementation, and finally evaluation. The relationships between one step and another are explicated. Planning is seen as an analytic approach that requires the performance of interactional tasks systematically related to each other.

The systems approach, however, is more than being systematic. The analysis of the planning situation in systems terms requires an ability to assess the systemic environment within which planning takes place. In Chapter 5, both the planner's agency and the service providers whom the planner may be attempting to affect are discussed in the context of their task environments. The task environment is described as having four elements: the providers of resources (inputs) into the unit or organization in question; the consumers of that unit's outputs or services; competitors for both resources and consumers; and those organizations or societal mechanisms that serve to legitimate and provide auspices for the unit in question.

Chapter 6 continues this train of thought by focusing on ways in which the planner can exert leverage over a target system by controlling access to or the direction of the flow of resources to that system.

Chapters 7 and 8 draw on systems theory in a different way. They focus on approaches to the assessment of environmental issues and the problems to be addressed in planning at the community level. In addition to the task environment, approaches to assessing the climate around a particular issue are explored. Also the implications of supportive, indifferent, and antagonistic environments are spelled out in reference to the appropriateness of one or another intervention strategy.

A number of planning and assessment tools are described in some detail. These draw on earlier approaches to operations, research, and applied systems theory. They include the use of program planning and budgeting systems, benefit/cost analysis, social indicators, functional job analysis, and force field analysis.

The final chapter of Part II describes the way in which planners use PERT, a program evaluation review technique. PERT is useful in planning the allocation of personnel and materials over time since it specifies the relationships between activities and events. By sketching these relationships on a network chart, lines of interconnection between one activity and another become immediately visible. It thus becomes evident how changes or delays in one aspect of the planning system may have direct consequences on another.

Our discussion of systems concepts will, of course, not be completed in Part II. We will continue to explore their implications for other aspects of the planning process in later sections of the text.

4

Planning as Systematic Problem Solving

In daily usage, the term "planning" often refers to a systematic and ordered method of problem solving. The implication is that planning is or ought to be a rational and analytic method of intervention. This is certainly true. Planning is oriented toward the *solution* (or at least amelioration or reduction) *of problems*. It is *systematic* in that various alternatives are examined prior to selection of either the goals to be pursued or means used to achieve these goals. It is an *ordered* process because it requires the performance of a number of activities which occur in a logical sequence, even if they tend to be performed somewhat out of sequence and sometimes simultaneously.

Planning is a *method of social intervention,* because it aims at influencing or modifying a social course of events, a social process, or a social structure. As the term "intervention" implies, it is often an act of mediation, a coming between parties or between what is and what is intended. It is a *rational method* of intervention because planners often use technical and highly rational means to gather information, weigh the costs and benefits of one approach to their intervention over another, evaluate the impact of the intervention approach selected, and so on.

But while these perceptions are all true, they do not tell the whole truth. A great deal of the social planning that occurs in this country is not all that rational. Many critics of rational planning point out that cause-effect relationships are insufficiently known or understood in the social sciences to warrant the assumption that one can rationally select the means to achieve desired ends. Both goals and means tend to shift in response to experience. Moreover, the ends or goals of a planning process tend to reflect a set of values that have been arrived at through some process of political consensus. There may be little or nothing rational in these values particularly when they represent individual preferences and biases or the power of one party over another rather than public interest.

Much of what planners do, in fact, is in the nature of transactions—bargains arrived at, negotiations engaged in, organizing efforts and campaigns managed—that lead to agreements on both goals and means. Planning, then, requires the performance of both interactional and analytic tasks. These can be logically ordered into five phases or stages of the planning process and grouped as follows: (1) defining the problem; (2) building a structure or network of relationships; (3) formulating a policy and selecting from among alternative strategies; (4) implementing plans or programming; and (5) monitoring, feedback, and evaluation.

Analysis is required for the selection of feasible objectives and the design of appropriate means for accomplishing those objectives. Interaction is required in order to gather information, build appropriate networks for action and change, and concert the resources required in order to effectuate the desired change. The accompanying table summarizes this process.

Problem Definition: Consumer Populations, Service Agencies, and Interorganizational Relationships

It may seem unnecessary to point out that the way in which a problem is defined may be critical in determining the outcome of a planning process. Clearly it is not just what the planner looks at but how he or she assays the problem that affects the planner's working definition. In practice, most social planners focus on problems inherent in: (1) a specific consumer or potential consumer population; (2) a service provider or complex of providers; or (3) the interrelationships between providers or between consumers and providers. Concern with one problem often results in consideration of the other two. Nevertheless, it is helpful to examine what might happen if a planner focuses exclusively on one or another of these three.

FOCUS ON CONSUMER POPULATIONS

If a planner's attention is focused only on actual or potential consumer populations, for example, youth offenders, drug abusers, the aging, the problem will generally be defined in terms of the consumers' (a) debilitating or

ANALYTICAL AND INTERACTIONAL TASKS BY STAGES OF PROBLEM SOLVING*

Stage or Phase	Analytical Tasks	Interactional Tasks
1. Defining and conceptualizing the problem	Studying and describing a situation in preliminary terms, conceptualizing the problem. Assessing what opportunities and limits are set by the agency employing the practitioner and by other organizations for effecting change.	Receiving and/or eliciting information and preferences from those experiencing the problem and from other relevant actors.
2. Building a structure or network of relationships	Determining nature of relationship with various actors, means of communicating with them, and type of structures to be developed (committee, task force, forum, etc.). Selecting people for roles as experts, communicators, influencers, etc.	Establishing formal and informal communication and recruiting participants into selected structures and roles. Developing wider awareness of problem selectivity.
3. Formulating policy and laying out alternative strategies	Analyzing past efforts to deal with problem and developing alternative goals, strategies, and resource requirements. Selecting from among alternatives for recommendation to decision makers in light of opportunities and/or opposition from various quarters.	Promoting expression and exchange of preferences. Testing out feasibility of various alternatives with relevant actors. Assisting decision makers to weigh alternatives and to overcome resistances.
4. Implementing plans or programming	Specifying in detail what tasks need to be performed to achieve agreed-upon goal, by whom, with what resources and procedures.	Presenting recommended specifications to decision makers, obtaining their committments or resources, and putting the resources into action. Enhancing volunteer and staff resources through training.
5. Monitoring, feedback, and evaluation	Designing system for collecting, feeding back, and analyzing information on operations. Analyzing consequences of change, specifying adjustments needed and/or new problems which call for action and planning.	Obtaining data from designated sources. Receiving or eliciting information based on experience of actors. Communicating findings and recommendations to appropriate actors.

*This formulation was developed by staff of the Community Organization Curriculum Development Project at Brandeis University and was first described in an earlier work by Robert Perlman and Arnold Gurin, *Community Organization and Social Planning* (New York: John Wiley and Sons, 1972).

inappropriate attitudes, values, or perspectives; (b) inability to organize on their own behalf or effectively present their message to political decision makers; (c) lack of awareness of services, programs, and facilities; and (d) absence of marketable social and economic skills.

The way in which the problems of a population are defined can have a significant impact on the methods a planner will use to initiate the process of service delivery. If the problem is viewed as a lack of marketable skills, for example, the planner's emphasis may be placed on increasing opportunities for on-the-job training or on preparing people for new employment roles appropriate to their situation. If the problem is defined as lack of awareness of available facilities and programs, then planning efforts may be aimed at providing outreach services or establishing information and referral centers. If the problem is defined as inability to organize, efforts may be made to develop self-help associations, to recruit volunteers from among the population so as to increase representation on the boards of service agencies, and to mobilize members of the population for political and social pressure.

FOCUS ON SERVICE AGENCIES

Other planners prefer to address problems they perceive as the various service delivery systems. These systems include many of the institutionalized providers of service described in the previous chapter as well as an extra-professional system sometimes referred to as a "lay service network" or "natural helping" system. It is made up of a complex network of constantly changing informal relationships among friends, relatives, neighbors, self-help groups, and of church and civic organizations. In looking at both the professional and extra-professional systems, planners may concentrate on problems of (a) availability, (b) accessibility, (c) responsiveness and accountability, (d) effectiveness, and (e) efficiency.

The problem of availability is frequently related to a quantitative lack of resources or services. The planner may assume that the means for dealing with an actual or potential problem are known, but that not enough staff, money, time, and other resources are currently being directed or allocated to such services.

A problem may also be defined as one of accessibility. Services may be located inappropriately—even outreach programs may be inaccessible to the physically handicapped or other target groups. Transportation and housing programs may involve architectural barriers which do not take into account slowness of step, weakness of eyesight, and other physical infirmities. Recreation programs, while available, may not be located where older people can easily take advantage of them, or they may be offered at night when many older persons are fearful of venturing out. Some services are inaccessible because of social and psychological barriers. "They don't treat black people with dignity," may be a complaint.

Even if available and accessible, some programs may not be acceptable to potential consumers. They may not be properly responsive to consumers' perceptions of their needs or to their wishes and interests. Protective and semiprotective services and dependence-producing health care services may be unacceptable to the aging who prefer to maintain freedom and independence at the cost of deteriorating health.

Clients or consumers of services rarely have much of a voice in determining what kinds of services an agency will provide. Few service providers include mechanisms by which they are made accountable to actual or potential consumers. Task forces and advisory committees established to give clients a voice in agency policy are almost nonexistent. The scarcity of services and the paucity of information about them, along with the near or actual monopoly held by some providers, make the notion of consumer choice little more than pious hope in many communities.

Even when no mechanisms for consumer involvement exist, however, service providers may be held accountable by funders, planning and coordinating bodies, or entities conferring their auspices—boards, state, local, and federal government bodies. These are an agency's "input constituencies"; on the whole, these are much more powerful than generally unorganized and dependent client populations.

Unfortunately, even those services that are available, accessible, and responsive are frequently ineffective. Sometimes a program is ineffective because complementary services do not exist. Volunteer recruitment and training programs, for example, may be stymied because there is nowhere to refer volunteers for placement. Job training is not effective if there are no available jobs, or no accessible public transportation. Programs aimed at rehabilitating mental patients represent little more than wasted effort unless supportive services exist in the communities to which the patients are to be returned.

Efficiency is lowered: (a) when services are unnecessarily duplicative; (b) when they are so fragmented that the availability of one service is cancelled out by the unavailability and inaccessibility of a necessary complementary service; (c) when costly manpower, facilities, and techniques are used instead of less expensive approaches; (d) when economies of scale are such that independent, uncoordinated approaches cause heavy and unnecessary drains on a service provider's resources.

FOCUS ON COORDINATION AND INTERORGANIZATIONAL EXCHANGE

Many planning agencies are mandated to coordinate the services of public, voluntary, and private providers of professionalized services. For this reason many planners define problems in terms of uncoordinated and poorly integrated service structures. Frequently they attempt to create more comprehensive and integrated service networks such as ad hoc or semi-permanent task forces, action coalitions, study groups, and federated or council-type structures of "member agencies and associations" organized to maximize exchange potential.

Many locality-oriented social planners spend a great deal of time in performing liaison functions between service providers or in mediating disputes between them. If necessary, they may apply pressure to get providers to cooperate or coordinate their efforts. At other times, they will attempt to manage the flow of resources between service providers so as to increase their interdependence and collaborative efforts on behalf of mutual client populations. The activities of various organizations may, of course, be at times complementary, at other times contradictory, forcing the planner to make constant assessments and choices.

Choice is central to any notion of comprehensiveness. Comprehensiveness is not synonymous with increasing "everything." It does require selection of those service components that will offer a multiplicity of choices to clients and consumers. Efforts at comprehensiveness in planning may require the development of integrated area "master plans" which set long-range goals and short-term objectives. They may also require that planners conduct periodic needs assessments and evaluative studies, and provide for information exchanges and referral services.

INFORMATION AND CONCEPTUALIZATION

One of the first steps in trying to understand a problem is to gather information on it. What parameters can be used to describe the problem? Whom does it affect? How badly? At what cost? Who cares about it? Who does not? Where is there likely to be support (or opposition) for various means of attacking the problem? Many social planners have developed exceptional skill at describing problems. They conduct surveys or use survey and census data. They find useful information in program reports, in available social indicators. But description without conceptualization is not sufficient. In order to take appropriate action the planner must be able to formulate the problem so that he or she can act on it effectively, and this may require some familiarity with the social service literature.

If the planner has decided that interorganizational exchange, for example, is the crux of the problem, he or she might examine the writings of such sociologists as Litwak, Thompson, and Levine and White for concepts that might help him to better understand this process.* Each of the concepts found in the literature might be applied successively, each yielding different insights, and each suggesting further areas for exploration. Those concepts not found useful can then be discarded. The process calls for a continual reevaluation of the problem in light of new information and data.

*See suggested readings at the end of Chapters 5 and 6.

The reader should not be led to believe that problem conceptualization and definition is entirely an analytic process. Not at all. The planner who sits in his office, or in the library, or in city hall poring over fact sheets or examining theoretical constructs without reference to the values, interests, and concerns of other community people faces the danger of developing utopian schemes, and of completely missing the mark.

In finding out what the problem is, the planner should involve knowledgeable people both for purposes of gathering information and in order to provide support in later planning efforts. Without such interaction, many of these people might otherwise engage in obstructionist behavior. Further, involving knowledgeable, concerned, and influential community people helps the planner to maintain perspective: to see the problem from their point of view and give them a stake in the development of an action strategy.

The Community Mental Health Board staff whose start-up period was described in Chapter 1 spent two weeks examining available data, interviewing local people and agency administrators, just to get a feel of the range of issues and problems to which they might address their efforts. The knowledge gained from these interactions was fitted directly into the analytic processes that took place at staff meetings. The long list of problems identified by staff shows the complex interrelationship of the difficulties faced by certain populations in the community. The isolation of some ex-mental patients, for example, is interwoven with problems in education, health, housing, and other fields. The planner and his or her constituents must thus define the scope of their intervention. Choices must be made. These choices are in the final analysis human preferences. There are no planning "tools" that can be used to make decisions, even though some may inform the decision-making process. Such tools may help in estimating feasibility or degree of interest, but the final choices will have to be made through some interaction with the individuals and organizations that will be called upon to commit resources to accomplish the objectives selected. Planning choices, after all, must reflect their interests, their wants, and their commitment. This requires establishment of channels of communication and structures for sustained interaction.

Building a Structure of Relationships

LOCATING SUPPORT

The development of a structure of relationships or a communications network may be thought of as phase two of the planning process. It is not a single act nor even a series of acts that takes place during a discrete period of time. The formation of informal as well as formal planning structures begins with the data gathering and analytic process of problem formation and extends throughout each of the phases of the planning process. Initial data-gathering activities should result in information about those elements in the community that can be expected to support a project or to block it.

This was implicit in the planning approaches of all three illustrations in Chapter 1. It was explicit in the director's instructions to the CMH Board's staff to "look for who might support or block any future efforts on our part." The planner in Illustration I who effectively involved senior citizens in projects on their own behalf clearly saw the building of structured relationships as concomitant with fact finding and information gathering. He worked with and through existing organizations of senior citizens, transforming his relationship to them in the process, and eventually building several structures for continued fact finding and exchange of information—a cable TV show with an action reporter, guides to services with instructions on how to obtain them, a more comprehensive semi-autonomous information and referral service.

The numerous relationships developed by a planner need not always be based on cooperation and mutual trust. Whether the planner engages in a cooperative venture or feels constrained to develop a set of adversary relationships will always depend upon the nature of the environment around an issue or set of issues or problems.

COOPERATIVE, CAMPAIGN, AND CONTEST STRATEGIES

According to Roland Warren,* analysis of the environment that surrounds a planning issue will suggest appropriate strategies. In a consensual environment, one in which everyone is generally concerned about solving a particular problem, it makes most sense to develop a collaborative strategy. Here the planner's task is to bring relevant parties together in order to explore the facts of the case, to reconcile viewpoints via reasoned discussion, and finally to reach a decision to collaborate or act upon the problem in a certain manner.

Frequently, the planner plays an enabling or facilitating role. He or she may act as a guide or catalyst, as a convener, a mediator a consultant, or even a coordinator. The planner may be a staff member or the leader of a committee, council, task force, or even a federation of interested parties. The planner may work toward an organizational structure that is formal and explicit, such as a commission or an agency board, or informal and ad hoc—perhaps an action group that serves for four or five weeks to raise money for a specific project.

The choice of structure is dependent not only on whether there is consensus in the community, but on the nature of the organizations or groups among which the planner is trying to establish communication. Linkages and exchanges between formal organizations generally require formal committees,

*See Roland Warren, "Types of Purposive Community Change," in the reference section at the end of this chapter.

councils, or federations. Sometimes they require only ad hoc groupings; at other times they need more long-range, long-term federated or interorganizational linkages. In working with informal organizations or voluntary associations and population groups, it may be more appropriate to develop loose, informal relationships between key persons in each organization.

At times, committees and task forces may be lopsided in that some members represent only themselves and their viewpoints, whereas others are the chosen delegates of certain organizations, associations, or agencies. The development of an effective organizational structure will depend in part on the planner's skill in achieving the right balance among participants. Often the planner will attempt to establish a variety of communications or action networks. Planners' reasons for using different structures are discussed more fully throughout the text.

The planner's behavior with regard to establishing communications networks may vary considerably if there is dissension or disagreement on either the issue or the strategy. He or she may employ what Warren calls a contest or conflict-oriented strategy, in which all efforts to arrive at consensus may be abandoned. Instead the planner may band together whatever forces exist in the community to support his or her point of view and launch a campaign against the opposition. The social planner as protagonist may need to use legislative action, financially coercive measures, or political pressures to attain "victory."

When a community is indifferent to the planner's objectives or statement of a problem, it may be necessary to devise a strategy for converting apathy to interest, and opposition to agreement or support. The first planner in Chapter 1, for example, used a "campaign" strategy in which educational techniques, mass media, endorsements of influential people, and testimonials were used to seek agreement on a particular perspective. In this case the planner will perform the role of persuader, promoter, salesman. Frequently, he or she will form ad hoc committees and voluntary associations designed to operate on a temporary basis; with some evidence of success they may be converted into more formal federations, councils, or permanent interorganizational committees.

Work on phase two of course overlaps with the third phase of the planning process—formulating objectives and strategy development.

Formulating Objectives and Developing a Strategy

FORMULATING A STRATEGY

A planner's strategy includes both the objective to be reached and the means toward the accomplishment of that goal. It can be formally stated, or implicit in a planner's behavior or the activities in which the planning organization engages.

The selection of a strategy also implies that decisions be made about the target of intervention: Is it to be a particular population in need? A service organization or network of service organizations? The private employment sector? Will it be limited to a particular geographic neighborhood, a total city, or a broader region? Is it to be limited to a particular sex, age, or ethnic group? Is the intervention to include a broad range of manpower services and approaches—job recruitment, job placement, job development?

Under whose auspices should the new service program be undertaken— the planner's agency alone, some other planning organization or service agency within the community, an ad hoc grouping of concerned citizens or business people, a newly established federation of organizations or agencies, a new citizen action group? How is the project or program to be funded? Will federal funds be required? Where will local matching funds be drawn from? What should be the mix of governmental and private funds? Should some of the consumer populations or client groups be taxed or charged a fee for service? Should they be paid in order to induce them to accept services?

In developing strategy, the planner should be concerned with the value implications of the various alternatives before him.

FEASIBILITY

The feasibility of accomplishing the objectives through another service deliverer must also be examined. Under what circumstances will the planner be more likely to achieve at least a part of his goals? At what cost? How rational or responsible is one approach versus another? The process of policy analysis requires a continual ends-means analysis in which ends and means are viewed as a chain of interaction. The planner's analysis aims at distinguishing between them and showing their interrelationships.

Strategic analysis also requires an understanding of the interaction between the various components of the social system that affect the problem. Who will benefit from a particular approach? Who will bear the costs? To what extent are costs and benefits interrelated? What resources are available to bear the costs of intervention? Which resources are renewable—for example, good will, or legislated funds and which are one-time benefits?

The process of strategy development is dependent in great part on the inputs of various constituencies. To assure support during the programming phase, the planner must involve members of both the formal and informal networks that he or she has constructed throughout previous planning phases. Effective strategic analysis and formation is thus as dependent on the planner's interactional as well as on his or her analytic skills.

Program Implementation

Frequently, the formulation of goals and development of strategy are only partially accomplished prior to the programming phase of the planning process. There are many who argue that the planner's role should end with program development, and that program implementation should be left to operational staff and administrators. The lines between program planning, development, and implementation are fine, and often quite obscure. Planning that is limited only to strategy development may result in abortive intervention efforts. To some extent, the planner must be involved in an on-going relationship with the structures he has developed in order to facilitate program implementation.

Program implementation involves mobilization of resources and their delivery to target populations. This requires logistical analysis and the continued application of planning throughout the programming phase. While planners and planning agencies may be charged with managing the flow of resources, the actual implementation of services or the creation of new facilities and programs will be undertaken by service providers and other organized groups within the community. The planner's task may thus be designated as "facilitating and monitoring the implementation process."

Monitoring, Feedback, and Evaluation

At the lowest level of involvement, the planner retains a relationship to program implementation as an overseer of the monitoring and feedback processes. These are continuous activities. Monitoring refers to a way of checking on the relationship between means and ends in the programming process. If the means are unequal to the task, they must be adjusted. If the ends are unrealistic, they need revision. Feedback refers to a systematic way of gathering information to be evaluated so as to make monitoring possible. Feedback requires an ongoing system of interaction, whereas monitoring efforts require analysis of data inputs and decisions about modifications in means or ends.

Both monitoring and feedback are components of the evaluation process. Evaluation, however, tends to be more comprehensive. It focuses on what happened, how it happened, and whether or not it should have happened. Although evaluation of planning activities is used by different groups for different purposes, its underlying rationale is almost always to receive information for future action. Findings can be used to improve ongoing planning operations, to modify, expand or terminate planning activities, or to justify current investments in terms of future gains.

The benefits of proper evaluation may be justification enough for the efforts invested. Yet social planners may have little choice over whether to evaluate or not, or what to evaluate. The requirements of a grantor, or of the organization employing the planner, and the expectations of others involved in the planning process may determine the nature of the evaluation. In general, planners evaluate planning inputs, planning throughputs, and planning outputs.

INPUT EVALUATION

Input evaluations place emphasis on the resources and processes used to accomplish planning results. Planning activities may be evaluated on the basis of the information gathered to establish planning objectives, the sophistication of the method used to gather the data, the expertise of the planners and others involved, the extensiveness of the involvement of relevant others (service providers, consumers, community influentials), the amount of money and other resources expended. Cost may be examined in terms of both time and money. The efficiency of the planning process may be a major concern.

THROUGHPUT EVALUATION

The evaluation of throughputs is often based on information gathered through the monitoring and feedback processes. Expository reports in nature, throughput evaluations focus on what happened and how it happened. They may include examination of the way in which problems were defined and objectives set, the nature of the planning structure built, and the implementation of the planning process. They describe the planner's efforts and those of others but do not purport to measure the extent to which objectives were met and at what costs. These concerns are the focus of output evaluations.

OUTPUT EVALUATION

The evaluation of outputs places emphasis on results—in terms of changes in the consumer population, in a service organization or complex of providers, or in the relationships among providers or among providers and consumers. Output evaluations begin by examining the planning objectives. They derive from the definition of the problem or problems the planning process was intended to attack.

Output studies are perhaps the most difficult of all three to conduct properly. They often require a level of sophistication rarely available to planners. Their cost may be prohibitive, rivaling or even exceeding the cost of designing the plan itself.

When inputs are related to outputs, the emphasis shifts to an examination of the relationship of costs to planning benefits. Cost/benefit ratios can be used to examine the relative merits of alternative planning approaches. This technique can be used to examine the extent to which a goal might be met by varying the amount of the investment; or, by keeping the desired benefit constant, the costs of alternative means toward goal accomplishment can be measured or projected.

Like the other phases of the planning process, evaluation requires the planner to engage in both analytic and interactional activities. Evaluation may require convening the original network of interested parties through whom the planner was able to identify the specific problem. It is not sufficient for the planner to be satisfied that something went well, or aware of where something went poorly. The other interested parties—those directly and indirectly affected by the problem or the intervention strategy—should also be consulted in evaluating the program or intervention strategy. It is at this point that they or the planner may discover new facets of the problem to be attached on new problems.

A Spiraling Process

Perhaps the reader has noted that the process of evaluation is very similar and in some ways identical to the process of problem identification and definition. In fact, the planning process seems to have gone full circle—from problem definition to the development of a structure, the assessment of policies and development of a strategy, through plan implementation, and monitoring, feedback and evaluation and back again to problem definition.

Although the planning process has been presented in a linear sequence, it might be best to think of it as a spiraling process in which the planner may be engaged in any one or all five of the phases at the same time. In essence, this is a logical description rather than a temporal one. No planning process follows sequentially from one phase to the other, although for analytic purposes it is useful to view it in terms of stages. The planner may enter the process at any phase and may be engaged simultaneously in structure building, policy analysis, plan implementation, problem definition, or evaluation.

Review: Planning as a Systematic Approach to Problem Solving

The planning process begins with the way in which a problem is defined. Some planners direct their efforts at correcting for some deficiency or inability in a particular population. Others may focus on deficiencies in the delivery of services expressed in terms of lack of availability, inaccessibility, nonresponsiveness, ineffectiveness, and inefficiency. Still others view the crux of a problem as inadequate coordination or relationships between providers and consumers.

Problem definition, however, is only the first of five stages in the planning process, which may be outlined as: (1) defining the problem; (2) building a structure of relationships; (3) formulating policy and developing a strategy; (4) implementing a program; and (5) monitoring, feedback, and evaluation. Success at any stage requires both analytical and interactional skills.

SUPPLEMENTARY QUESTIONS AND ACTIVITIES

The following activities may be helpful to the reader as he or she progresses through other chapters in this text.

1. Review the stages or phases in the planning process. In view of your own experiences, do they seem logical? You might want to contrast this description of the planning process with the concepts discussed by some of the authors in the reference section. Some noteworthy approaches appear in (a) Davidoff and Reiner, "Choice Theory of Planning;" (b) John Freedman, "The Transactive Style of Planning;" (c) Alfred Kahn, "Theory and Practice of Social Planning," Chapter 3; (d) Charles Lindblom, "The Science of Muddling Through;" (e) Morris and Binstock, "Feasible Planning for Social Change;" and (f) Franklin M. Zweig and Robert Morris, "The Social Planning Design Guide."*
   Which of these articulates most closely with your own approach to planning? Lay out a sequence of steps for planning which you find personally useful. If you currently have a planning assignment, think through what you do on the job. If you do not, try to devise a planning sequence you would be comfortable using. Use this sequence as a personal checklist for the future and modify it when the need arises. Review your sequence periodically over the years to be certain you're doing all the things you consider important.

2. Develop a personal bibliography on planning. Don't be limited by the items found in this book. Look to the literature of allied professions, such as business, urban planning, and regional planning. Are there libraries and resource centers in your community that might be of help?
   Put your name on the list of one or two clearinghouses and information

---

*These and other articles describing stages or steps in the planning process are found either in the Cox reader or in the collection by Gilbert and Specht listed in the reference section.

centers. The National Clearinghouse for Improving the Management of Human Services, for example, publishes a journal of human services abstracts and a bibliography series. Write to Project Share, P.O. Box 2309, Rockville, Maryland. Are there other clearinghouses in your area of interest? Alcoholism? Mental health? Corrections? Check them out. Your state agency or federal regional center should be helpful.

Recommended Readings

PERLMAN, ROBERT, and ARNOLD GURIN. *Community Organization and Social Planning.* New York: John Wiley and Council on Social Work Education, 1972, chaps. 3, 4, 8 and 9.
Perlman and Gurin describe the practice of social planning and some of the problems inherent in that practice. This was a landmark book in that it contrasted social planning with community organizing in an effort to provide greater understanding of practice problems, of the ways in which those problems are addressed, and of the growing body of knowledge that can contribute to more effective solutions. A major thesis is that the organizational context of planning will significantly determine the tasks of the practitioner. The authors examine the characteristics of three major organizational contexts: the voluntary association; the direct service agency; and the planning organization. Chapter 4 presents and discusses the basic "analytic interactional" planning model which is elaborated upon in this chapter.

Suggestions for Further Reading

COX, FRED, et al. (Eds.). *Strategies in Community Organization, A Reader.* Itasca, Ill.: F. Peacock Publishing Co., 1973 edition.
DAVIDOFF, PAUL, and THOMAS A. REINER. "A Choice Theory of Planning." *Journal of the American Institute of Planners,* May, 1962.
DEMONE, HAROLD W. "The Limits of Rationality in Planning." *Community Mental Health Journal.* Winter, 1965.
ECKLEIN, JOAN LEVIN, and ARMAND LAUFFER. *Community Organizers and Social Planners.* New York: John Wiley and Council on Social Work Education, 1972. See especially chaps. 1, 2, and 8.
EMERY, F. E., and E. TRYST, "The Causal Texture of Organization Environments." *Human Relations,* February, 1965.
FRIEDMAN, JOHN. *Retracking America: A Theory of Societal Planning.* New York: Doubleday Anchor Books, 1973.
GILBERT, NIEL, and HARRY SPECHT (Eds.). *Planning for Social Welfare: Issues, Models, and Tasks.* Englewood Cliffs, N.J.: Prentice-Hall, Inc., 1976.
HORTON, GERALD T. (Ed.). *Readings in Human Services Planning.* Atlanta, Ga.: The Research Group, 1975.
KAHN, ALFRED J. *Theory and Practice of Social Planning.* New York: Russell Sage Foundation, 1969. (Chapter 5 appears in the Gilbert and Specht text.)

KRAMER, RALPH, and HARRY SPECHT (Eds.). *Readings in Community Organization Practice.* Englewood Cliffs, N.J.: Prentice-Hall, Inc., 1973 edition.

LASSEY, WILLIAM R. *Planning in Rural Environments.* New York: McGraw-Hill Book Company, 1977.

LINDBLOM, CHARLES. "The Science of Muddling Through." *Public Administration Review,* Spring, 1959. (This also appears in Gilbert and Specht).

MAYER, ROBERT. *Social Planning and Social Change.* Englewood Cliffs, N.J.: Prentice-Hall, Inc., 1972.

MICHAEL, DONALD N. *On Learning to Plan and Planning to Learn.* San Francisco: Jossey-Bass, 1973.

MORRIS, ROBERT, and ROBERT H. BINSTOCK. *Feasible Planning for Social Change.* New York: Columbia University Press, 1965.

ROSSI, PETER. "Theory, Research and Practice in Community Organization," in *Social Science and Community Action,* Charles P. Adrian et al., (Eds.) Michigan State University Press, 1960.

ROTHMAN, JACK. *Planning and Organizing for Social Change: Action Principles From Social Science Research.* New York: Columbia University Press, 1974.

SCHEFF, JANET. *The Social Planning Process: Conceptualization and Methods.* University of Puerto Rico Press, 1976.

WARREN, ROLAND L. "Types of Purposive Community Change at the Community Level." Brandeis University, *Papers in Social Welfare,* No. 11, Waltham, Massachusetts, 1965. Reprinted in Roland L. Warren, *True, Love and Social Change.* Chicago: Rand McNally, 1971.

ZWEIG, FRANKLIN, and ROBERT MORRIS. "The Social Planning Design Guide." *Social Work,* April, 1966. (This also appears in the Kramer and Specht text).

5

Resource Control
and the Planner's Leverage

Service and Service Providers

Planners are well aware of the fact that they would have little leverage over those they hope to influence without access to or control over the flow of resources. To begin with, planners need money, time, ideas, and other resources just to do their jobs. Equally important is the fact that those agencies, government structures, and other organizations that social planners attempt to influence are also dependent upon resources. No organization can accomplish its mission without access to the minimally required resources. A system's outputs cease—or are severely disrupted—shortly after its inputs are terminated. A change in the number or kind of resources may also influence an organization to expand or modify its programs or service.

THE AGENCY AS PROVIDER OF SERVICE

Because so many of the social services in this country are provided by social agencies, and all of them depend on outside suppliers for their essential resources, planners often find themselves attempting to influence these agencies indirectly by influencing the source or flow of resources to them. Some planners, in fact, may spend the bulk of their efforts to affect the policies, programs, and procedures of these agencies by redirecting the resources available to them. This requires an understanding of how organizations behave and why, and what inducements might be effective in bringing about change.

Social planners, however, are not interested in change for change's sake. Their interest in effecting changes in service agencies and the complex system of interrelationships among those agencies derives from their concerns with the development and delivery of human services. Their relationship to social agencies and other institutionalized or professional service providers is based on their assessment of (1) the availability of services to designated populations; (2) the accessibility of these services; (3) the responsiveness of providers to the interests and wishes of its actual or potential consumer population; (4) the extent to which the available services are effective or efficiently provided; and (5) the extent to which the service providers hold themselves and are held accountable to their consumer populations.

An overriding question for many planners is whether there are adequate resources to assure that human services are available, accessible, responsive, effective, efficient, and accountable. A second question focuses on who has access to those resources necessary for the provision of services, and how they can be better concerted to accomplish the objectives of a more equitable service system. Are there means by which the planner can influence the way resources flow to agencies, and consequently the way agencies provide services, and for whom?

RESOURCES

Discussion of agency resources are frequently limited to capital or physical facilities and to financing. But resources can be *any of the commodities or means which permit an organization to accomplish its objectives.* While money and credit and physical facilities may be essential to a particular service, they certainly are not sufficient in and of themselves. Money is overly sufficient, for example, to purchase the manpower resources with the requisite knowledge and skill required for successful practice.

While other resources may be more ephemeral and elusive than money or facilities, they are just as essential to organizational survival and service provision. These include political influence; social standing and prestige; charisma, popularity, and esteem; legitimacy and legality; personal or organizational energy. These resources are conferred by individuals and organizations. Though not easily purchased, they may be exchanged for other resources.

The greater the monopoly of any supplier over resources, the greater the power of that supplier over the consumer—unless the consumer also maintains control of some resources essential to the supplier. Organizations are dependent on various elements in their environment for the input of resources. This dependence is often greatest when an organization is unable easily to obtain resources from alternative elements of the environment. Planners who can direct the flow of essential resources to and from an agency, or manage the exchange of resources between organizations can be particularly influential.

On Feasibility and the Use of Resource Pathways

ANATOMY OF FEASIBILITY

This term was coined by Robert Morris and Robert Binstock in their book, *Feasible Planning for Social Change*. The feasibility of any planning objective, they point out, varies according to the nature and extent of the influence possessed by the planner. Influence is dependent on access to resources. Often, for example, the problem before the planner is to overcome an organization's resistance to policy change. Planners must be aware not only of the forces within the target organization that will resist change, but the kinds of resources that can actually be mobilized and the methods by which those resources can be used to influence key decision makers.

If the planner's objectives (Morris and Binstock call this a *preference goal*) are in fundamental conflict with the primary concerns of an agency's dominant faction, the planner's objective is not feasible without some revision. However the planner's objective is rephrased, there continues to be the likelihood that there will be some resistance to the planner's change objective. Overcoming resistance requires effective utilization of resources.

TYPES OF RESOURCES

As has been suggested, resources that may be available include such elements as money and credit; professional knowledge and expertise; personal energy; popularity, esteem, and charisma; social standing; political influence; control over information; and legitimacy and legality. However, resources by themselves are of little value unless the planner can effectively utilize them. Morris and Binstock talk about "pathways to influence," including obligation, friendship, rational persuasion, selling, coercion, and inducement.

PATHWAYS

Without clear access to decision makers in the target agency, it is exceedingly difficult to employ resources in such a way as to influence its leadership. Much of the planner's success will depend on his or her skill in managing the resources and negotiating a pathway to the decision maker.

Typically, planners expend a great deal of effort on rational persuasion; sometimes they resort to "selling" or calling in a community representative with some social standing or political influence. They may also try to cash in on previous obligations or on friendships. In seeking to influence policy makers, planners rely, perhaps too heavily, on their expertise, knowledge, access to information, their personal energy, and on the esteem in which they may be held. These resources are effective only when the dominant faction in an agency is open to rational persuasion or selling. Unfortunately, the planner may too often rely on such approaches when they are clearly ineffective with certain decision makers.

While the ability to control appropriate resources is essential to the planner's success, his or her capacity to do so may be severely limited. Resources such as money and credit, political influence, legitimacy and legality may be unavailable to the planner. In fact, the possibility of his or her success may so threaten existing relationships that pressure will be brought to bear on the planner or the planner's agency to pull back or to go more slowly.

The Agency and Its Environments

Many planners attempt to influence a service agency's policies—that is, the way it uses or allocates its resources—indirectly, by influencing the suppliers and consumers of those resources. This requires a clear understanding of the agency's relationship to its environment.

While all organizations exist simultaneously in a number of environments, they are most significantly affected by their *task environments.* According to Levine and White,* a task environment is composed of those elements in the general environment which most directly impinge on the agency's ability to accomplish its objectives: (1) its *suppliers* of resources (i.e., personnel, funds, equipment, and work space); (2) the *consumers* of the agency's output or services, including both the users of those services and the distributors of the services; (3) *competitors* for both resources and service markets; and (4) those *regulatory groups* which provide auspices, legitimation, domain consensus, or legislative rules and procedures regarding the agency's operations.

SUPPLIERS

Suppliers are those organizations, groups, and individuals who provide an organization with the resources necessary to produce its product, give its services, or maintain itself. A state agency, for example, might be the conduit through which the local agency receives funds or special services for the aging. A Community Mental Health Board or a United Fund might be an alternative or additional supplier of funds. A local volunteer bureau might be the supplier

*See the reference section at the end of this chapter.

of supplementary manpower. A nearby university might provide the local agency with the necessary expertise to assess a need, evaluate a program, or provide a new service.

CONSUMERS

Generally, people needing service are defined as an agency's actual or potential consumers. These direct recipients of an agency's service or product might be clients in a welfare agency, patients in a nursing home or hospital, users of a bus service for the handicapped, members of a Golden Age Club, or participants in a city recreation department's summer crafts program. In some cases, one agency is the consumer and subsequently the distributor of another agency's services. An agency that receives technical assistance from a welfare council, or volunteers from a volunteer bureau, is the consumer of another's services. It also distributes those services to another user population.

COMPETITORS

In any situation in which there is a scarcity of resources, there is also likely to be competition for those resources. A limited supply of volunteer manpower or of funds for services to the developmentally disabled may cause competition among service providers. Conversely, when services are in abundant supply and there is insufficient demand, agencies may compete for consumers. While situations in which supply exceeds demand in the human services are rare, there are occasions, for example, when recreation or group work agencies compete for participants and members or nursing homes for patients. Some manpower agencies have been known to compete for trainees with the greatest potential for rehabilitation and placement. At times, agencies compete for a particular clientele with certain attributes based on racial, ethnic, or socioeconomic characteristics.

REGULATORY GROUPS

Most institutional providers are responsible to boards of directors, legislative bodies, governmental agencies, or other bodies under whose auspices they operate. At the local level, an agency's board of directors may provide it with both auspices and legitimacy. In addition, some agencies are regulated by local, state, or national agencies. For example, family service agencies are licensed and legitimated through voluntary affiliation with the Family Service Association of America, which also imposes certain regulatory constraints on its member agencies. Many other voluntary agencies, such as Jewish Community Centers, YMCAs, and settlement houses, are also responsible to regulatory groups or those providing auspices. It is not unusual for them to be further regulated by local health and welfare councils.

All agencies under governmental auspices as well as many private agencies must meet governmental standards in order to continue to operate. Nursing homes and convalescent centers, for example, are periodically inspected and licensed by state agencies. An Area Agency on Aging must be responsive not only to its local advisory panel or board of directors but also to the state agency which established it. It is regulated in part by procedures and guidelines established by the Administration on Aging which are derivatives of the 1973 amendments to the Older Americans Act. Area plans must be consistent with state plans, and state plans must be consistent with federal regulations established in accordance with the Commission on Aging.

Relationships between an agency and the various elements of its task environment can be complex. Each element in that task environment—suppliers, consumers, competitors, and regulatory groups—operates within its own task environment. All are thus engaged in a constant shift in demands and expectations. Each agency and the members of its organizational set are further embedded in the larger environmental context, which includes society's complex of norms, values, and cultural patterns, as well as larger organizations and groups which may not affect the particular agency directly, but which may do so indirectly by affecting other elements in its task environment.

MULTIPLE TASK ENVIRONMENTS

To complicate matters further, most agencies have multiple objectives and thereby live in a plurality of task environments. Consequently, in attempting to influence an agency, the planner must seek out those elements in the agency's task environment that are likely to have the greatest impact on the agency. In an earlier day, many social agencies were dependent on a primary or single source of funding. The planner who could influence the flow of those funds might have considerable influence over policies, especially if those dollars could be converted into other needed resources—public acceptance, appropriate technology, needed manpower. Today, however, most agencies have multiple funding sources. The planner is often hard put to know which funding source to influence.

The complexities facing the planner as well as the agency administrator were highlighted at a recent University of Michigan symposium on grant writing for agency administrators. "It was less exciting, but easier in the early '60s," reported the director of a family agency. "We used to get an allocation each year from the United Fund. We could expect more money if the campaign was successful or if we were good at selling a new idea or expansion of service. Of course, this was pretty risky too. We had to do what we were doing as well as possible and hope the funding source would remain stable or expand. Then came the poverty program, the state's mental health act, and now all kinds of purchase-of-service agreements from the public welfare people. We're getting our money from seven different state and federal agencies. The wider the variety of financial inputs, of course, the more interesting things we can do. And if we lose one source of funding, there are still plenty of others. We can make readjustments without too much difficulty."

"It's not always that easy," disagreed the director of a neighborhood service agency. "First of all, multiple funding means you become accountable to many masters. You fill out more forms, you are subject to more regulations. Still, the temptation of new funds to do significant new things is pretty strong. We first enlarged our operation with the development of a state-financed community mental health center in a public housing project. Later, we got a $600,000 grant from the city's public housing administration. From a $100,000 operation, we grew to a payroll of over $1 million a year. Then the city lost a sizable chunk of its federal funds, cut the housing program, and we had to eliminate almost fifty percent of our employees in one fell swoop."

"Shifts in funding priorities have affected our operation, too," added the administrative director of a nursing home. "The availability of Medicare and Medicaid funds changed the nature of our patient population. Then new restrictions were put on Medicaid, and we had to change our services or lose money. Now if those planners concerned with the aging are really serious about developing personal care services, we're going to have to try to get people rehabilitated enough to be able to manage on their own in the community. Frankly, I don't think we can do it. It doesn't matter how much money they put into it. Where are we going to find the qualified staff?"

"He'll do it, all right," observed a planner, "with or without qualified staff. If he doesn't, others will. There will be plenty of people ready to take the dollar to provide services even if they haven't got the organization or the manpower to do it. That nursing home administrator will be hustling against his competitors in no time."

Despite this planner's insistence that competition for available funds would be a strong inducement to change, this is not always the case. For one thing, some agencies may perceive change as inconsistent with their missions. For another, as the nursing home administrator pointed out quite correctly, shifts in one element of the task environment may not always be complemented by shifts in other elements. Thus, for example, the availability of nurses and paramedicals supplied by training agencies may in no way correlate with the availability of funds to support the expansion of nursing home services.

Nevertheless, the planner quoted above was not being entirely unrealistic. "If we have to, and I'm sure we will," he added later, "we'll train nursing home staffs so that they can do the jobs that we're supplying them with money to do." This, however, brings up another sensitive issue: To what extent should planners target funds or projects to agencies that do not currently have the technical or manpower resources to provide specified services? Do planners have a responsibility for helping agencies deal with their internal manpower problems when they press those agencies to expand services or to provide new ones?

It is no secret that the supply of trained manpower has not kept up with the phenomenal growth in most of the human services. For this reason, planners have increasingly addressed themselves to the need to develop new types of professional and ancillary personnel, and to the need for in-service training of currently employed personnel. The ability of a professional agency to provide a needed service may require a mix of professional personnel from a variety of occupations with nonprofessionals, sub- or paraprofessionals, volunteers, interns, and lay care-givers. The mix itself may result in a new or changed service.

Planners need more than skill in assessing resources available to service agencies. They must also be prepared to balance those resources so that they complement one another rather than cancelling each other out. If funds are available, the planner may have to concentrate on the development or the importation of personnel with knowledge or technical expertise. If personnel are already available, he may have to concentrate on finding new sources of funding. When both funds and knowledge are available, but a service agency is still unwilling to provide a necessary service, the planner may try to induce the flow of client referrals to more willing social agencies. In the sense that clients are required for an agency to provide its service, they too may be seen as resources.

Resources and the Planner's Leverage

INFLUENCING THE FLOW OF RESOURCES FROM SUPPLIERS

The planner's leverage over service providers may be increased to the extent that he or she has control over the flow of resources needed by them. This may require an indirect approach in which the planner tries to influence one organization so as ultimately to influence another. Most service agencies, as has been noted, are dependent upon a variety of individuals, organizations, and groups for the input of resources and for their auspices or legitimacy.

"When we can't influence an agency directly through rational persuasion or through offering them new sources of funds," reported a planner, "we may try to apply a little leverage obliquely. We'll try to influence some group or organization that has control over resources they need badly." She went on to give examples of this technique: (1) changing the regulations of a state agency so that greater credit was given to agencies for rehabilitation rather than custodial services; (2) getting a university's School of Social Work continuing education program to emphasize community-based services in a seminar on grant writing for administrators of nursing homes and custodial facilities; (3) specifying in a milage proposal that fifty percent of all new library funds would go to services for the disabled; (4) consulting with an architectural firm on the design of a new hospital wing for the elderly, thereby influencing the flow of services to the elderly patients as well as the patterns of interaction among service agencies within that wing.

A planner may also attempt to influence other agencies that compete with an organization for resources, and those populations and organizations that are the actual or potential consumers of its outputs. These competitors and consumers may be other service providers. For example, a home for the aged may utilize the services of a recreation department or of a group work agency. To the extent that recreation services become a crucial component of the nursing home, and the nursing home is dependent on the recreation department to provide that service, the recreation department becomes the supplier.

Relationships between providers and consumers may result in modified behavior by one or another of the parties to the exchange. A rehabilitation agency, for instance, may provide diagnostic services to a manpower agency concerned with retraining older adults with occupational or social disabilities. In the process of interaction, modifications may be necessary so that policies of the consumer and the provider become more compatible. This may require mutual readjustment or capitulation by one of the collaborating agencies.

At times, planners are successful when they increase competition rather than engage in interagency collaboration. "The Substance Abuse Center has been providing emergency services for three years to kids in the northeast section of town. We couldn't get them either to expand to other neighborhoods or to add a counseling and referral program," explains a planner. "It wasn't until we threatened to fund the Catholic Family Service to do just that, that they got interested. They didn't want competitors for prestige especially from an 'establishment agency.' " Not only can agencies sometimes be induced to change or modify their services through the threat of competition, but actual competition may itself induce experimentation and innovation.

"Up until now," explains a planner from the Southwest, "we funded agencies on the basis of the programs they promised to provide. Now we're instituting a new approach by which they will be funded not just on the basis of what they say they'll do, but by a formula which takes into account the number of contact hours with clients. In a sense, we've shifted the direction of competition. The old way, they competed with each other for program resources. Now they'll also be competing for clients. The clients, not just the funders, will be involved in deciding which services are good."

While facilitating exchanges or competition among service providers may increase the likelihood that clients will receive better services, there are times when social planners will choose a radically different approach—that of enabling clients themselves to increase their influence over service providers. Providers are not always responsive to the interests of consumer groups, nor do they always consider themselves accountable to them. Generally speaking, clients have little voice and little influence over agency policy.

Warren points out that clients are usually viewed as an agency's "output constituency." A constituency is any group, organization, or collectivity to which an organization has some form of obligation. In the case of a service agency, the output constituency is generally the group to which the agency is obliged to provide service. "Input constituencies" are those groups or organizations which an agency sees as having a legitimate influence over it in determining policies and programs. These constituencies may include agency suppliers as well as providers of auspices and regulatory goups.

Output constituencies are rarely as powerful as input constituencies. However, agencies cannot stay in business without clients. For this reason, some planners employ a strategy of converting client populations from output to input constituencies. The voucher payment mechanism, for example, turns the client into a funder. Alone, one client may have little influence, but to the extent that they make their interests felt collectively, clients using voucher payments can influence agency service through market mechanisms.

Consumer education programs and effective information and referral systems enhance the potential client's choice. In other instances, planners may support the development of self-help groups like neighborhood associations and others made up of persons with common problems. As these groups become aware of service alternatives, they may exert collective influence through demands for certain services and rejection of others. The history of social action in the 1960s is replete with attempts by clients to exert political pressure and "consumer control" over professionalized service providers. Consumer input has been built into most of the social legislation of the 1970s.

Planners can also help consumers to redefine themselves as providers by formalizing aspects of the lay service network. Self-help groups, volunteers, and "junior partner associations" are examples of consumer organizations that engage in cooperative or collaborative ventures with professionalized providers.

INFLUENCING REGULATIONS

Frequently the most influential elements in an agency's task environment are those which have regulatory power. When a planning, coordinating, or funding body sets up standards or guidelines for service agency performance, it performs a direct regulatory function. When it trains agency boards or mandates greater power to professional organizations that exert influence over agency services, it is operating indirectly. When it influences the policies of agencies like health and welfare councils and United Funds, or achieves agreements on policies or regulations with other federal, state, and local agencies, it exerts its influence both indirectly and directly.

"Let's face it," argues a health planner, "we're not in this alone. There's not much sense in trying to develop an independent policy on appropriate services without closely articulating that policy with the State Department of Mental Health and the local Community Mental Health Board. Mental health regulations affect which people stay in state hospitals, which are released, and which ones will be provided supportive services in the community.

"The welfare people are in on this too. It's absolutely crazy for the mental health people to operate under one policy and the public welfare people to operate under another. After all, the welfare people support many ex-mental patients in the community. In our state, they've got the licensing power over group home care facilities, day care centers for older people, and even some nutritional programs. We've been delegated licensing power over other nutritional programs, and the mental health people can license certain kinds of after-care facilities. What with competing regulations and guidelines coming down from the federal and state offices, it's our job in the Department of Public Health to try to promote some consistency at the local level."

Planners Use Their Leverage: Illustrations from Practice

COMMON EFFORTS WITH COMMON CLIENTS

While influencing the providers or consumers of resources will engage a great deal of the planner's time, an equal amount of energy may be needed to manage the process of resource exchange or to increase the effectiveness of that exchange.

"Putting rehab counselors who knew something about people in their mid 50's in JOBS, Inc. [a manpower agency which had previously concerned itself with training youth and placing young people in jobs] did not have a remarkable effect by itself," reported one planner to his advisory committee. "Although we'd arranged an agreement between the Voc Rehab people and JOBS, Inc., and were partially funding the joint effort, we soon found that the rehab counselors and the job trainers were not talking to each other. The trainers resisted working with older people. They showed many of the fears and prejudices about age that we find elsewhere in society. To make things worse, they didn't like having people from another agency looking in on their work. Conversely, the rehab counselors were suspicious of the job trainers who they felt didn't understand rehabilitation principles.

"This was one of the first times we had brought two agencies together to work on a common task with a common client population. In order to insure success, we contracted with the community development people at the state university. One of their staff came in and conducted sensitizing sessions with the rehab and job training staffs. For one of the sessions, we arranged to have on hand two retired workers who had reentered the job market and one employer who made extensive use of older people. Within several weeks, the anxiety and distress had been dispelled. Both agencies are working well together now. The job training agency currently includes 23 percent older trainees (over the age of 55) in its other programs, up from three percent last year." The planner's utilization of educational resources complemented his earlier efforts at introducing new service staff, ultimately increasing the host agency's effectiveness.

MANAGEMENT OF RESOURCE EXCHANGE

The management of resource exchange requires considerable skill. Many planners may require outside help to understand where and when intervention will be most useful.

"This resource exchange concept was a new one to me," admits the new executive of an Information and Referral center. "I knew I needed some help with it, so I invited a sociologist from the Public Health School to come in and talk with my staff about it. She pointed out that some agencies try to reduce their dependency on other agencies by increasing their control over their environment through incorporating resource providers into their own operations. That's why some hospitals and family service agencies are willing to develop their own home helper and home visiting services, and why some nursing homes develop their own laundry facilities. She pointed out that it's sometimes cheaper and more economical for everybody if agencies expand their services. At other times, it creates monopoly situations leading to an inefficient use of funds. Planners, she suggested, might want to increase or decrease an agency's dependence on its environment.

"We got to thinking about it, and decided to study the kinds of exchanges that occur between agencies in our service area. Our sociologist consultant stayed with us as study project director. We focused only on those items we thought might be important for us as planners to know about. We found that some agencies had few exchanges with others, some dominated exchanges to the detriment of others, and that in a few cases the exchanges helped everybody, including the client. Our consultant told us that by understanding how such exchanges take place, and by managing some of them, we could increase our leverage. She was right."

The agency staff engaged in this analysis made some interesting discoveries. They found that the greater the similarity of goals and functions between an agency and the elements in its task environment, the greater the competition among them. This situation further reduces an agency's degree of decision-making autonomy, especially when all elements of the task environment are operating at something less than capacity. If the service area was generally short of clients or some other resources, charges of duplication of services were often made. However, competition tended to be less keen when both the agency and the elements in its task environment operated at near capacity, or when sufficient resources were available for each to maintain or expand its operation.

Frequently, the larger the number of elements in an agency's task environment, the greater its autonomy seemed to be. For this reason, agencies are often willing to expand their service programs. Like two of the agencies whose administrators were quoted earlier, they find that expanding their services and their resource bases makes them less dependent on any particular element in their task environment.

INTER-AGENCY EXCHANGES

Agencies interested in reducing their competition for scarce resources may try to do so by engaging in a variety of inter-agency exchanges such as staff consultation, use of physical facilities, or sharing printing and equipment costs. Planners can be helpful in identifying the areas in which such exchanges might take place and the advantages of such exchanges. They might also reward such exchanges through special grants to these agencies, or by facilitating their access to funding sources.

Inter-agency cooperation can also be increased through increased interaction between personnel or by sharing staff. "Boundary personnel," as they are sometimes called, function at many levels. Administrators may interact through community-wide task forces or through health and welfare council committees. Public welfare caseworkers may interact with family agency workers and with proprietors or allied health personnel in nursing homes. However, cooperation among lower level personnel may be effectively nullified by internal administrative requirements, or by conscious refusals to cooperate from those at higher levels. Planners are not always aware of these problems, nor do they always have sufficient time to deal with them.

Nevertheless, increased interaction at each level may result in a development of complementary or similar perspectives. As workers engage in dealing with common problems, they may come to view the needs of clients in a similar manner. Of course, this can create tensions within their separate agencies. Depending on their objectives, planners can take advantage of this knowledge by increasing or decreasing the likelihood that boundary personnel will interact with each other.

Sometimes boundary personnel are not paid staff people. They may be volunteers who perform service or administrative functions, or who serve on boards, task forces, and policy committees. Overlapping board and policy committee memberships frequently increase the likelihood that agencies will cooperate or attempt to accommodate their differences. These kinds of exchanges are not necessarily free of friction. They may result in conflicts of loyalty, and in contradictory pulls and tugs. Planners can be helpful in explicating the conflicts so that they become understood by those so affected.

In general, the greater the similarity of functions between agencies, the greater the likelihood that they will compete, unless overlapping memberships mitigate against that competition.

REDEFINING OUTPUT CONSTITUENTS AS INPUT CONSTITUENTS

One of the interesting findings by the aforementioned Information and Referral (I and R) agency staff had to do with the relationship between input and output constituencies. The I and R staff considered itself an input constituency to many agencies for both funds and information. The client populations in the community were defined as the output constituency of these agencies —a position with relatively little clout.

But after a number of consumers had participated with the agency staff in a planning task force, they were no longer thought of as powerless. As a result of their information gathering and other voluntary activities on the task force, they were treated with new respect by agency workers. "All a person has to do, it seems," observed a planner, "is to introduce himself as a member of one of our task forces or policy committees, and he gets preferential treatment in almost any agency that we fund. The client's identification with us puts him in a special position vis-à-vis the agencies that get money from us. Without realizing it, the I and R agency has become like an old-fashioned political ward."

To the extent that planners have control over the redistribution of resources, they may very well exhibit some of the characteristics of ward politicians. Unlike some old-time ward heelers, however, they are hopefully less concerned with maintaining their influence than with using it for the accomplishment of specific objectives. Of course, since these objectives may require changes in a social agency's policies, procedures, and programs, some of the planner's efforts are sure to meet resistance.

Review

In any particular community, services may be unavailable, inaccessible, unresponsive to consumer needs or interests, just plain ineffective and inefficient, or unaccountable to certain minority groups or to their representatives. Planning is an attempt to correct such deficiencies or inequities in the service system. For these reasons, planners frequently orient their activities toward modification of service agencies' policies, programs, and procedures.

This may require management or control of resources necessary to the agency's survival or to the accomplishment of its objectives. Such resources may include money and credit, physical or capital facilities and goods, manpower, knowledge and skill, political influence, social standing, charisma, legitimacy and legality, personal and organizational energy, and time.

Planners try to influence professional service workers both directly and indirectly. They attempt to influence a service provider indirectly through its task environment, which includes all those elements in an organization's "set" that directly affect its ability to accomplish its objectives or to fulfill its function. These are (a) the providers of resources (personnel, money and credit, regulatory agencies, and so forth); (b) competitors for those resources; (c) consumers of the agency's service (clients and members); and (d) those elements in the immediate or broader community which provide an agency with auspices and legitimacy.

Direct efforts may be aimed at the key decision makers in an agency or at those staff members engaged in service delivery. The planner may try to (a) influence the composition of agency staff to reflect more innovative ideas and relevant service technologies; (b) facilitate continuing education, staff development, and information exchanges among agencies; (c) promote the range and frequency of inter-agency cooperation or interorganizational exchanges between "boundary" personnel at all levels. These exchanges may include personnel, knowledge and technology, resources and clientele.

SUPPLEMENTARY QUESTIONS AND ACTIVITIES

1. Draw up a list of the major suppliers, consumers, providers of auspices, and competitors of an agency which does planning in your community. Which of these play several roles—that is, may be located under more than one category?

2. If you were a planner looking at a service agency and its task environment, which elements in that environment might you try to manipulate so as to influence the agency? Select an agency you are familiar with and write its name in the middle box on the following chart. Fill in the boxes in its environment, indicating by their location if they are providers of services or of legitimacy, competitors or consumers. Do some organizations fit into more than one category? Does the fact that some of the elements in the planning agency's task environment are the same as some in the service agency's environment suggest anything to you?

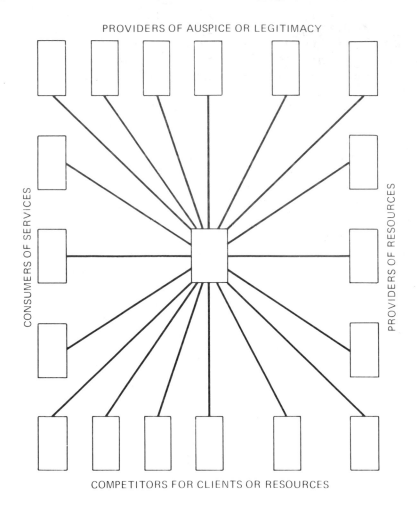

PROVIDERS OF AUSPICE OR LEGITIMACY

CONSUMERS OF SERVICES

PROVIDERS OF RESOURCES

COMPETITORS FOR CLIENTS OR RESOURCES

3. Which three agencies in your community are among the least likely to be influenced by manipulating elements in their task environments? Why? Which are the most vulnerable to such change?

4. Which three agencies in your community are you least likely to be able to influence because the elements in their environment are relatively immune to external pressure by a local planner?

5. If you are a planner or working in a planning setting, inventory the types of resources actually or potentially at your command. How can you beef up those categories in which you are weak? Who else has access to these resources? What kinds of reinforcements or trade-offs are possible? Around which issues?

Recommended Readings

Levine, Sol, and Paul E. White. "Exchange as a Conceptual Framework for the Study of Interorganizational Relationships." *Administration Science Quarterly,* March, 1961.

Levine and White explain the relationship among social welfare agencies in terms of a system of interorganizational exchanges. This process is defined as "any voluntary activity between two organizations which has consequences, actual or anticipated, for the realization of their respective goals or objectives." The article identifies elements in the organization's environment which impinge on its ability to accomplish objectives. Under conditions of scarcity, the authors point out, an organization can seldom accomplish its goals—or obtain the resources, labor supply, and clients it requires—without establishing relationships with other organizations.

Morris, Robert, and Robert Binstock. *Feasible Planning for Social Change.* New York: Columbia University Press, 1965.

The word "planning" connotes a wide variety of thoughts and actions. A major premise of this book is that discussions of planning must be somewhat circumscribed if they are to be useful. The authors therefore concentrate on a few major aspects of planning. As the title suggests, a major portion of the book discusses the factors that determine the feasibility of planning goals and ways of revising unfeasible goals. Relevant chapters include: "The Anatomy of Feasibility," "Organizational Resistance to Planning Goals," "Overcoming Resistance through Influence," and "Evaluating the Feasibility of Goals." Of particular interest is their discussion of resources.

Warren, Roland L., Stephen M. Rose, and Ann F. Bergunder. *The Structure of Urban Reform.* Lexington, Mass.: D. C. Heath and Co., 1974.

Disenchantment with urban reform efforts of the '60s and early '70s has been fairly universal. The authors provide some major guidelines by which current methods of addressing urban problems can be assessed. Their book describes some major urban structures and processes that reform attempts must acknowledge and overcome in order to be effective. Chapter 6 introduces the concepts of input and output constituencies.

Suggestions for Further Reading

Evan, William. "The Organization-Set: Toward a Theory of Interorganizational Relations," in *Approaches to Organizational Design,* James D. Thompson (Ed.). Pittsburgh: University of Pittsburgh Press, 1966.

Joiner, Charles A. *Organizational Analysis: Political, Sociological and Administrative Processes of Local Government.* East Lansing: Michigan State University, Institute for Community Development and Services, 1964.

Litwak, Eugene. "An Approach to Linkage and Grassroots Community Organization," in *Strategies of Community Organization: A Book of Readings,* Fred M. Cox (Ed.). Itasca, Ill.: F. Peacock Publishing Co., 1973.

Litwak, Eugene, and Lydia Hylton. "Inter-Organizational Analysis: A Hypothesis on Coordinating Agencies," *Administrative Science Quarterly,* June, 1966.

LITWAK, EUGENE, and HENRY J. MEYER. "Balance Theory of Coordination Between Bureaucratic Organizations and Community Primary Groups," *Administrative Science Quarterly,* June, 1966.

LITWAK, EUGENE, and JACK ROTHMAN. "Toward the Theory and Practice of Coordination Between Formal Organizations," in *Organizations and Clients: Essays on the Sociology of Service,* William R. Rosengrin and Mark Lifton (Eds.). Columbus, Ohio: Bobbs Merrill, 1970.

THOMPSON, JAMES D., and WILLIAM J. McEWEN. "Organizational Goals and Environments: Goal-Setting and an Interaction Process," *American Sociological Review,* February, 1958. Reprinted in Mayer N. Zald, *Social Welfare Institutions.* New York: John Wiley and Sons, 1965.

WARREN, ROLAND. "Interaction of Community Decision Organizations: Some Basic Concepts and Needed Research," *Social Service Review,* September 1967. Reprinted as "Planning Among the Giants: Interaction of Community Decision Organizations," in Roland L. Warren, *Truth, Love and Social Change.* Chicago: Rand McNally, 1971.

———. "Model Cities' First Round: Politics, Planning and Participation." *Journal of American Institute of Planners,* July, 1969.

Overcoming Resistance to Change

Organizational Resistance to Change

A central fact of organizational life is that organizations find it easier to keep busy with routine tasks than to take on new functions or to change accustomed modes of behavior. Planners are often dismayed when some service agency personnel show a calculated opposition to change and others demonstrate a complete inability to change. While service agency administrators do not always verbalize their true feelings, their actions may suggest that they generally prefer to maintain their current structures or modes of operation even when a change will obviously enhance the accomplishment of the organization's stated goals or mission.

PLANNERS VERSUS AGENCY ADMINISTRATORS

In fact what is desired by the planner may be anathema to the agency administrator. "Every time a new planning agency hits this town, they come with a bunch of new ideas and a bunch of dollars and expect us to change who we are," complains the director of a sheltered workshop. "We know darn well who we are. We've been performing an important function in this community for 25 years."

"I've met that attitude many times," confides a planner. "We could probably put pressure on lots of agencies to take on new clients, or to change the focus of their services. But we're not always going to be able to make them do it even when such a change helps them accomplish their objectives more easily. Sometimes we have to try to convince them, cajole them, or tempt them into changing. If we force somebody into doing something they don't want now, no matter how much money we've got, we won't be able to get them to do something for us later. We've got to go slow, and keep the agency administrators on our side at every stage in the game."

REASONS FOR RESISTANCE

The reasons for resistance to change are many. Being pressured into change by outsiders may result in some loss of face. Under such circumstances, financial incentives to individuals and to agencies may be insufficient inducements, particularly if a change once adopted might result in embarrassment or loss of stature in the event of failure.

Agency administrators may perceive change as an imposition on their personnel and thus disruptive to the management process. Agency personnel may be intent on protecting the advantages they receive from keeping things as they are. Change may require learning new skills and modifying accustomed ways of behaving. Some professional staff members may fear that change will result in an erosion of standards, or will require them to perform tasks that could better be performed by others. Frequently, defenders of the status quo do so in what they perceive to be the public interest. Distinguishing between self-interest and public interest is sometimes extremely difficult.

There are significant psychic costs to change. For some personnel, changing established patterns of practice or adding new functions may mean becoming novices again. It takes a long time to become a master craftsman. Most changes require immediate risks. While not changing may result in eventual erosion of influence or service efficiency and effectiveness, at least that erosion is gradual.

For many professionals and allied staff, precedent is a valuable guide because it defines a safe, if narrow, path. Planners would do well to cite precedent and previous experience in their efforts to induce change. In many agencies, following well established procedures is more important than accomplishing the stated aims of the agency. This insularity reinforces inflexibility and sometimes results in a ritualism imbued with an almost fundamentalist quality.

THE IMPACT OF NEWNESS

Newer organizations and newer employees are more apt to take risks. As agencies grow older, they frequently institutionalize innovations. They establish procedures and formalized rules to ensure predictable behavior and to consolidate whatever gains they may have made. Staff become increasingly concerned with the survival and the growth of the organization rather than with finding new or even more effective means to reach goals.

While new staff people tend to be more innovative than those with established positions, this is not always the case. Many well-established agencies continue to innovate and seek creative solutions to emerging problems. Unfortunately, this is more the exception than the rule.

Still, newness is no guarantee that innovation will happen. Nor, of course, is innovation to be equated with good service. "We had a plan by which we thought we could shake up the service system," recalls a planner on the West Coast. "With new funds coming into the area, agencies would be employing lots of new staff. New staff, we reasoned, would bring in new ideas. To make certain that they were the right people, we established a recruitment system right within our planning agency. We figured to attract good people and screen out the bad. We sure were naive.

"First of all, even some of the young people we recruited and who were hired by local agencies came with their creativity already bred out of them by professional training. Trained incapacity, I call it. There just weren't that many topnotch prospects, even when we recruited directly at the universities. Besides, recruitment is a costly and time-consuming process.

"Secondly, no matter how good we were at screening, the agencies seemed to think they were better. We can only suggest standards, not insist an employer take our recommendation. We found that some agency directors chose people who were congenial by temperament, personality, and philosophy. They didn't seem as interested in seeking persons with the best objective professional qualifications. One executive told me that he was looking for a program director who would fit in and not rock the boat."

Organizational analysts are well aware of this tendency of agencies to program employee behavior by "weeding out" or containing those staff members who might suggest new or unorthodox approaches. Some planners are no different. They may systematically ignore those agencies and associations that rock the boat, challenge existing patterns of behavior, or threaten other agencies in the planner's constituency.

RESOURCE LIMITATIONS, SUNKEN COSTS, AND OBLIGATIONS

There are, of course, other obstacles to change, some of them inherent in the system and rather insidious. An agency may agree to the need for change, but be unable to mobilize necessary resources. At times, resources are rendered inadequate by overly rapid expansion, or by an agency's assumption of commitments beyond its capacity to fulfill. Some agencies are limited by lack of access to new ideas and new technologies. Planners can be particularly helpful in facilitating relationships between service providers and those elements in the environment which can provide necessary resources.

In addition to resource limitations, there sometimes are sunken costs which limit an agency's ability to move from the status quo. Investment in equipment, as in a medical clinic, or in certain kinds of staffs whose specialized training has made them tenured employees, represents commitment to previous conceptions of mission. This investment makes adaptation to more appropriate missions almost impossible.

Agencies may also accumulate both obligations and commitments that constrain their behavior. Over the years, they may have made promises to other service agencies, to consumers, and to providers. The expectations of others may make it extraordinarily difficult for service agencies to change their procedures, their programs, or their services without endangering existing relationships. Needless to say, when such relationships are endangered, an organization is less likely to achieve its goals, and its very existence may be threatened. Change invariably alters the pattern of relationships between agencies and elements in their task environments. New relationships may engender anxiety and mistrust between the organization and elements in that environment.

Some Strategies for Increasing the Likelihood of Agency Innovation and Change: More Illustrations from Practice

Agencies that do not experience rapid turnover of staff or multiple pressures from a changing environment tend to move toward conservatism rather than innovation. In such cases, planners can try to increase the range of agency staff exposures to new or different ideas and practices. Several approaches have proven successful.

EDUCATION FOR CHANGE

Staff training workshops, professional development seminars, and skill laboratories may be used to introduce providers to new approaches. Such continuing education activities are particularly useful when (a) the students themselves are involved in selecting the learning objectives; (b) they come away from the experience with a set of practical ideas or skills; (c) they receive on-the-job reinforcement for using their new skills. In order for agency administrators properly to reinforce these employees, planners may have to provide leadership with complementary consultation and to encourage support for the new approaches among funders and service consumers.

Inter-agency exchanges can be encouraged and facilitated by planners. Case conferences, periodic visits between agency staffs, and occasional newsletters are minimal but nonetheless effective exchange mechanisms. More significant is encouragement of interorganizational cooperation in which "boundary personnel" collaborate on projects of mutual concern.

ADAPTING TO SHRINKING RESOURCES

When agencies are threatened with a drastic reduction of resources—or extinction because of the curtailment of their original social function—they may be expected energetically to seek new functions. Even in such circumstances, they will tend to develop those functions or services that will enable them to survive with as little shrinkage or change as possible. Agencies that cannot adapt may find the shrinkage excessive.

REDUCING INCENTIVES TO OPPOSE CHANGE

"We know it's not easy to make agencies change. There are too many barriers," explained a planner at a recent professional symposium. "Instead of inducing them to change, we try to reduce their incentives to oppose change. I'll tell you what I mean. Promising an agency more resources if it initiates a new service may get you a negative answer. However, it's another matter to promise more staff and more money for current projects if the administrators agree to take the kind of staff you want to locate in the agency. Suppose, for example, you increased an agency's staff capacities by adding paraprofessionals and volunteers who have gone through *your own* training program. Then you add some accountability measures, say, reporting forms the directors are required to fill out. Pretty soon you may find agency policies reflecting the ideological and value positions of the new staff members, reinforced by your own well thought-out reporting requirements. Of course," he concluded, "you've got to be sharp enough to know if they are 'conning' you with their use of nomenclature. A rose by any other name. . . ."

INCREASING RATES OF CHANGE IN THE ENVIRONMENT

An organization's rate of innovation can be expected to vary directly with the rate of change in its task environment, and also with the need for new technical expertise. As services to the aging become more complex, they may increasingly require staff with specialized skills in health and related care, in organization and coordination, and in environmental management. The greater the external pressure for change, the greater the diversity of activities that will be undertaken by the agency, and frequently, the greater the interdependence of these activities.

While many agencies tend to conserve their gains and accomplishments, they are also caught in the pressures to increase the variety and innovation of their services as they strain toward greater and more inclusive relationships with elements in their task environment.

"All too often, well established agency personnel seem to be hiding with their heads in the sand, refusing to see that new knowledge and new techniques exist that would result in markedly improved practice," reported a planner. "We see our job as inducing the agencies to want to change. We've developed some simple techniques, but they work. We know that there's little incentive to change if you're a big shot in an organization, supervising a certain kind of program for which you're the recognized expert. So we go about completely redefining the situation. We provide a 'consultation' service to those agencies that we envision as capable of being improved. Sometimes we even kick some money into the pot. I'll give you an example.

USING A CONSULTANT TO INCREASE THE LIKELIHOOD OF SELF-GENERATED INNOVATION

"The psychiatric director of the geriatric ward in the state hospital was fighting the transfer of older patients back into the community on every ground possible: they were too badly damaged; they'd been in the hospital too long; there were no supportive services in the community. In a sense he was right. But he refused to look at any other alternatives to simple discharge. Now we could have gone in there and told him how they did it at another institution, but he and his staff would have just rejected our suggestions outright. They would have told us that the local situation was different. So we decided to have them tell us what needed to be done. Our consultant went in there with a graduate student from the university. He met with the director of the geriatric ward, the nursing director, and the hospital administrator.

"He told them that he knew something about community resources, and something about effective programs in other communities. But, he said, he didn't know what would work in this area because he wasn't familiar with the hospital, its program, or its patients. Nobody, he continued, could design a more effective patient-release program than the three people in that room.

"He then explained that he would have to make a report to the state unit on aging and the State Department of Mental Health. But he didn't feel that he could write this report himself. He wanted to write it on the basis of the recommendations that the three hospital people made. He had an idea. He had a sharp graduate student who would pull together some of the literature on releasing geriatric patients. He would also put together a file on community resources, and get the reports on some other programs from around the country that had been successful. He would then lay out a list of questions, for the hospital people to use as a guide in going through all the material. Since he was getting a consultation fee, and didn't feel he was fully earning it, he wanted to split it equally among the four people in the room, including himself. He explained that this was perfectly legitimate and could be construed as their consulting on a plan. It had been done elsewhere.

"After some deliberation, the three hospital people agreed. Now let me tell you, it worked this time and it works every time. Our consultant doesn't exactly go into those places blind. He selects those articles on releasing geriatric patients very carefully. The graduate student is told exactly what to dig up and how to package the materials. Frankly, anybody reading through a packet of our consultant's material would have to come up with a similar conclusion. The packages point only to certain limited ranges of alternatives.

"When the hospital people turned in their reports, the consultant wove them together into a final report, and checked it back with his 'consultants.' The key people in the hospital had made the recommendations; and they felt those recommendations were their own. After that kind of involvement, we're not too worried about whether they'll follow through. And we give them plenty of recognition in our newsletter and in the media for their efforts. They're still the experts, but now they're the experts on a new program."

SHAKE-UPS TO INDUCE CHANGE

In some agencies change is not produced that easily. It may require a major shake-up in the allocation of jobs and assignments for a large proportion of the staff. It may mean bumping some people into dead-end jobs, or releasing others into positions where they have a greater chance to innovate. A shake-up is no guarantee of permanent change. It is intended only to loosen up the system a bit, allowing for some restructuring and retooling to accomplish new and different objectives. Those standing in the way of new programs or services may be reassigned to different offices throughout the agency, or co-opted through involvement in the structural redesign of the agency or in the design of a new program, much as the 'consultants' were in the previous illustration.

LOANER STAFF

Linking the personnel of two agencies through the loan of a staff member with particular expertise may eliminate some mental blinders through juxtaposing different approaches to the provision of services. Sometimes it is possible to bring together people who have radically different ideological and value positions, or who employ very different methods. Some planners encourage agencies to "loan out" their staffs to other agencies in efforts to share their expertise, build a bridge of understanding between agencies, and improve exposure to different service systems and client populations.

An important consideration is the compensation of the "victims" of change for their losses. This may mean giving certain staff reduced caseloads or increased time to do their work, or offering them special recognition. Experienced planners are aware that agency administrators often must be appealed to in terms of their self-interest. They help agency administrators recognize other people's self-interest by approaching agency staff as well.

The quick influx of new "blood" or new ideas is no guarantee that an organization will continue changing. When individuals with new ideas are brought into an agency and promoted into higher positions on the basis of their outlook, values, or expertise, they may quickly form an avant-garde clique. Feeling themselves kindred spirits in the attempt to reform the system, they may be fired by a sense of shared mission.

MOVERS AND CONSERVERS

Effective "movers," however, usually guard their flanks quite well. A few years after making some major changes, they may be employing the same techniques the "conservers" in their organization used to employ. The movers may be foot-dragging, evading direct confrontation of issues, and refusing to comply with approaches they consider "nonprofessional."

"I visited one local service agency," declares a researcher from a New England university, "and I'll bet you there were at least three 'old guards.' The oldest of these groups simply shuffled along and did their thing. They were so beaten down that, except for an occasional murmur of resistance, they could be expected to carry on as they were told. Here and there you could find one who had been given a position of token importance. Then there were the 'young turks' of ten years ago. They came in with the poverty program, got themselves identified as the whiz kids, and were pretty dominant until about '68 or '69. A shake-up at that time brought in a group of consolidators who cut back on ineffective programs and built up proven activities. Now, with a new administration in Washington, pretty soon there'll be another bunch of young turks coming in. In the meantime, the crowd from the mid-60s are pretty well entrenched and will be digging in their heels, trying to stop any radical new departure."

In many agencies, the introduction of change may call forth an immediate reaction to isolate, contain, and bureaucratize it. Since any change has unanticipated consequences and unintended side effects, even organizational innovators may put the damper on certain developments, and thus in some ways diminish their own innovations. Too often, the spontaneity and exuberance of innovators are completely absorbed into the fabric of ongoing activities, or so routinized as to reduce the uncertainty of risk. In most agencies, tolerance for unpredictability and uncertainty is very narrow, and these human frailties are reflected in the extent of change actually achieved.

ACCOMMODATING BOTH CONSERVATION AND CHANGE

Since not too many things can be changed all at once without destroying a working system, planners must be clear about those issues which are most important to them, and those practices or procedures or policies they are most interested in changing. Even those planners who advocate drastic and sweeping changes must tolerate continuation of many established practices. In every community, there must be an accommodation between the proponents of change and the guardians of tradition. What may seem a massive and sudden change to one, may seem infinitesimal to the other. Even the most conservative elements in the service system can accept modifications in their operations if these modifications do not threaten the particular continuities which have special importance for them. Tradeoffs will have to be reached, compromises made.

SERVICE AGENCY EFFORTS TO INFLUENCE THE PLANNING AGENCY

Just as area planners are involved in fostering multiple exchange relationships with service providers, so will these organizations try to influence a planner or planning agency. Service agencies may attempt to mobilize support for their ideologies, programs, or clientele from elements in the planning agency's input constituencies.

They may anticipate the planner's intervention by entering into formal and informal agreements for the exchange of services, personnel, facilities, and resources. Frequently, service agency administrators expend considerable energy on inducing *planning staff* to engage in planning efforts on behalf of some population the agency is unable or unwilling to serve; that is to shift accountability to the planner and ultimately to some other body in the community. "The trouble with our current notion of accountability," a planner in San Francisco confides, "is that it emphasizes only the services currently being provided. Agencies should be held accountable for those services they do not provide. Too many low-income and oppressed minorities are just not served by anyone."

Despite agency resistance to change, planners should not assume that they have all the answers and that agency people are unaware of the circumstances. Just the contrary. "We came in here like gangbusters," admits a planner, "figuring that we knew best for everyone; that we were the only ones after the golden fleece. We learned quick enough that if you want to know what is going on in town, and what changes are feasible, you check with your key agency administrators. They know what's going on, and they can make things happen . . . and they do. Most of the time they are more than willing to make changes, to add new services or to expand in needed directions. Most of the time they know better than the planner does."

"We really grooved on the idea that there was to be a new planning agency for the aging," testifies the director of a mental health center. "We'd wanted to expand our services to the elderly for some time but needed some legitimizer or facilitator to help us coordinate efforts with other agencies. Then in comes this character who calls himself a planner and stirs everything up. Organizes the elderly against us, puts us in trouble with the County Board of Supervisors, makes accusations left and right about our lack of interest, skill, and commitment. We were ready to welcome a colleague, only to find ourselves with a new adversary."

In their zeal to get things done, planners too often engage in adversary relationships with service agency people, when collaborative and cooperative relationships are needed. Part of assessing the "issue environment" involves feeling out the extent to which agency personnel are receptive to and take the leadership in program development and service coordination. "We're in the business of providing services. The better they are, the better we feel about what we're doing," concludes the mental health center director. Yet many people still fall "between the cracks," underserved by some agencies, overserved by others. The problem may have nothing to do with the unwillingness or unresponsiveness of service providers. Rather, it may be based on the inadequacy of the mechanisms for cooperation, collaboration, or exchange between agencies.

Implications for Social Planning at the Community Level

LIMITED ACCESS TO RESOURCES

Because the social planner has only limited access to fiscal resources, he or she must rely heavily on such other resources as knowledge and expertise, political influence, diplomatic skills, charisma, and so forth. Such intangibles are not always easy to acquire. It has been too often assumed that the network of "untapped resources" (agencies and other service providers) can readily be activated and their services coordinated in some effective and efficient manner. The planner and student of planning should be disabused of any notion of quick and simple solutions to complex problems. The providers of services have their own agendas. Consumers have theirs. Funders have theirs. And planners may have theirs. Often the goals and objectives implicit in these agendas are contradictory. Often they are fuzzy and unclear. The planner must be clear about just how much clout he or she has—and when and how to use it.

Review

Much of the planner's energy is directed at overcoming resistance to those changes he or she attempts to induce. Change efforts require not only carefully designed strategies but in most cases skillful management of scarce resources. By itself, access to resources is insufficient. The planner must be able to concert these resources and to float them down the appropriate channels by influence, selling, appeals to friendship, rational persuasion, coercion, and so on. Needless to say, the planner must be well versed in the negotiation process and in stimulating and managing the exchanges of benefits among both providers of services and consumers.

The reasons providers of service resist change are many. Change may be expensive in terms of temporary loss of prestige, giving up accustomed and routine patterns of operation, sunken costs in facilities and equipment. It may be costly in terms of personnel retraining, reassignment, or acquisition. While education is an often used tool, it must be implemented by other resources, and by other supports.

Change is of no value in its own right. Agency administrators are often quite correct in questioning the utility of an innovation. Even when a change is very much warranted, it may be resisted unless the costs of change—in terms of time, effort, and psychological discomfort as well—can be reduced. Practically, this means reducing incentives to oppose change and increasing rewards for successfully implementing change.

SUPPLEMENTARY QUESTIONS AND ACTIVITIES

1. Identify a problem that requires a change in the way in which a service agency operates. Who might support the change you feel is warranted? Who might oppose it?

2. Now identify all the resources that might be mustered to support change. Who has access to them? What resources might be mustered to oppose change? Who has access to these?

3. What is the issue environment; that is, to what extent is there agreement, disagreement, or indifference to the needed change? What does this suggest in terms of an intervention strategy?

Recommended Reading

LIPPIT, RONALD, JEANNE WATSON, and BRUCE WESTLEY. *The Dynamics of Planned Change.* New York: Harcourt, Brace and World, Inc., 1958.

Planned change—that is, change derived from a purposeful decision to improve a personality or social system—is a subject of great concern in the human services. In this book, Lippit, Watson and Westley have undertaken a comparative study of the principles and techniques employed by various professional change agents in the field. The authors attempt to answer some fundamental questions on the nature and principles of planned change. Chapter 4, "Motivation of the Client System," offers a good general discussion of reasons for resistance to change and innovation.

DOWNS, ANTHONY. *Inside Bureaucracy.* Boston: Little, Brown and Co., 1967.
In a provocative, serious book written with a good deal of humor, Downs lays out a number of organizational "laws" and expounds on a larger number of propositions. He discusses different types of bureaucrats: the climber, the conserver, the zealot, and others. The response of each to innovations is fully explained. Conditions under which changes are most likely to occur are laid out.

KURILOFF, ARTHUR. *Organizational Development for Survival.* New York: American Management Association, 1972.
Kuriloff systematically examines the reasons why organizations must change yet resist doing so. Of special interest to the social planner is the discussion on reducing the costs or penalities of change.

ROTHMAN, JACK, JOHN L. ERLICH, and JOSEPH G. TERESA. *Promoting Motivational Change in Organizations and Communities: A Planning Manual.* New York: John Wiley and Sons, 1976.
The authors draw from a four-year study of the application of scientifically derived principles to social action and planning. The book is written in manual form, making explicit suggestions to the practitioners on what to do and how when a specific goal is desired. Of particular interest are Chapters 2, "Promoting an Innovation," and Chapter 3, "Changing an Organization's Goals."

Suggestions for Further Reading

LIPPITT, GORDON L. *Visualizing Change: Model Building and the Change Process.* LaJolla, Calif.: University Associates Press, 1973.

MOORE, WILBERT E. *Social Change.* Englewood Cliffs, N.J.: Prentice Hall, Foundations of Modern Sociology Series, 1963. See esp. Chap. 3, "Small Scale Changes."

MORRIS, ROBERT, and ROBERT BINSTOCK. *Feasible Planning for Social Change.* New York: Columbia University Press, 1965.

PERROW, CHARLES C., and J. MEHINA. "The Reluctant Organizations and the Aggressive Environment." *Administrative Science Quarterly,* 1965, 10 (2), 229–257.

PERROW, CHARLES C. "Organizational Goals." *International Encyclopedia of the Social Services,* Vol. II. New York: MacMillan Press, 1968.

PRICE, JAMES. L. *Organization Effectiveness: An Inventory of Research.* Homewood, Ill.: Richard D. Irwin, 1968.

STARBUCK, WILLIAM H. "Organizational Growth and Development," in *Handbook of Organizations,* James G. March (Ed.). Chicago: Rand McNally, 1965.

ZALD, MAYER, and PETER DENTON. "From Evangelism to General Service: The Transformation of the Y.M.C.A." *Administrative Science Quarterly,* 1963, 8 (2).

ZOLTMAN, GERALD, ROBERT DUNCAN, and JONNY HOLBEK. *Innovations and Organizations.* New York: Wiley-Interscience, 1973.

7

Assessment and Evaluation

Assessment occurs at virtually every stage of the planning process. The identification or definition of a problem requires assessment. Decisions about the kinds of planning structures to be built and how long they are to last requires preliminary as well as ongoing assessment. Decisions about goals and means require an assessment of costs and benefits and a determination of what might be feasible in a given set of circumstances. The programming or implementation phases of the planning process require ongoing monitoring, another form of assessment.

Because many of the methods and planning tools used in the assessment process are similar or identical to those of the evaluative process, the two terms are sometimes used interchangeably. This is an error. Assessment and evaluation are conceptually distinct. Assessment focuses on an examination of what is, what may occur in the future, or what ought to be. It also includes an examination of what might be needed in order to achieve desired ends. Evaluation focuses on what happened, how it happened, whether it might have happened better or more efficiently, and whether it should have happened at all.[1]

[1] I am indebted to a colleague, Louis Ferman of the University of Michigan for helping me crystallize this distinction.

Assessing the Environment and the Issues to be Addressed

In applying assessment techniques, planners are generally concerned with the problem to be addressed, the process by which it is to be addressed, and the likelihood that the problem can be dealt with successfully. Success depends in part on the skills of the planner or planning agency. It also depends on what is happening in the multiple environments around the problem or issue to be addressed. The "issue environment" was discussed in Chapter 4. Around any issue or problem, there may be consensus, disagreement, or disinterest on the part of significant persons and organizations. When there is general consensus that intervention is necessary and some agreement on goals and on the means of achieving those goals, the planner is led to a cooperative strategy. This may entail simply allowing those parties with common interests to work out the details of their collaboration. It may require providing technical assistance on plan making or on the location and acquisition of resources.

However, when there is disagreement or conflict over the ends, the means, or the definition of the problem to be addressed, a different strategy is called for. The planner and his or her supporters may have to overcome resistances that are often synonymous with organizational procedures themselves. A contest or conflict-oriented strategy may be required, in which resources are redirected from one organization to another. Political and coercive tactics may be employed to influence decisions or to nullify the opposition. A somewhat different set of strategies may be required when the general attitude can be summed up as indifference toward the issue.

In circumstances of either disagreement or disinterest, a campaign strategy may make the most sense. The planner may try to sell others on the need to do something about a particular problem, first by raising the public awareness of the existence of a problem, then by emphasizing the need to do something about it. The selection of both goals and means may require the development of coalitions of potentially interested parties. Opposition, if any, may be ignored or contained.

Whatever the issue, the choice of a cooperative, contest, or campaign strategy will depend first of all on the planner's assessment of the environment around that issue.

Integral to the assessment of the issue environment may be the assessment of various task environments. These were discussed in Chapter 5. Planners need to know what resources are currently or potentially at their disposal. To what extent can they expect an appropriate supply of resources from their suppliers? Who else may have access to those resources and compete with the planner or the planner's agency for their acquisition? Do the planner, the planner's organization, and the plan itself have sufficient legitimacy to receive needed support? And is this legitimacy adequate to assure implementation of the plan? Is the plan's legitimation dependent at least in part on the support of those who may be the recipients of services should the plan go into effect?

In addition to examining the planner's or planning agency's own task environment, it is necessary to pose the same questions about the environment around the organization or the institutional arrangements that may require changing. This assessment will enable the planner to make decisions about intervention points at which some leverage may be applied.

The planner often assesses a situation as it exists now and contrasts it with its projected appearance some time in the future. When the planner's assessment suggests a lack of community support, he or she may decide temporarily to shelve a project. Depending on the circumstances, perhaps action on an issue of lesser importance is warranted, because it is relatively certain that such action will be successful. Successes in one or more efforts are likely to lead to success in others.

Thinking in terms of both the present and the future is also important in examining the issues or problems to be addressed.

Problem-Focused Assessment

Problem-focused assessment can be current, anticipatory, or normative in its orientation. The planner's focus may be on the consumer of a particular service, on the providers of services, or on the relationships that exist among service providers and between providers and consumers. These points of focus were also described in Chapter 4. The planner may approach each aspect of the problem differently, however, depending on whether his or her orientation is toward current problems, future problems, or the correction of deficiencies based on some normative view of what ought to be. Current or anticipatory assessments begin with the recognition that something is or soon will be troublesome. Tackling this situation, the planner or planning agency may pose the following questions:

What is (will become) the problem?
Who is (will be) affected by it?
How does (will) it hurt?
Who else cares (or will care) about the problem?
How frequently or broadly does (will) the problem express itself?

When the problem is located in the present, the planner may use a number of analytic as well as interactional techniques to assess it. These include force field analysis, the nominal group approach, the use of surveys and questionnaires, consumer analysis, and others. When the problem is anticipated for the future, the planner may use a number of trend analysis techniques, social indicators, Delphi panels, and other projective techniques.

When the planner uses a normative lens, however, he or she does not focus on what is or what is likely to be, but on what ought to be. In normative assessment, the end or goals of the planning process do not emerge from an examination of the problem. Instead, the problem emerges from an assessment of the gap between what is and what the planner conceives as an ideal end state. In essence this approach to planning requires the development of a "competency" model. This model represents someone's idea of good practice, of appropriate or effective services, or of who should be served at what level.

Some of the same techniques, for example, Delphi panels, force field analysis, and benefit/cost analysis, can be used in assessing the gap between what is and what ought to be. But now the planner uses the model to establish clear standards of behavior and performance—norms that, once agreed to, become the basis for behavioral guidelines. Moreover, these same standards become the basis for evaluating the effectiveness of the planning process, which is defined as the extent to which there has been movement from the actual to the ideal.

Because many normative-oriented planners have relatively clear and distinct objectives, they are frequently able to develop an ordered sequence of interventions, each leading to a closer approximation of the ideal. This is quite different from the focus on current or anticipated problems, which requires no notion of an ideal end state. The more pragmatic approach of problem-oriented planners allows them to be satisfied with reductions in the consequences of problems and, consequently, to shift their energies from one problem to another as the means for dealing with each become available or as the issue environment permits.

Analytic and Interactional Approaches Used in Assessment

Social planners use a large number of techniques for assessing both their environments and the situations they seek to ameliorate. Among them are (1) interviews; (2) agency and other public records; (3) public meetings; (4) surveys; (5) social indicators; (6) consumer or client analysis; (7) benefit/cost analysis; (8) program planning and budgeting systems; (9) input-output analysis; (10) the Delphi conference; (11) functional job analysis; (12) force field analysis; and (13) nominal group technique.

INTERVIEWS

Perhaps the most common techniques in assessing a situation, interviews can be formal or informal. Planners often use interviews for preliminary assessment, to get the lay of the land, to get a sense of who cares about what, or to identify the dimensions of a current or emerging problem.

Interviews may be conducted in person or by telephone. The telephone interview is less expensive, easier to administer, and apt to reach a large constituency. There are drawbacks in using the telephone, however. People may not feel as compelled to answer questions when they are not in a face-to-face situation. It may be difficult for the interviewer to probe or to catch nuances that appear only in facial expressions or body movements. When telephone interviews are used as part of a formal interviewing process with standardized questions, several cautions need to be considered. First, certain populations may be underrepresented. Lower income people may not have telephones. Others may not be available when called. Second, most people find spending more than 12 to 15 minutes on the telephone irritating, either to themselves or to others who may wish access to the phone.

Although much more expensive, person-to-person interviews tend to be more informative. They permit longer periods for probing and for following leads. Person-to-person interviews can be conducted individually or in small groups. When the latter method is employed, there may be some danger that more charismatic, more verbal, or more powerful persons will dominate. Nevertheless, such a "brainstorming" technique may result in a greater amount of data.

SURVEYS

Surveys are usually conducted through the use of questionnaires (although telephone and personal interviews may generate similar information). Questionnaires have certain advantages over interviews. They tend to generate fairly uniform responses; they can be administered in person or through the mails; and their results can be tabulated and processed mechanically by hand or machine.

In general, mailed questionnaires are among the least expensive methods of generating information. Particularly if they are anonymous, they may give rise to some candid and honest responses. On the other hand, the return on questionnaires may be poor, either in terms of numbers or in terms of quality of response. People frequently fill out questionnaires as rapidly as possible, feeling they have completed their obligations if they have answered each question, even if the answers are not thoughtful or in depth. Moreover, some populations are more comfortable in using and responding to questionnaires than others. People from low-income backgrounds, especially those who have low levels of literacy, may find it uncomfortable or impossible to respond to a questionnaire.

There are, of course, a number of other advantages and disadvantages to the use of the survey material. Surveys are not terribly useful in evaluating complex relationships or the impact of complex service systems. Responses on surveys are often superficial. Because most surveys are administered during a limited time period, they tend to pick up feelings or perceptions that exist at the present time. It is extremely difficult to design a survey that will give some indication of changes in perception. In addition, some surveys are designed so that they generate the kinds of results that the user is hoping to find.

A final cautionary note: The construction of both the survey instrument and the sample requires technical expertise not always available to the planner or planning organization. When this happens, the results may be invalid and therefore somewhat less than useful. Surveys designed by persons who lack expertise and experience often generate more data than are necessary for planning purposes but leave large gaps of requisite information unfilled. The designer of a survey instrument must therefore know beforehand how the information is to be used.

PUBLIC MEETINGS

Planners frequently arrange public meetings with representatives of consumer populations, agency representatives, and with the public at large, as in a public hearing or town meeting type of situation. This assessment approach also includes both formal and informal give-and-take sessions with the memberships of church, fraternal, and civic associations. Meetings have certain disadvantages when compared with survey and interview techniques. They tend to generate more heat than information, and when facts are forthcoming, most are not replicable. Too often, meetings are so unstructured as to generate inappropriate information or expectations that are unreasonable. This is particularly true when an issue is hot, when it is strongly felt, or when it generates heated controversy. Then, too, participants are self-selected. For all these reasons, meetings may be generally said to be more helpful in assessing the community's interest or support for a plan or action than in specifying the nature of the problem to be addressed.

AGENCY RECORDS

Agency and other public records are often underutilized in assessing either the needs for or the possibility of change in some desired direction. Most agencies maintain records of who was served and how they were served and —to a greater or lesser degree—information on the effects of those services. Records that specify who was served, by inference, specify who was not. When agency records are scant, incomplete, or inconsistent, this in itself may suggest the existence of a problem.

When examined periodically, agency and other community records can indicate shifts or changes in population characteristics or in population needs. Birth, marriage and mortality records, for example, tell a great deal about the nature of the population living in a particular area. Police records might provide indications of changes in public morals, in public safety, or in public perceptions of what is legal and illegal.

Unfortunately, although agency records may provide a great many clues, they're not always able to provide definitive data. The data collected by one agency may not be comparable to the data collected by another. Even within the same agency, statistics may be gathered inconsistently over time. Because planners are not always able to bank on the validity of agency records, they are making increasing use of social indicators.

SOCIAL INDICATORS

Social indicators are quantitative measures that facilitate concise, balanced, and comprehensive judgments about conditions in the social environment. Their use presumes that selected problems or conditions can be quantitatively measured. National, state, and local indicators may deal with such measures as health; social mobility; income distribution; poverty; the physical environment; public safety; the growth of science, technology, art; or participation and alienation.

Unfortunately, indicators tend to vary from community to community and from state to state. Lack of consensus on the phenomena to be measured, and on the meaning of those measurements, reduces their utility. Difficulties in finding a common measure that might unify diverse components into a meaningful aggregation reduce the utility of social indicators.

Meanings not only differ from community to community, but from one time period to another within a particular community. This gives social indicators much less utility for planning than their proponents would admit. Nevertheless, they make available a set of data which outlines the social condition of a community or a particular population and has the potential for measuring social conditions over time.

CONSUMER OR CLIENT ANALYSIS

Consumer or client analysis can be used as a partial corrective to an unsatisfactory market system. Since the consumer of services rarely has a range of choices, market factors are not particularly useful in weeding out inappropriate services or facilities. Planners sometimes use techniques borrowed from the field of market analysis to identify actual or potential consumer populations, and to determine the reasons why only a proportion of the potential consumers actually become agency clients.

Those variables which increase the use of services for some and those which deny services to others are isolated and the effects of manipulating one or another are examined. Projections are made on a two-, three-, five-, or even ten-year basis to determine the impact on potential clients of changes in such variables as financial and other resources, administrative procedures, location of services, public education, and establishment of alternative service programs.

BENEFIT/COST ANALYSIS

Benefit/cost analysis refers to techniques of measurement that planners use to assist them in the choice of alternatives and in the evaluation of program impact or effectiveness. Alternative benefits are examined, ideally, in terms of their total costs, and the efficiency of one approach or another may be determined. Whether used by itself or as part of a larger program and budget process, benefit/cost analysis is becoming increasingly central to the assessment process in social planning.

PPBS

Program Planning and Budgeting Systems includes the use of cost/benefit measures. Based on elements of operations research and of earlier approaches to systems analysis, PPBS requires the appraisal of an organization's current activities and comparison of those activities with its stated objectives. Analysis includes the designation of a program structure in which the relationships among the organization's composite elements, its accomplishment of goals, and the range of its activities are documented. The resultant "program chart" may be contrasted with more traditional "organizational chart," which shows how administrators think the organization is structured but which may not take into account the actual (formal and informal) networks of communication and decision making within the organization.

PPBS also includes a projection of the organization's activity over time and a comparison of its capacity to perform a needed social function with the ability of other organizations or several components of disparate agencies to perform the same function. This may lead to a revision of the organization's programs, its objectives, and its structure.

INPUT-OUTPUT ANALYSIS

Input-output analysis is an analytic tool used extensively in the field of economics. It has not yet been applied in any major way in social planning, although a number of planners have attempted variations of this approach. Input-output analysis begins with the assumption that each element in a system is related directly or indirectly to all other elements in that system. A service agency, for example, is involved in relationships with resource providers, other service agencies, and with consumers. Each party to the relationship may provide some output to the other or may require some input from it.

By creating a chart (similar visually to a mileage chart) with a column for inputs and a row for outputs, it becomes possible to specify from whom an agency receives inputs and to whom it gives outputs. The chart shows how, where, and to what extent changes occur. Similar charts for each of the agencies in a system should make it possible to identify functional sub-systems.

However, creating charts manually is an extraordinarily time-consuming process. For this reason, input-output analysts have begun to use computer simulations and statistical measures to identify relationships and to measure the strength of those relationships over time. Computer simulations are perhaps among the most sophisticated assessment techniques. By manipulating elements that affect either input or output, a planner can experiment with a model of reality in ways that are impossible in the real world. At the present time, however, there is lack of both sufficient data and trained manpower to conduct such analyses. Eventually, though, this conceptually and mathematically refined tool may be of much more significance to state planning systems and at the local level.

THE DELPHI CONFERENCE

The Delphi conference is a tool adapted from the field of technological forecasting. Through a multi-staged, highly structured questionnaire, the Delphi user asks respondents to make assessments about the desirability, probability, or feasibility of policies or events. Delphi panelists (respondents) receive immediate feedback in the form of summary statements arrived at by adding up the judgments of all other respondents. Planners can use the Delphi technique in the first stage to identify those items on which there is agreement and those where considerable difference of opinion exists.

Should everyone agree, for example, that a policy or event is highly desirable, the planning direction becomes clear. If everyone agrees that it is desirable but highly unlikely, the planner knows he or she must seek further to identify the blocks to goal accomplishment. Or suppose there is a great deal of difference of opinion over whether an event is desirable, or a sizable gap between assessments of feasibility by respondents in one location over and against those from another location. In such instances, successive questionnaire "waves" are sent to the Delphi panelists after the planner has had time to analyze the data of each preceding wave. Each successive questionnaire probes deeper and deeper into those areas that the planner identifies as problematic.

Delphi conferences have several advantages over more traditional surveys, consultations, and public meetings. By making issues highly specific, by reducing the danger of group contagion, and by allowing the respondent to be anonymous, Delphi questionnaires encourage openness and honesty.

FUNCTIONAL JOB ANALYSIS

Functional job analysis, like Delphi, can be used to assess both current problems and anticipated problems, as well as to develop a competency model to serve as a goal. FJA can be used to examine either what individuals within an organization do or what organizations within a larger service system or network are expected to do functionally. It requires that tasks be broken down into three categories—those that involve people, those that involve material, and those that involve ideas. Each task is then described and recorded on a card.

Task cards include such factual information as a description of the task; minimal experiential or educational requirements for the person performing the task (or minimal standards for the agency assigned the task); minimal levels of acceptable performance; and identification of steps that might be used to improve performance. A task bank for human service agencies was developed by Sidney Fine and his associates from the Upjohn Institute in Washington, D.C. This bank includes some 600 tasks, each outlined on a McBee card.

Since Fine's work, a number of planners have attempted developing similar sets of McBee cards to describe inter-agency functions; that is, the tasks of a number of agencies that interact at the community level. The agencies that return such McBee cards to the planning organization indicate whether they perceive the various functions identified on the cards as being appropriate to them. By means of such feedback, planners can determine to what extent agencies meet minimal requirements for the performance of certain tasks within the larger community. Functional gaps can then be identified, and these will serve as a basis for developing planning goals and strategies.

FORCE FIELD ANALYSIS

Another technique employing face-to-face contact is force field analysis, which tends to focus on problems in the here and now. This tool has been used for organizational development purposes as well as interorganizational or community problem solving. Primarily, it attempts to identify problems in need of rapid intervention as well as those forces which might either prolong the problem or support change efforts. In using FFA, the planner would bring together those persons whose opinions he or she values, including social agency administrators, representatives of consumer groups, community influentials, funders, and others. The participants in an FFA process are generally divided into small subgroups of no more than five to eight persons, each organized in accordance with some commonality of interest or functional similarity. Each subgroup is then instructed to identify specific problems within the range that merit attention. Generally the planner has already determined the limits of the discussion, either through an announcement of the purpose of the meeting or through the selection of the participants. Once a problem or problems have been identified, forces that might be activated or employed to ameliorate it are also identified. These are categorized as "driving" or "restraining" forces. They are sorted into three categories—those over which the participants have no control, those over which someone else within the organization or community has some control, those over which no one locally seems to have control.

The forces over which the group is perceived as having some control are then ranked in terms of potency and acceptability. Strategies for overcoming the problem are devised and implementation procedures are tentatively designed. A similar analysis is then directed to those forces under someone else's control. The main advantages of this technique is that it begins the action process at the very same time as the planner is engaged in assessing the problem and possible strategies to overcome it.

NOMINAL GROUP TECHNIQUE

Like FFA, the nominal group technique also employs personal contact, but within a more structured framework. Participants in the meeting that uses a nominal group technique are asked to identify either needs, interests, problems, or objectives on a small card. The planner or group leader then collects and groups together those cards that evidence similar concerns. These are tacked up according to categories already identified on a bulletin board at the front of the room.

The planner then leads the group in a discussion of each card in turn. Participants are allowed to explain only what they intended by what they wrote on the card; evaluation and argumentation is delayed to a later time.

If several cards within a designated category seem to overlap in content or meaning, the contents are compressed into a smaller number of items. These are then ranked according to their priority through a voice or hand vote of participants. Once priorities are set within each category, categories are ranked in relationship to each other. Now decisions about how to proceed are made against feasibility criteria, such as costs, readiness, motivation, acceptability, unavailability of other resources. Like force field analysis, assessment and the beginning intervention process are linked in this technique. Like the Delphi method, the nominal group technique permits the weighing of a number of alternatives according to a large number of criteria. Unlike the Delphi technique, anonymity is lost and the sharpness of perspectives that exists in Delphi can be blurred through group interaction. On the other hand, the nominal group approach requires less direction and management by the planner, and permits greater responsibility to be assumed by the participants for their collective actions.

Most social planners will make use of one or more of the tools described here. They may find them useful in working out "a plan for planning" and in sorting out and ordering the data they need as a basis for decision making. The preliminary assessments can, of course, also be used to monitor a planning agency's progress and to evaluate its accomplishments. Insofar as many of these techniques are used to involve others in the planning process, they are used in a positive or offensive way.

The planning tools can also be used for defensive purposes. Social planners are not alone in their access to assessment tools, which can just as well be used by persons hostile to the planner's objectives. "We know the state agency wants us to put all our proposals in systems language," reports a director of a community mental health board, "so we use all the technical terms necessary to justify our requests. We put all our stuff in cost effectiveness terms. We have to. We wouldn't get funded otherwise."

Program and Planning Evaluation

A great deal has been written in recent years about the techniques and methods of program evaluation, and their uses for program development, plan making, and for holding planners and service providers accountable. The richness of this literature makes it unnecessary and perhaps unwise to recapitulate it in the limited space available. A list of suggestions for further reading appears at the end of this chapter.

The reader may also find the following excerpt of an interview with an experienced planner instructive. "People often confuse evaluation with cost effectiveness measures. The way I see it, evaluative research should be a diagnostic tool. It helps you understand why some things occurred or did not occur. The big question in evaluative research is what happened and why, not how much did it cost. I find evaluative research important in planning because it can help you switch strategies when you need to make programmatic adjustments.

"A good evaluator will help the program people think through what they're doing in relationship to their objectives. A bad evaluator will justify a weak program by picking only those aspects which look good, or he will destroy a program which he may be opposed to for political reasons. There always is a danger of using the guise of scientific objectivity to fool the public. I've seen some agencies stalling a decision about a controversial matter, pending the outcome of an evaluation. The outcome may never be made public, but the storm blows over. Some people use evaluations to shift attention away from failure in a program toward some aspect of it which looks good.

"On the other hand, good evaluative research can be used to mobilize public support for needed change in programs that don't work, or to highlight programs that do work in order to expand them or get more support.

WHO WANTS WHAT OUT OF THE EVALUATION?

"Not everybody will be seeking the same thing from an evaluation process. The agency director might be concerned with how well the program is achieving its goals, and which components are most effective. Or he might simply want to justify a pet project. Program staff might want to justify their biases about the program's operations, or enhance the prestige of their particular service against other services provided by the agency. Often everyone will resist an outside evaluator. They will be resentful, fearful, and skeptical about the possibility that the researcher doesn't know what is important.

"Of course, the researcher may *not* really know what's important. His criteria for success may be quite different from the staff's because he may not fully understand the program objectives and goals. This may not be the researcher's fault, especially when the agency is unclear and hasn't spelled out its program objectives.

"Chances are that most consumers will have little or no interest in evaluations. Their interests are in the availability, accessibility, quality, cost, and variety of services. This is unfortunate. Any evaluator worth his salt will try to involve consumers in evaluating an agency.

"In my own experience, the most effective evaluations are those which involve representatives of line staff, administration, policy members, and consumers. While there will probably be tensions among these parties and between them and the evaluator, their involvement and support will increase the probability that changes will happen even before the evaluation is complete. Some evaluators think that involving the staff is sufficient. Not so. Agency staff are notoriously myopic in their views of what is important. They need the pressure of outsiders to see what they're doing from someone else's point of view. Too often, I've found staff evaluating a particular service very positively or very negatively only to discover that policy makers or consumers have an entirely different point of view."

Review

Assessment informs and accompanies all stages or phases of the planning process. It can be used to assess the planner's capability of effecting change as well as the need or desire for those changes. When focusing on the planner's capability, it may be used to examine the climate or issue environment, or the task environment around the planner's organization or around those other organizations that may be targets of change.

When focusing on issues to be addressed, assessment may be used to examine the extensiveness or severity of current or anticipated problems, or to assess the differences between the current situation and one that may be considered more desirable. A variety of assessment techniques were briefly described.

Several of these will be dealt with in greater depth in the following chapter. For this reason, a list of supplementary questions and activities as well as an expanded list of recommended and suggested readings will be deferred until the end of that chapter.

Suggestions for Further Reading*

ASSESSMENT

Assessing the Need for Human Services. Human Services Bibliography Series, No. 2. Washington, D.C.: Project Share, Department of Health, Education and Welfare, 1976.

Assessing Human Needs. Sacramento, Calif.: League of California Cities, 1972.

Assessing Social Services Needs and Resources. Washington, D.C.: Booz-Allen Public Administration Services, Inc., 1975.

BANG, STEPHEN, and JOHN STEVENS. *Information Systems How-To Guides.* Cincinnati: Information Systems Center, 1975.

BAUMHEIR, EDWARD C., and GRETCHEN A. HELLER. *Analysis and Synthesis of Needs Assessment Research in the Field of Human Services.* Denver, Colo.: University of Denver Center for Social Research and Development, 1974.

ELLIOTT, DELBERT S., et al. *Research Handbook for Community Planning and Feedback Instruments,* Vols. I and II. Boulder, Colo.: Behavioral Research and Evaluation Corporation, 1976.

HALPERT, HAROLD P., WILLIAM J. HORVATH, and JOHN P. YOUNG. *Administrator's Handbook to the Application of Operations Research to the Management of Mental Health Systems.* Ann Arbor, Mich.: The University of Michigan Mental Health Research Institute, 1974.

WARHEIT, GEORGE J., ROGER A. BELL, and JOHN J. SCHWAB. *Planning for Change: Needs Assessment Approaches.* Gainesville, Fla.: University of Florida Department of Psychiatry (Box 722), 1974.

PROGRAM EVALUATION

CARO, FRANCIS (Ed.) *Readings in Evaluation Research.* New York: Russell Sage Foundation, 1971.

*See also the suggestions at the end of Chapter 8.

DORNBUSCH, SANFORD M., and W. RICHARD SCOTT. *Evaluation and the Exercise of Authority.* San Francisco: Jossey-Bass, 1975.

FERMAN, LOUIS A. "Some Perspectives on Evaluating Social Welfare Programs." *Annals of the American Academy of Political and Social Sciences,* September, 1969.

FRANKLIN, JACK L., and JEAN H. THRASHER. *An Introduction to Program Evaluation.* New York: John Wiley and Sons, 1976.

GLASS, GENE V. (Ed.). *Evaluation Studies Review Annual,* Vol. I. Beverly Hills: Sage Publications, Inc., 1976.

GOTTMAN, JOHN MORDECHAI, and ROBERT EARL CLASEN. *Evaluation in Education —A Practitioner's Guide.* Itasca, Ill.: F. Peacock Publishing Co., 1972.

ROSSI, PETER H., and W. WILLIAMS. *Evaluating Social Programs.* New York: Seminar Press, 1972.

SUCHMAN, EDWARD A. *Evaluative Research.* New York: Russell Sage Foundation, 1967.

SZE, WILLIAM C., and JUNE G. HOPPS. *Evaluation and Accountability in Human Service Programs.* Cambridge, Mass.: Schenkman Books, 1974.

TRIPODI, TONY, PHILLIP FELLIN, and IRWIN EPSTEIN. *Social Program Evaluation.* Itasca, Ill.: F. Peacock Publishing Co., 1971.

8

Assessment Tools

Tools as Instruments of Rationality

If planning is the rationalization of the political process, as some say it is, planning tools may be the instruments of that rationalization. Jacques Ellul, the French philosopher, predicts that political decisions may eventually be made in an arena of competing technologies. Those who can apply the winning technology become the most influential.

Over the past thirty years, a number of tools have been developed in the fields of management science, social economics, and technological forecasting which have direct applicability to social planning, and in particular to the assessment process. Some of these tools, such as PPBS, and benefit/cost analysis, are well known. Built on operations research and systems analysis, they have had a significant impact on the design and evaluation of human services.

Unfortunately, many community-based social planners may be only dimly aware that some of these tools exist. Fewer still may be skillful enough to use them. Even though social planners have accumulated a good deal of experience in the use of these tools, little of their experience has been adequately documented in the literature. For this reason, the experiences and insights of the planners interviewed for this chapter may be of considerable interest to the reader.

Some of the assessment tools described have just recently entered the lexicon of social planning. Others are well established and have been the subjects of many books. Nevertheless, each tool described will include one excerpt from an interview with a social planner who has found it particularly helpful in his or her practice. In most instances the planner describes how the tool was used and under what circumstances it was found to be either functional or dysfunctional.

The reader should beware, however, since many of these tools are still primitive. This point is made clearly by the planner who discusses his experience with PPBS. Other planners may claim more for their tools than is warranted. There is always the danger that over-enthusiasm might lead to the erroneous belief that the tools are available to do almost anything desired and that any problem can be solved if the right tool is found.

In a number of situations, several of these tools might be used together. Juxtaposing the experiences and opinions of the planners quoted suggests an amazing confluence. PPBS, of course, is inseparable from benefit/cost analysis. Both focus on the relationships of means used to outcomes expected.

Conversely, client analysis and social indicators (as described in this text) both put a greater focus on the client, whose objectives become the measure of program success. The actual or potential consumer of services determines whether the quality of life or availability of services is satisfactory. Services and their impact are then evaluated against changes in consumer perceptions.

Six tools are described: Delphi, PPBS, benefit/cost analysis, input-output analysis, social indicators, and client analysis. They are selected for their representativeness, not because these six are more important or more useful than any others that might have been described. Although their treatment is far from exhaustive, the reader should be able to get a glimpse of how they're used and for what purposes. The rather exhaustive bibliography at the end of the chapter is designed for the reader who wants to gain a working knowledge of these and other assessment tools.

The Delphi is no Oracle

Delphi is a method of eliciting expert opinion through the use of successive questionnaires administered to individual panelists, who are selected on the basis of their perceived expert knowledge or opinion. They are asked to respond anonymously to a number of statements, perhaps to evaluate the statements' accuracy, likelihood, desirability, or cost. Their responses may also include statements of their own or reasons for their assessment.

The results of individual responses are tabulated and fed back to all the panelists in a succeeding questionnaire. This feedback takes the form of a summary of the points of agreement or disagreement among the experts. Where differences of opinion are identified, the Delphi design team probes for the reasons for these differences through a refinement of the statements presented for panel response.

The Delphi method is generally considered to be fast, inexpensive, and easy to administer. This is not always the case, however, as respondents who have been participants in a poorly designed Delphi process are likely to point out. There are generally two types of Delphi questionnaires: those that attempt to forecast or predict the likelihood that some event or process is likely to occur; and those which are oriented toward an assessment of the best or more feasible policies to take.

Predictive or projective Delphis require the involvement of panelists who are exceptionally knowledgeable about the substantive area being examined. Although their opinions may differ, it is expected that they will nevertheless be well informed. In a policy Delphi, participants are generally those who might be in the best position to evaluate the impact of one or more policies or program priorities. These may include representatives of consumers, providers, or regulatory agencies who are influential in the policy-making process. The policy Delphi is no more intended to arrive at a consensual policy statement than the predictive Delphi aims at forecasting the future. Instead, both aim at achieving clarity even if consensus is impossible. It is therefore crucial that the panelists represent as broad and diverse a group of experts as possible. Also, as indicated previously, respondent anonymity permits a greater degree of risk taking and obviates the possibility of "group think."

The Delphi concept is one of the many by-products of defense industry research. An Air-Force-sponsored Rand Corporation study entitled "Project Delphi" was conducted in the early fifties. It was initially used to estimate the probable effects of a massive nuclear attack on the United States. Later, particularly during the 1960s, the Delphi technique was applied to long-range technological forecasting. Although the method tends to be associated with Norman Dalkey and Olaf Helmer of the Rand Corporation, it has been used extensively in the mid- to late '70s in a variety of human service assessment studies. In the vignette that follows, a health planner describes his use of the Delphi method at the local level. Note that he has combined the Delphi method with the use of task forces. As in many of the examples given in the previous chapter, this planner integrates assessment completely into the other planning phases.

"If we planners could have it the way we want it, we would consult the oracle of Delphi every time we need information or want to predict the future. But there is no oracle. It disappeared with the ancient Greeks. What's more, the old oracle gave bad advice from time to time. Why trust a single source?

What I look for is a way of spreading the risk when I want informed advice. That's where the twentieth-century Delphi comes in. It's a technique, not a place.

"The Delphi technique is little more than a method for systematic collection of informed judgments on a particular topic. In a way it owes its origins to the British jury system rather than to the Greeks. It's a comparatively new technique, developed originally by the Rand Corporation and used heavily in the field of technological forecasting. But it's got applicability to our field as well.

WHEN I USE IT

"I use the Delphi technique when there is a need for a meaningful communications structure among individuals and groups around a particular issue. For example, before our area-wide health task forces were established, there'd been almost no communication about any issues pertaining to health needs among hospital personnel, private practitioners, or concerned citizens, influential public officials, and community lay persons.

"I knew from the histories of the community action program, of the Model Cities program, and of our Community Mental Health board, that my community is badly divided. Unless task forces are all composed of like-minded individuals with similar backgrounds, they promote fireworks and then either bomb out or fizzle out. It was clear to me that I had to build some sort of communications structure and identify an agenda before I could allow our task forces to meet face to face. The agenda had to be based on informed opinions, hopefully the opinions of future task force members and other influential community people.

"Now don't misunderstand me. I don't use Delphi as a substitute for empirical data or for committee meetings. I use it to supplement them, especially when one or more of the following conditions prevail:

> when adequate information is unavailable and would take too long or be too costly to get
>
> when the informed opinion of significant parties, including consumers or potential consumers, may be as important as or more important than hard data
>
> when the problems at hand or the tasks to be performed are so broad that more individuals are needed to share opinions than can interact in any kind of face-to-face exchange
>
> when disagreements among individuals are so severe that the communication process must be structured and refereed
>
> where time is scarce and it would be difficult for the individuals I need to involve to get together for frequent group meetings

where a supplemental group communication process helps to increase
the efficiency and effectiveness of face-to-face meetings

HOW IT WORKS

"The Delphi technique uses a structured series of questionnaires which
are distributed sequentially at various time intervals. The first Delphi questionnaire is usually exploratory in nature. You can involve a relatively large
number of respondents at one time—as many as 50 or 60—and you don't have
to bring them all together for a meeting.

"Before convening our area-wide task forces, I designed a Delphi with
20 issue statements. I sent them to everyone we had invited to become a task
force member. If I remember correctly, two of the statements went something
like:

The public transportation system with neighborhood and house-to-house pick-
ups as required should be established for disabled persons needing transportation
to health care facilities.

A center for health services should be built in each neighborhood with service
inputs from all relevant agencies.

"I asked the respondents to rate each of the items according to a number of
dimensions on a five-point scale. For example, I asked them to indicate
whether the proposed policy was 'highly desirable,' 'desirable,' 'neutral,' 'undesirable,' or 'highly undesirable.' I then asked them to rate each statement
according to their 'estimate of cost,' 'probability of support,' 'probability of
opposition,' and 'feasibility within three years,' also on a five-point scale. I left
space at the bottom of the questionnaire for respondents to add as many as
five additional policy issues, if they wanted to.

"I then summarized the responses from each task force and from the
total group. That way, task force members could see whether there was consensus or a variety of opinions on issues in their own task forces. They could
also see how members of other task forces felt. We were also able to identify
those issues on which preliminary consensus existed and those where disagreement was widespread.

"These preliminary inputs from task force members helped cut down the
confusion that usually prevails at first meetings when people are jockeying for
position and power and find it difficult to deal with substantive issues. Before
the first task force meeting I sent out the collated responses along with a second
questionnaire, and used this second set of responses as the basis for the agenda
of each task force's first meeting.

"The reason for the second wave of questionnaires is an interesting one;
this is what makes Delphi such a useful way of structuring inputs. When the
first questionnaires were returned, there was nothing left to probe for regarding

those items which everyone rated as desirable or highly desirable, and which respondents predicted would command a high degree of support or could be feasibly completed within the next three years. We could just go ahead and act on these items. Why waste task force time rehashing them? Concensus existed.

"However, many items were rated as highly desirable by some and highly undesirable by others. It *was* a divided community. I took each item of this kind and broke it down into its component parts so that in the second questionnaire I could probe for an explanation of the differences in opinion. In some cases, the clues for these differences came from the items the respondents had added at the bottom of the first questionnaire. In a few instances, on the second wave, I asked respondents to explain the reasons they felt something was desirable or undesirable or why they thought it was desirable but not feasible.

THE ADVANTAGES OF DELPHI

"I guess it would be possible to use a Delphi as a substitute form of communications. Frankly, the care and feeding of task forces and committees takes up so much time and energy that I've sometimes been tempted to replace them all with a Delphi. It's a hell of a lot neater and, in terms of getting informed opinion, it's a hell of a lot more effective. Its major advantages are that respondents can remain anonymous, and are therefore more apt to take risks in their responses and to be more honest about their thoughts and feelings. Further, Delphi minimizes the phenomenon of 'group-think.' Since people aren't in face-to-face interaction, they don't wait to find out how someone else is going to feel before forming their own opinion, and they aren't swayed by group pressure or charismatic leadership.

"Delphi also has a built-in feedback mechanism: respondents can compare their own answers to those of other equally anonymous respondents. Of course, you can tell people who the other respondents are as a group without allowing anyone to know how a particular individual responded. There are, however, some limitations to Delphi.

THE LIMITATIONS OF DELPHI

"First of all, it doesn't replace the committee or task force process. It complements it and structures it but doesn't replace it. Certain issues have to be fought out in public. Decisions have to be made in a political arena. They can't be made on the basis of data or informed opinion alone. If decisions are to stick, they must often be made by convincing, buying off, compromising with, or defeating the opposition. That requires a face-to-face process. You've got to know who's for you and who's against you, and how much they've got at stake.

"Decisions are going to stick if public opinion or the support of key individuals and organizations is behind them. But these decisions are best reached when the areas of agreement or disagreement can be identified and specified dispassionately. That's where Delphi comes in.

"However, Delphis aren't easy to conduct. I've seen them fail when: (a) the designers didn't know the issues well enough to select or design important items for inclusion in the questionnaire; (b) they used poor techniques for summarizing and presenting group responses or common interpretations; (c) they failed to explore disagreements. This disheartens dissenters, or encourages them to drop out, creating an artificial consensus."

The Politics of Rationality and the Rationalization of Politics: PPBS

Like many of the other tools described in this chapter, PPBS (Program Planning and Budgeting System) was developed by the Department of Defense. In 1965, by an executive order, it was adopted by other branches of the federal government. Although PPBS is more than an assessment tool, its principal and perhaps lasting use is in assessing the difference between what is and what might be. Like other analytic tools based on systems theory, it tends to define functions and then to determine what might be necessary in order for those functions to be optimized.

As adopted by HEW in fiscal year 1966, for example, it required the development of program and financial plans for a five-year period in each of the following four program categories: education, health, social and rehabilitation services, and income maintenance. PPBS's introduction was not an unqualified success. Many critics felt that too much was attempted too soon. PPBS is a "rational" management system in that it attempts to connect planning, managerial control, and operational control to the budgetary and financing system. It requires comparing inputs (defined in terms of cost) to outputs (defined in terms of dollar benefits). It then requires the making of time-line projections for the accomplishment of particular benefits. Some planners argue that there is not a single PPBS method; that PPBS is really a state of mind or a way of looking at things.

This is perhaps the best way of approaching PPBS. As a rational tool it falls short because the requisite variables are hardly ever under the planner's control. It does, however, tend to impose or add rationality to the planning and programming as well as to the budgeting processes.

Both the problems and the promise of PPBS are described in the vignette that follows.

"I found that probably the biggest problem in using the program budgeting approach is that it really puts administrators, bureaucrats, and politicians on the defensive. Any system that will force an organization into a public evaluation of its objectives and means is going to put a crimp in its traditional ways of operating. I've never seen PPBS introduced into an agency where a significant shift in power didn't happen as the result. And it usually causes an equalization or redistribution of power within the organization.

"A lot of people say that PPBS is an overrated tool, that it didn't work in HEW and it won't work here. Maybe too much was claimed for it. Maybe they tried to take on too large a system at HEW. PPBS is not an infallible tool.

"Still, PPBS is a fact in this state. The Governor's office uses it, and the appropriations committee judges all state department budgets on the basis of how well defined they are in program budgeting terms. It may not be the last word in program development or in budgeting, but it is the latest one.

"Most people don't know that the United States has gone through three budgetary phases since 1920. First was the 'control' phase, which emphasized organizational control of specific tasks. It began the use of the line-item budget, the one most of us were trained in. This was followed by the 'management' budget, identified with the New Deal. Focusing on the effective use of resources, it was later called the 'performance' budget. PPBS was developed by the Rand Corporation as a way of articulating performance budgets with systems concepts. Its central feature is the development of benefit/cost analyses on alternative ways of accomplishing objectives. The costs of various means are weighed against their relative effectiveness and program outputs.

WHY USE IT?

"A knowledge of how PPBS works is for me essential for survival. Whether you like the system or not, you are at a tremendous disadvantage if you don't talk the right language. I myself find the system extremely helpful. Of course, it's taken some study and a few mistakes on my part. My basic initiation came from some university consultants. In most communities, there's usually somebody around who can be helpful, in the city manager's office, the county hospital, or in some nearby college.

STEP 1: APPRAISING CONTRIBUTIONS OF EACH UNIT

"In Program Budgeting you start out by *appraising the contributions of every unit within the system in terms of that unit's objectives.* If you looked at all the providers of service to the elderly as comprising a system of services, you would identify what each of the service providers does for older people. I'll have to be honest with you: Social welfare people have the hardest time doing this sort of thing. They tend to specify their activities by administrative units. They'll tell you that a geriatric unit in a large hospital does this and that. Or they'll describe what the special services division of the public transportation agency does. But they won't specify what these units *do* for older people, what difference they make.

"Somehow they haven't moved off the old line-budget notion to a performance budget. That makes it particularly difficult to get them to adopt a program budget. First you have to get them to specify their performance objectives and their goals. Then you can get them to categorize all their activities that lead toward goal attainment and those which militate against it. Pretty soon, the agencies discover that what they're actually doing may not have any bearing on what they thought their objectives were.

"Hopefully this encourages agency leadership to reexamine organizational objectives, bringing goals into line with actual performance. Or perhaps program directors may explore the possibility that what they're doing is inappropriate in relation to their goals. By extending this notion to the whole system, they can begin to identify those units which are engaged in activities that nullify or block the successful achievement of other units. In other words, you begin to identify those places where the system breaks down. You also find out whether there are any conflicting goals or objectives among the units involved.

STEP 2: SPECIFYING OBJECTIVES

"Arriving at some consensus on objectives can be a difficult job, one which requires constant hammering out through task forces and policy boards. Once you've got consensus you determine how those objectives might be reached with a minimal expenditure of resources.

"Here, in step two, you try to *account for both future program needs and fiscal costs as well as realistic fiscal constraints.* In other words, you try to guess what the maximum is you can get for any given objective or any given program at a given time. But you've got to look at other resources as well: manpower, expertise, good will, and the like. You go back to the first step. You look for budget distortions where money spent for one objective is actually accomplishing another or subverting the first one.

STEP 3: LISTING PROGRAM ALTERNATIVES

"This leads you to a third step: *examination of program alternatives projected over time.* You have to think through all the possible ways of getting to where you want to go. And you should free your thinking of all constraints, ignore tradition and past experience, if you can. But then get hard nosed. Up to this point, most planners with a little savvy and a good ability to develop relationships could probably carry the analysis and specification of objective steps analysis on their own. But evaluating alternative approaches may require special technical expertise. At this step you may need to bring in your outside consultant; someone who knows about benefits and costs and how to figure them.

STEP 4: BENEFIT/COST ANALYSIS

"Good design requires that you have indices of effectiveness and efficiency. For example, how many psychiatric patients in a geriatric ward have been placed successfully in the community? Counting the number of placements is easy, but quantifying the meaning of success is a little more difficult. Once you've done that, you calculate the efficiency of one kind of placement over another and contrast that with keeping elderly patients in back wards. Anyway, you've got somehow to *weigh your costs in relationship to the extent to which you accomplish your objectives.* It's a question of effectiveness. Then you have to make some pretty hard choices.

"If an expenditure of $13,000 per patient will buy you 75 percent effectiveness, and an expenditure of $14,000 will buy you 99 percent effectiveness, the choice is easy. You go the extra $1,000 per patient. And if the cost of moving from 75 percent to 99 percent effectiveness is double the original cost requiring that you cut the numbers of patients you can help in half, the choice is again relatively easy. But sometimes the alternatives are not that simple. The ranges are different. For example, the cost of placing black people may be much higher than the cost of placing white people. Your choices then may be more political than they are economic.

"A benefit/cost analysis of this sort is actually valid only when you compare the efficiency of one means with the efficiency of another, or the effectiveness of one program with the effectiveness of another. The trouble is, it doesn't compare apples and oranges. You still don't know whether to put your dollars into a transportation program or a multi-service center—or perhaps a home handyman program.

STEP 5: MAKING POLICY OR PROGRAM CHOICES

"Your economic calculations through PPBS only provide you with additional data. They don't make the choice for you. *Decision-making is still a political process.* Only the analysis of the relationship of costs to benefits is a technical process. Don't ever let anybody tell you that technical analysis is a substitute for value judgments.

STEP 6: PROGRAMMED BUDGET REVIEW

"OK, you try to reach a compromise among objectives, cost, political acceptability, and availability of manpower with sufficient expertise to do what your group of agencies wants to have done. You specify your objectives, and choose the program to accomplish those objectives. You now move on to the sixth step—*an ongoing process of program and budget review.* This includes listing target dates for the achievement of program objectives and sub-goals, figuring your costs over time.

"In essence, this is what most people call 'a plan.' It serves as a guide to action, evaluation, and monitoring. At various target dates, you can see how many of your objectives you've accomplished or whether you or some other person or organization has thrown obstacles in your path. If so, you might want to reconsider your objectives, figure out ways to overcome apparent resistance. At your completion date, you determine whether you've accomplished your objectives—how effectively and at what cost.

"In order to do this, you have to make sure you've got a well designed evaluation system that supplies you with the relevant data about program effectiveness and cost. The biggest problem you're likely to meet is in deciding on the essential variables, and then on how to weigh each factor in your information system. Retrieval is the simplest part. It is a technical problem. It can be solved with or without computers. But deciding what to put in and when, that's the tricky one.

SOME CAUTIONS

"As I pointed out earlier, PPBS can be pretty threatening. It has a new language, and it requires at least a certain amount of technical expertise. But the mystique can be dispelled with a little experience. What's most threatening is that it transfers power by making new information available. This can be a threat to bureaucrats and politicians. I can't think of too many agencies who want their program effectiveness measured and the reports made public. I don't know of many departments or units within an agency that want to be evaluated on the basis of whether they contribute to the overall agency goal.

"When people complain that PPBS is primitive and therefore useless, I remind them that the tomahawk is more primitive than the jeweler's mallet, but they both can be used to crack open stones. You have to be careful with a primitive tool. You don't apply it to the wrong kind of stone, expecting it to accomplish what it is not refined enough to do. As I see it, you've got to practice with your tomahawk, refine it. Discover all its possibilities. It's the same for using a tool on any system.

"Another problem is that there's no single model for PPBS. Anybody who's made even a cursory review of the literature must come out spinning. You've got to stay with it, and recognize that PPBS is still more of an art than a technical tool, despite the fact that some aspects are technical. You bring in outside experts to help where they can. Still, your biggest problem will probably be in assigning values to your ends and means. Whatever approach or model you use, you've got to make sure that value judgments and resistances

are explored early and openly. That's why the first step—the nontechnical one
—is perhaps the most important.

"In the long run, probably the greatest argument for using PPBS is that
it forces the parties involved in the process to think through their program and
policy alternatives. It forces them to become problem- and goal-oriented. It
forces them to assume a strategic stance in all their decisions."

Costing Out the Benefits of Service Programs

At the heart of the program planning and budgeting system is benefit/cost
analysis, essentially an economic tool that can be helpful in deciding what
benefits are achievable in relationship to certain costs. From the planner's
point of view, he might want to:

maximize benefits, given costs remain stable
minimize costs to achieve any given level of benefits (cost-effectiveness)
find an optimal level at which point one gets the greatest benefit for the
    least cost

As the following vignette demonstrates, there is considerable difference
in outcome when one applies a benefit/cost analysis in contrast to a net present
value analysis. NPV is equivalent to the benefits accrued minus the costs
involved to achieve those benefits when measured over time. Benefit/costs,
however, are expressed in ratio terms; that is, benefits accrued or desired in
relation to required costs. The advantage of using a ratio is that different
benefit/cost ratios can be compared in terms of absolute numbers. A ratio of
3/2, for example, would be better than a ratio of 5/4. Using benefit/cost
analysis as an assessment device thereby can enable the planner to make
choices between one form of intervention or one kind of service and another.
It may not be all that easy, however. Some rather difficult questions have to
be answered.

First, the planner has to be able to specify the ends or benefits sought.
Then these must be quantified (reduced to dollar terms) so that benefits can
be compared to each other as well as against the costs of attaining them.

But what are costs? Which costs are to be counted and how are they to
be quantified in dollar terms so as to allow comparisons?

The development of useful benefit/cost ratios requires that externalities
be taken into account. In economic terms, externalities are all those inputs and
outputs which may affect the planning process or service program but which
have been excluded from the cost/benefit analysis. They are includable only
if they make no real difference for purposes of calculation. Unfortunately, it

is sometimes almost impossible to determine whether a variable is truly an externality or whether it should have been included in the equation to begin with.

As the reader who may be interested in pursuing cost analysis will discover, even the terms "benefits" and "costs" tend to be somewhat slippery. The word "benefit" is often modified by prefixing it with the words "direct," "indirect," or "social spillover." Direct benefits are those that accrue directly to the participant of a program or project. Indirect benefits are those that accrue to various other elements in the community—to the taxpayer, for example, if the unemployed are retrained and placed in permanent jobs. The social spillover might include an even broader benefit, for example, to the overall economy, which benefits from increased production and a larger tax base.

Costs are also complicated by adding such prefixes as "average," "direct," "fixed," "marginal," "real," "total," and "opportunity." Direct costs are those which a funder must provide in order to carry a program (for example, federal appropriations for job training and placement). The average costs might be determined as the number of dollars required to train and place a single unemployed worker on the job. Fixed costs are those that do not vary with output. They'll be the same if output is 20 placed workers or 200 placed workers. They generally reflect overhead and general administrative costs which are difficult to reduce. The real cost is the dollar cost adjusted for changes in prices. This measure thus aims at pinpointing the cost of a program in terms of its output rather than in purely monetary terms. The word "total" means just what it says, the numbers of dollars required for producing a given level of output. To these should be added the social spillover costs, which may include losses incurred by some people not involved in either the production or the consumption of the benefits—for example, opportunity costs, those opportunities left unexplored because funds and other resources were allocated to the particular project in question.

The reader without a strong economic background should not be discouraged if these terms sound a bit obscure. It is not necessary for all planners to be able to conduct benefit/cost analysis. It is important, however, that they understand the strengths and limitations of B/C A, what it does, and how it differs from other approaches. The following example may add some clarity to this discussion. It is somewhat technical and less conventional than our other interviews. This is as it should be. C/B analysis is technical and planners need to be familiar with the language used by those conducting cost/benefit analyses.

"It would be terrific if we had a standard system of measurement to determine the economic returns of programs and services. I'm afraid we're still far from it, but we do have a variety of cost/benefit and benefit/cost models which move in that direction. Of course, not everything is measurable. Trying to quantify every value would just diminish the overall credibility of any benefit/cost study because such quantification would tend to be overestimated and spuriously accrued.

HOW IT WORKS

"Benefit/cost analysis is not the only method of economic evaluation of programs in nonprofit systems. It can be understood by contrasting it to the net present value approach. NPV rates alternative programs according to the differences between the present values of the sum of all benefits and cost. Its general formula is:

$$\text{Net Present Value} = \frac{\Sigma}{t} \frac{\text{Benefits}}{(1 + r)^t} - \frac{\Sigma}{t} \frac{\text{Costs}}{(1 + r)^t} *$$

where

t = time over which the benefits and costs accrue

r = cost of capital or social time preference rate

Benefit/cost ratio, in contrast, ranks projects according to their benefit/cost ratio which is the total benefits divided by the total costs. Its general formula would appear as follows:

$$\text{Benefit/Cost Ratio} = \frac{\underset{t}{\Sigma} \text{Benefits}}{\underset{t}{\Sigma} \text{Costs}}$$

"The difference between the methods is significant. For example, holding the instant rate at a constant zero, assume that the benefits in project A are $3,000 and its costs total $1,000. According to the net present value method, the difference between the two gives you an NPV of $2,000. Using a benefit /cost ratio, you would divide 3,000 by 1,000 and get a benefit/cost ratio of 3.

"Let's take a different set of figures. In project B, let's say the benefits are $8,000 and the costs $5,000. The NPV would be 8,000 − 5,000 or 3,000; the benefit/cost ratio would be 8/5 or 1.6.

"Now, if you had to make a choice between the projects using a benefit-/cost ratio, you would take project A because its benefit/cost ratio is greater than that of project B. But if you use a net present value approach, you would select project B which gives you 3,000 as against project A which gives you only 2,000. So, the project you choose depends on the technique you use.

"Planners should be aware that the NPV is biased toward larger projects. The larger the project, the higher its net present value. What's more, this

*Σ refers to "The total of"

method doesn't provide you with any way of ranking projects on the basis of output achieved per unit of input. Thus its approach is inadequate when resources must be allocated across several projects or programs, or when a total program has to be evaluated in terms of its return per dollar cost. Since this is almost always the case in social services where there are serious budgetary constraints, the net present value approach is inapplicable as a decision-making tool when you want to implement programs that have the highest return per unit of resource utilization.

"Of course, benefit/cost ratios are also biased, but only in favor of those projects which have the greatest percentage of their costs in future time periods. The more future the costs are—that is, the longer you delay the costs—the higher the ratio you can get. The most important thing is that by using a benefit/cost ratio approach, you can rank projects on the basis of return per dollar of expenditure."

Input-Output Analysis

The planner interested in economics may also find the next vignette on the use of input/output analysis in the assessment process of interest. It draws from a tool developed in macro-economics but uses it in much the same way as sociometrics are used to measure relationships. It is useful in assessing the environment and in particular the exchange relationships that occur between the providers of service in a given geographic area. The vignette speaks for itself.

"I studied economics as an undergraduate and remember running across a macroeconomic analytic tool developed by Leontief, the economist who won the Nobel prize a few years back. It's a way of charting market transactions within a country or across national boundaries. I've never seen it referred to in the social welfare literature, but it seemed like a natural way to chart the relationships between social agencies in a community. If one of the things social planners are concerned with is coordinating programs and services, they've got to have some way of analyzing the nature of exchange relationships between the providers of services.

CONSTRUCTING AN INPUT-OUTPUT CHART

"Constructing an input-output chart is as simple as constructing a mileage chart. In fact, it looks quite similar. You list the names of all social agencies in your area in a column on the left-hand side of a piece of paper; then you list them in the same order in a row across the top. By drawing in the matrices, you wind up with hundreds of tiny boxes. You might start off with a chart like this:

	State Hospital	Mental Health Center	Nursing Home	Family Agency	School Counseling Service	Vocational Rehabilitation
State Hospital						
Mental Health Center						
Nursing Home						
Family Agency						
School Counseling Service						
Vocational Rehabilitation						

"Now, on a scale of one to five, indicate the extensiveness of the interchange between the agencies listed, to the best of your knowledge. In doing so, it might force you to think through which units in each of the agencies are involved in the exchange. In the mental health center, for example, perhaps the division that deals with community placements has exchange relationships with the state hospital, whereas its crisis center might relate to the family service agency. The more you think through the relationships the more complex the chart gets, and you might want to consider building several charts. Much of the time, of course, you won't have factual information on which to do your rating, and you'll have to arrange to have the legwork done. Too often, you'll discover that the exchanges between agencies are limited or nonexistent. That might suggest areas for you to explore encouraging exchanges.

"Essentially, the input-output chart gives you a map of the linkages that exist between organizations. What you might want to do is develop a directional map. Once you've established that exchanges take place between two organizations, you might then want to explore what is exchanged and by whom.

"Suggesting the kinds of questions to be asked is the great value of input-output analysis. Does one agency give more than it receives? Do agencies exchange clients? Do they also exchange staff and other resources? Does one party to the exchange provide the other with money while the other assumes programmatic or service responsibilities? Could the giving and taking involved be expanded to include other organizations? Within the total system of exchange, are there some sub-systems or sub-units? Do there exist the sort of natural clusterings like those that crop up in a sociogram? Are there ways in which those clusterings can be expanded or made more inclusive?"

Social Indicators

Social indicators have been variously defined as:

> ... a system of social accounts which give measures of the use of human resources in four fields:
> (1) the measurements of social costs in relation to net returns of economic innovations, (2) the measurement of social ills, (3) the creation of performance budgets in areas of defined social needs, and (4) indicators of economic opportunity and social mobility.

> measurements of social phenomena whose movements indicate whether a particular problem is getting better or worse relative to some common goal.

> statistics of direct normative interest measuring some state of welfare and if it changes in the right direction, it can be interpreted as things got better or people are better off.

> social statistics that:
> (1) are components in the model of social systems, (2) can be collected at various points in time and can be accumulated into a time/series, and (3) can be aggregated or disaggregated to levels appropriate to the specifications of the model.

Most social indicators are constructed by public commissions on a national, regional, state or local level. There are indicators of health, of social stability or instability, of mental health, of levels of education, and so on. Any data can be aggregated so as to provide measures relative to a particular field of interest or population.

What's important in the construction and use of social indicators is that the same measures be applied from year to year. For example, it makes no sense to try to get an indicator of change by comparing the numbers of persons who seek treatment for respiratory diseases in one year with those who report in a survey that they feel that they have respiratory diseases in another year. In the first case one is using as an indicator of illness the fact that certain persons seek treatment; in the second case, one is asking the entire population whether or not they feel they have a certain illness. The figures are not comparable and no inference can be made by trying to compare them.

Even when the data are comparable, their interpretation may be subject to a variety of external considerations. The numbers of persons seeking treatment for respiratory illnesses may have little to do with the numbers of people actually suffering from respiratory diseases. It may relate to the awareness of the existence of such diseases, the availability or accessibility of effective services to treat respiratory illnesses, or to the fact that costs are borne by public agencies.

Nevertheless, as imprecise as they sometimes are, social indicators can be of great help to the planner at the local level. In the vignette which follows, a planner describes how a survey instrument designed to gather comparable data from year to year became an effective tool in the assessment of both needs and wants at the community level.

"One of the most useful planning guides I've seen in a long time is the questionnaire designed for the Administration on Aging by the Institute for Interdisciplinary Studies of the American Rehabilitation Foundation. Every state unit on aging has a copy. It's a guide for obtaining information on the status of the elderly in each community throughout the state.

WHAT INDICATORS DO

"The indicators highlight the most common deficiencies among services for the elderly. They make it possible to make more intelligent allocations of funds, resources, personnel, time, facilities, and so on. Social indicators are quantitative measures of those conditions which affect the elderly: housing, neighborhood and social relations, satisfaction with life, economic well-being, independence, health. By measuring these qualities from year to year, it is possible to make balanced and comprehensive judgments about various aspects of the social environment, thereby highlighting those issues that planning should be concerned with and pinpointing the targets.

"Without these indicators, we have an intelligence gap. There'd be no way to measure the changes in the social condition of the elderly from year to year. There'd be no way to judge how well or how poorly we're doing in any of our planning, coordinating, or programming efforts. But I don't want to overclaim.

"Social indicators complement other kinds of information, but they don't substitute for them. For example, they don't describe the kinds of services being offered or the scope of those services. They don't tell you about the kinds of resources that are available or those being expended on behalf of the elderly. They do tell you what the actual social conditions of older people are, either as individuals or by demographic groups. And they will tell you the status of the *entire elderly population* in a particular community, not just that segment of it using available resources or services.

HOW TO CONDUCT A SOCIAL INDICATOR SURVEY

"Your first step is to decide what you want your indicators to measure. The IIS guide for state agencies is a good place to begin. Drop the items you don't need, include others that you think are important. You should have both objective and subjective criteria for each category. Sometimes you can combine the two. For example, an objective indicator of health might be the older person's self-evaluation about whether he has difficulty going up and down the stairs, washing, bathing, or eating solid foods; or the number of days he has spent in the hospital in the past six months. A subjective indicator would be his own opinion of whether his health is better or worse than that of other people of the same age.

"After you've constructed your survey instrument, you've got to select your sample. You might want a representative sample of the entire area and decide to use some form of probability sampling or random selection of dwelling units within the entire community. Or you might want to select samples from different neighborhoods or different ethnic populations.

"The third step is to administer your questionnaire. Personal interviews are a must for several reasons. The questionnaire will be too long for most people to answer over the phone. Then, too, many potential respondents are incapacitated for health or psychological reasons. Others won't be able to read or write. This means gathering a manpower force.

"If you've got the money, contract with some national survey outfit like the Institute for Social Research at the University of Michigan or the Yankelovitch people in Cambridge. If you don't, you'll have to recruit and train volunteers. It shouldn't be too difficult. There are any number of volunteer groups in each community, and many are made up primarily or extensively of senior citizens. Older people are much less fearful of answering questions from people of their own age.

"The final step is to process the data. That means scoring it and tabulating it. That's a technical procedure but a rather simple one. Any competent researcher can show you how to do it.

HOW I USE INDICATORS

"I make heavy use of social indicators in my community. They help me document the existence of particular social conditions or conditions that require correction. Also, by comparing the social indicators in this community to those in others, we can measure ourselves against both the state and national standard. By repeating the survey, we can monitor changes in social conditions over a period of time. It also helps us to identify differences in life styles among distinct social or ethnic groups.

"Once a planner has the data in terms of hard figures, it's difficult for people either to magnify a problem or to deny its existence. Voters can't argue with figures, especially if they are well constructed and they include assessments by the elderly themselves about what their problems are. By providing the public with factual information, you can increase the likelihood that there will be significant advocacy on behalf of the elderly in general or certain groups of the elderly in particular."

Maximizing Consumer Choice Through Client Analysis

In the vignette that follows, a planner describes how she uses an assessment of what is likely to happen in the future, both in terms of available services and consumer needs, in order to make decisions in the here and now. She points out that without consideration of the future, decisions in the present may become nonoperational or counterproductive in short order. She also points out that by planning ahead one corrects for the lack of a free market in the social services field. By assessing future needs, however, one can compensate for the fact that services tend not to be in direct response to consumer demand; in effect, one is using a social marketing approach to planning.

"There is no real marketplace for social services. Most services are publicly sponsored. They live on because clients are stuck with a monopolistic system. The people who argue for consumer sovereignty and for putting money and vouchers into the hands of consumers forget that the market system has not created the best and the safest products in other fields.

"Besides, big business does not invest in a new product unless someone has reason to think the public has some interest in or real need for the product. I decided the next step was to survey professional market analysts to find out how they go about convincing their clients to develop new products or markets. The first and most important thing I learned was that market analysts don't go to their business clients and ask them what they think the public needs or wants. They go directly to the public. Too often social planners determine needs by some abstract criteria or on the basis of some expert opinion. Then they design programs to meet those needs. A good market analyst knows who his expert is—the consumer.

"But things aren't that simple in the social services. First, the consumer rarely knows what the range of available or potentially available services might be. Second, the range is always limited by public law, or by history and tradition as in the case of voluntary agencies. Thus, public analysis in the social services must begin with an examination of the current programs offered by service agencies along with the collection of data on consumer wants.

STEPS IN CLIENT ANALYSIS

"The first thing to do is examine the mandate of the agency providing the service. According to the law, who is to be served? Or, according to the policy established by the agency's directors, who are the clients? How do administrators' regulations limit the impact of the legislation or modify policy? Will these regulations further limit the client population?

"Now, calculate the potential client population—the total number of people in a particular area who might qualify for the agency's programs or services. Third, look at the agency's actual clientele. Who is being served? Chances are that only a small proportion of the potential consumer population is actually served. Then, compare the potential to the actual clients. This is generally done on the basis of demographic characteristics such as race, socio-economic status, neighborhood, age, and length of stay in the community.

"Now comes step five, the tricky one. Why the differences in numbers or types? Does the agency formally or informally impose selection standards that limit the proportion of the potential client population actually served? Have these standards been imposed intentionally? Who designed them? Do they help the agency meet its maintenance needs? Do location, training and background of the staff, and their attitudes toward clients influence the extent to which clients will make use of that service? To find all that out, you've got to ask the consumers themselves. You ask them a lot of other questions, too.

"In the sixth step, you find out how clients feel about the services they're receiving. Do they feel they are benefiting? How do they rate the services actually received? Do they meet minimal expectations?

"Now you've got some ideas about why people use or ignore services, how the agencies create obstacles for certain clients, and how they open clear pathways to others. This leads you to step number seven: figuring out how much it would cost to eliminate some of the roadblocks to different segments of the population. How much would it cost to reach 100 percent of your potential clients? This would give you some idea of differences in cost between a fully responsive service system and the one you've currently got.

"Next, calculate how many clients might be served on some future date —say, three, five, or ten years from now. This requires knowledge of demographic trends in your community—for example, how many older people with certain kinds of problems you can expect three, five, or ten years from now. Then determine for this *future population* how much it would cost to serve the same proportion of your clientele that you are serving now. *Ask how much it would cost if you eliminated some of the roadblocks over a three-, five-, or ten-year period.* If your costs seem astronomical, and public support at that level seems completely unthinkable, then ask what the cost might be if you added or created some new regulatory provisions.

"Finally, find out how your consumers would react to these new road-blocks. Who would object the most? Are reactions related to particular demographic characteristics, or do they reflect particular health or social needs?

SOME PROMISES AND SOME PROBLEMS

"The neatest thing about this kind of client analysis is that both consumers and providers of services know where the information is coming from. On the other hand, this type of analysis has been done so rarely that we have very little experience in conducting it properly. Furthermore, even those experts who have applied client analysis in the marketplace are unfamiliar with its use in the human services. We ought to develop a dialogue with market analysts in the business world.

"Of course, even if we knew what we were doing, the necessary data might not be available. Usually they're not. Don't let that stop you. You never have enough information. Start asking the right questions, and you might get the right data."

SUPPLEMENTARY QUESTIONS AND ACTIVITIES

1. If you were to employ a Delphi technique,

    What issues would you be concerned about?
    Who would be your respondents?
    Would you use it in conjunction with a committee process, or in its stead?
    Would a Delphi conference be useful in selecting among policy and program alternatives? When using PPBS?

2. Check whether or not a form of PPBS is employed in your state. What is it called? How does it differ from the process described in this chapter? How could it be modified for use in a practice setting you are familiar with?

3. Under what circumstances would application of benefit/cost analysis be useful in your work? Could you use it in selection of goals? Or in the selection of means to achieve these goals?
    Where would you go for additional help in the application of benefit/cost analysis?

4. Can you chart the input-output relationships between agencies in your community? Begin by charting relationships between service sub-systems (e.g., housing, health care, transportation, and so on). Now take specific agencies within each sub-system and identify the input-output relationships.
    Look over the descriptions of linking mechanisms in Chapter 11. Where input-output relationships exist between service providers, what is the linking mechanism that makes exchange possible?

5. Become familiar with the social indicator system used in your state or community. If none is being used, why not?

6. Do you agree with the planner quoted that client analysis is an appropriate substitute for a nonexistent or malfunctioning market? Why or why not?

Are there other functions for consumer analysis even in a market in which consumers do have a voice?

Recommended Readings

DELPHI

TUROFF, MURRAY. "The Design of a Policy Delphi." *Journal of Technological Forecasting and Social Change,* 1970, *2* (2).
Turoff has written what may be the most comprehensive and easy-to-read overview of the use of the Delphi technique and its design as a policy assessment instrument. He defines the procedure and discusses its uses and abuses, its benefits and potential liabilities. The use of the Delphi conference is contrasted with the use of face-to-face conferences. A step-by-step procedure for designing and managing a Delphi conference is given.

PPBS

HOVEY, HAROLD A. *The Planning-Programming-Budgetary Approach to Government Decision Making.* New York: Praeger, 1968.
Nearly a decade later, this book continues to stand as a major contribution to the field of PPB analysis. It describes the PPB approach in terms most readers will find relatively easy to understand, and it uses valuable examples from past government activities. The problems which arise from budgetary procedures that fail to indicate the total impact of government action are carefully examined.

LYDEN, FREMONT J., and ERNEST G. MILLER. *Planning, Programming and Budgeting: A Systems Approach to Management.* Chicago: Markham Publishing Co., 1970.
The political as well as the technical aspects of implementing planning, programming, and budgeting systems are reviewed in this anthology. Readings in the first chapter present an historical overview and discussion of PPB in the organization. Chapter 2 discusses budgeting and its relation to the political process. The planning and evaluation base of PPB is then described, followed by a discussion of issues involved in implementation. The final chapter presents critiques and future prospects of PPB. The book offers a general, readable treatment of the topic.

BENEFIT/COST ANALYSIS

CHASE, SAMUEL B., JR. *Problems in Public Expenditure Analysis,* Studies of Government Finance Series. Washington, D.C.: The Brookings Institution, 1968.
Of greatest interest to the planner at the local level may be the paper by Burton A. Weisbrod, "Income Redistribution Effects and Benefit Cost Analysis," and comments on it by Robert Haveman and Ruth P. Mack, and its appendix entitled "Concepts of Cost Benefit Analysis."
The Weisbrod article defines and differentiates efficiency and equity, describes problems and solutions to their integration. It involves some economic technical ingredi-

ents. However, in the appendix the author provides a concise explanation of these terms for those who do not have any economic background. It distinguishes "real" from "pecuniary" effects and points out the analytically valuable dichotomy between allocative efficiency and distributional equity.

HINRICHS, HARLEY H., and GRAEME M. TAYLOR (Eds.). *Program Budgeting and Benefit/Cost Analysis: Uses, Text, and Readings.* Pacific Palisades, Calif.: Goodyear Publishing Co., 1969.
A simple yet thorough primer, this book presents a logical framework for understanding benefit/cost analysis. It begins with a discussion of the rationale and theory behind this form of analysis. Readings and case examples of benefit/cost analysis in the field are presented next. Finally, an extensive treatment of program analysis itself is offered, including sections on comprehensive program evaluation, monitoring, and the multiple purposes of budget systems.

INPUT-OUTPUT ANALYSIS

LEONTIEF, WASSILY W. "The Structure of the U.S. Economy." *Scientific American,* (April, 1965).
Input-output analysis, according to Leontief, is a technique that assesses "intermediate economic transactions"—that is, transactions that carry goods and services "from industry to industry, from manufacturer to distributor and on to their final purchaser in the market." In this article, Leontief presents the basic components of input-output analysis and discusses the past application of this technique to the analysis of the American economy. While it does not discuss the use of the technique in social planning, the article offers a good, clear discussion of basic input-output principles.

SOCIAL INDICATORS

FITZSIMMONS, STEPHEN J., and WARREN G. LAVEY. "Social Economic Accounts System (SEAS): Toward a Comprehensive, Community-level Assessment Procedure." *Social Indicators Research,* 1976, *2* (4).
Much of the past research on social and economic indicators has adopted a national perspective. In contrast, these authors present a comprehensive, community-level Social Economic Accounts System (SEAS). The SEAS system is designed to aid social scientists, program developers, and public policy officials to understand the effects of public investment upon (1) the quality of life of individuals, (2) the relative social positions of groups of people, and (3) the social well-being of the community.

CLIENT ANALYSIS

REINER, JANET, et al. "Client Analysis and the Planning of Public Programs." *Journal of the American Institute of Planners,* November, 1963.
Recognition of conflicting interests in the community forces the planner to relate a wide range of public activities to various populations with distinct preferences and needs. The authors describe and illustrate a method of analysis that appears to be appropriate for addressing such diversity. Essentially, client analysis is viewed as a technique for examining: (1) people's wants, (2) the recognition of these

wants as needs, (3) eligibility to receive services or goods to address these needs, (4) actual receipt of services, and (5) the benefits derived from service. Implicit in the client analysis approach, according to the authors, is the assumption that the appropriate decision makers are the members of society.

PROGRAM EVALUATION

WEISS, CAROL H. *Evaluation Research.* Englewood Cliffs, N.J.: Prentice-Hall, 1972.
This is a concise, easy-to-read book that deals with the application of research methods to the evaluation of social programs. The basic theme of the book is that the evaluator uses methods and tools of social research but applies them in an "action context" that is basically inhospitable to them. Thus, a principal aim of the book, according to the author, is to "acquaint the reader with the realities of evaluation life." The book includes sections on the purposes of evaluation, formulating the evaluative question, the design of evaluation, and utilization of evaluative results. Chapter 6, "Utilization of Evaluation Results," is especially relevant to planning, as it discusses evaluation as a diagnostic tool for programming.

GUTTENTAG, MARCIA, and ELMER L. STRUENING. *Handbook of Evaluative Research.* Beverly Hills: Sage Publications, Inc., 1975.
An exhaustive two-volume anthology, the *Handbook* offers specific, comprehensive guidance in understanding both the theory and the practice of evaluation research. Volume I focuses upon the development and design of evaluation studies and includes sections on collecting and analyzing data and communicating evaluation results. Volume II applies the techniques of evaluation research to selected content areas (for example, mental health, compensatory education) and examines the politics, values, and cost/benefit factors unique to evaluation research.

FERMAN, LOUIS, KAREN KIRKHART, and JOE MILLER. *Program Evaluation.* Beverly Hills, Calif.: Sage Publications, Inc., 1978.
Especially written for the planner or human service administrator who does not intend to be a technical expert in the evaluation process, this volume provides a nuts-and-bolts guide to who uses evaluation, for what purposes, and how. Nothing else like it exists. It is written entirely from the user's point of view.

Suggestions for Further Reading

DELPHI

BRIGHT, JOHN (Ed.). *Technological Forecasting in Government and Industry.* Englewood Cliffs, N.J.: Prentice Hall, Inc., 1968.
BROWN, B., S. COCHRAN, and N. DALKEY. *The Delphi Method, II: Structure of Experiments.* Santa Monica, Calif.: Rand Corporation, RM-5957-PR, June, 1969.
CLARK, LORRAINE H., and SAMUEL W. COCHRAN. "Needs of Older Americans Assessed by Delphi Procedures." *Journal of Gerontology,* 1972, 27 (2).
DALKEY, NORMAN C. *The Delphi Method: An Experimental Study of Group Opinion.* Santa Monica, Calif.: Rand Corporation, RM-5888-PR, June, 1969.

DALKEY, NORMAN C. *Studies in the Quality of Life: Delphi and Decision-Making.* Lexington, Mass.: Lexington Books, 1972.

HELMER, OLAF. *The Use of the Delphi Technique in Problems of Educational Innovations.* Santa Monica, Calif.: Rand Corporation, P-3499, December, 1966.

MITROFF, IAN I. "On the Design of Enquiring Systems," in the *Proceedings* of the First General Assembly of the World Futures Society, Washington, D.C., May, 1971.

MOLNAR, DANIEL, and MARSHALL KAMMESUD. "Developing Priorities for Improving the Urban Social Environment: A Use of Delphi." *Socio-Economic Planning Science,* 1975, 9, (Reprinted in N. Gilbert and Harry Sprecht, *Planning for Social Welfare: Issues, Models and Tasks.* Englewood Cliffs, N.J.: Prentice-Hall, Inc., 1976.

QUADE, EMMET. "The Systems Approach and Public Policy," in *Whatever Happened to State Budgeting?,* Howard and Grizzle (Eds.). Lexington, Ky.: Council of State Governments, 1972.

RIESENFELD, MARK J., ROBERT J. NEWCOMER, PAUL V. BERLANT, and WILLIAM A. DEPSEY. "Perceptions of Public Service Needs: The Urban Elderly and the Public Agency." Paper presented at the 24th annual meeting of the Gerontological Society, Houston, Texas, October, 1971.

SCHEELE, D. SAM, et al. *GENIE* (Government Executives Normative Information Expediter), Governor's Office, State of Wisconsin, 1971.

TUROFF, MURRAY. "Delphi and Its Potential Impact on Information Systems." *Conference Proceedings,* Vol. 39, International Federation of Operations Research Societies Meeting on Cost Effectiveness, Washington, D.C., May, 1971.

PPBS

A "P.P.B.S." Approach to Budgeting Human Service Programs for United Ways. Alexandria, Va.: United Ways of America, 1972.

CARLSON, JACK. "The Status and Next Steps for Planning, Programming, and Budgeting," in *Public Expenditures and Policy Analysis,* Robert Naveman and Julius Margolis (Eds.). Chicago: Markham Publishing Co., 1970.

CRECINE, JOHN P. *PPBS Implementation: Some Considerations Based on the Federal Experience.* Ann Arbor: University of Michigan, Institute of Public Policy Studies, 1972.

DOH, JOOAN CHIEN. *The Planning-Programming-Budgeting System in Three Federal Agencies.* New York: Praeger, 1971.

HATRY, HARRY B. *Program Planning for State, County, City.* Washington, D.C.: George Washington University, 1967.

MEREWITZ, L., and S. H. SOSNICK. *The Budget's New Clothes.* Chicago: Markham Publishing Co., 1971.

MOWITZ, ROBERT J. *The Design and Implementation of Pennsylvania's Planning, Programming, Budgetary System.* Pennsylvania State University: Institute of Public Administration, 1970.

NOVICK, DAVID. *Current Practice in Program Budgeting.* New York: Crane-Russak, 1973.

RIVLIN, ALICE. "The Planning, Programming and Budgeting System and the Development of Health, Education and Welfare: Some Lessons from Experiences," in *Public Expenditures and Policy Analysis,* Robert Haverman and Julius Margolis (Eds.). Chicago: Markham Publishing Co., 1970.

SCHICK, ALLEN. "A Death in the Bureaucracy: The Demise of Federal PPB." *Public Administration Review,* 1973, *33* (2).

SCHULTZE, CHARLES L. *The Politics and Economics of Public Spending.* Washington, D.C.: The Brookings Institution, 1968.
The Subcommittee on National Security and International Operations. *Planning-Programming-Budgeting.* Washington, D.C.: U.S. Government Printing Office, 1970.

BENEFIT/COST ANALYSIS

BAUER, RAYMOND A., and KENNETH J. GERGEN. *The Study of Policy Formation.* New York: The Free Press, 1968. (See especially chaps. 1, 2, and 3.)
CONLEY, RONALD W. "A Benefit/Cost Analysis ... Vocational Rehabilitation Program. *Journal of Human Resources,* Spring, 1969.
CURCHETTI, CHARLES J. *The Trans-Alaska Pipeline: A Benefit Cost Analysis and Alternatives.* Chicago: Aldine Publishing Company, 1973.
FROST, MICHAEL J. *How to Use Cost Benefit Analysis in Project Appraisal.* Halsted Press, 1975.
HAVEMAN, ROBERT H., and JULIUS MARGOLIS. *Public Expenditures and Policy Analysis.* Chicago: Markham Publishing Co., 1970.
KLARMAN, HERBERT. "Present Status of Cost/Benefit Analysis in the Health Field." American Public Health Association 94th Annual Meeting, San Francisco, 1966.
LEFTWICH, RICHARD H., and ANSEL M. SHARP. *Economics of Social Issues.* Dallas, Texas: Business Publications, Inc., 1974.
NOROZHILOV, V. V. *Problems of Cost/Benefit Analysis in Optimal Planning.* International Arts and Sciences, 1970.
RIVLIN, ALICE M. *Systematic Thinking for Social Action.* Washington, D.C.: The Brookings Institution, 1971.

INPUT-OUTPUT ANALYSIS

EVAN, WILLIAM. "The Organization Set: Toward a Theory of Interorganizational Relations," in *Approaches to Organizational Design,* James D. Thompson (Ed.). Pittsburgh: The University of Pittsburgh Press, 1966.
LINEBERRY, R. L. "Who is Getting What? Measuring Urban Service Outputs," *Public Management,* 1976, *53* (3).

SOCIAL INDICATORS

AGORS, CAROL. "Social Indicators, Selected Readings." *The Annals of the American Academy of Political and Social Science,* March, 1970.
The Annals of the American Academy of Political and Social Sciences, Parts I and II, 1967.
BAER, WILLIAM C. "Evolution of Housing Indicators and Housing Standards: Some Lessons for the Future." *Public Policy,* 1976, 24.
BAUER, RAYMOND (Ed.). *Social Indicators,* Cambridge, Mass.: MIT Press, 1966.
BELL, DANIEL. *Toward a Social Report.* Washington, D.C.: Department of Health, Education, and Welfare, January, 1966.
CAMPBELL, ANGUS, and PHILIP CONVERSE. "Monitoring the Quality of American Life." Ann Arbor: University of Michigan, Institute of Social Research, 1970.
DWOBKY, BERNARD, and ROBERT WILSON. "Social Indicators for the Aged," in *The Social Welfare Forum.* New York: Columbia University Press, 1972.

Fox, Karl A. *Social Indicators and Social Theory Elements of an Operational System.* New York: John Wiley and Sons, 1974.

Galtung, J. "Towards New Indicators of Development." *Futures,* 1976, *8.*

Gerson, E. M. "On Quality of Life." *American Sociological Review,* 1976, *41.*

Institute for Interdisciplinary Studies, American Rehabilitation Foundation, *Social Indicators for the Aged: A Guide for State Agencies on Aging.* Washington, D.C.: Administration on Aging, U.S. Department of Health, Education, and Welfare, 1971.

Osborne, Parker T. *Review of the Literature on Social Indicators.* Denver: University of Denver Social Welfare Research Institute, 1975.

Sheldon, Eleanor, and Wilbur T. Moore. *Indicators of Social Change: Concepts and Measurements.* New York: Russell Sage Foundation, 1968.

Shonfield, Andrew, and Stella Shaw (Eds.). *Social Indicators and Social Policy.* Chicago: Crane-Russak, 1972.

Simon, Herbert A. "Research for Choice," in *Environmental Policy for the Next Fifty Years,* William R. Ewald (Ed.). Bloomington, Ind.: Indiana University Press, 1968.

"Symposium on Social Change and Social Indicators," *American Journal of Sociology,* 1976, *82.*

Van Dusen, Roxann. *Social Indicators, 1973: A Review Symposium.* Washington, D.C.: Center for Coordination of Research on Social Indicators, 1973.

CLIENT ANALYSIS

Bean, Louis. *The Art of Forecasting.* New York: Random House, 1966.

Bloedorn, Jack C., et al. *Designing Social Service Systems.* Chicago: American Public Welfare Association, 1970.

Chisholm, Roger, and Gilbert Whitaker. *Forecasting Methods.* Homewood, Ill.: Richard D. Irwin, 1971.

Jones, Manley Howe. *The Marketing Process, An Introduction.* New York: Harper & Row Publishers, 1965.

Matthews, John. *Marketing: An Introductory Analysis.* New York: McGraw-Hill Book Company, 1964.

Rewoldt, Stuart H. *Introduction to Marketing Management.* Homewood, Ill: Richard D. Irwin, 1969.

Stern, Mark E. *Marketing Planning: A Systems Approach.* New York: McGraw-Hill Book Company, 1966.

OTHER ASSESSMENT TOOLS

Arnfield, R. V. *Technological Forecasting.* Chicago: Aldine Publishing Company, 1969.

Avis, Warren E. *Shared Participation: Finding Group Solutions to Personal, Corporate and Community Problems.* New York: Doubleday, 1973.

Delbecq, Andre L., and A. H. Van de Ven. "Nominal Group Techniques for Involving Clients and Resource Experts in Program Planning." *Academy of Management Journal,* 1974, *12* (4).

Fine, Sidney A., and Freda D. Bernotavicz. *Task Analysis: How to Use the National Task Bank.* Kalamazoo, Mich.: The W. E. Upjohn Institute for Employment Research, November, 1973.

FINE, SIDNEY A., and WRETHA W. WILEY. *An Introduction to Functional Job Analysis: A Scaling of Selected Tasks from the Social Welfare Field.* Kalamazoo, Mich.: The W. E. Upjohn Institute for Employment Research, September, 1971.

FLANAGAN, JOHN F. "The Critical Incident Technique." *Psychological Bulletin,* 1954, *51* (3).

LEWIS, KURT. "Group Decision and Social Change," in *Readings in Social Psychology,* T. Newcomb and E. L. Hartly (Eds.). New York: Holt, Rinehart and Winston, 1947.

VAN DE VEN, ANDREW H., and ANDRE DELBECQ. "The Nominal Group as a Research Instrument for Exploratory Health Studies," *Journal of the American Public Health Association,* March, 1972.

VAN DE VEN, ANDREW H., and ANDRE L. DELBECQ. "The Effectiveness of Nominal Group, Delphi and Interacting Group Decision Making Processes." *Academy of Management Journal,* 1974, *17* (4).

WARHEIT, GEORGE J., ROBERT BELL, and JOHN J. SCHWAB. *Planning for Change: Needs Assessment Approaches.* Washington, D.C.: National Institute of Health, Education and Welfare, 1974.

9

Getting Things Done
Systematically*

*Many of the step-by-step instructions found in this chapter are drawn from a paper developed by Joe R. Hoffer and edited by Thomas Morton and Armand Lauffer when they worked on Project TAP, a national effort to *T*rain *A*rea *P*lanners in the field of aging conducted at the University of Michigan. Sections of the Hoffer article are to be found in greater detail in Cox et al. reader referred to at the end of this chapter.

Perking Up with PERT: A Planner Talks About Getting Things Done

WHAT IT'S ALL ABOUT

"I'm not a chart man or even a very organized person, but I've used PERT—the Program Evaluation and Review Technique. I'll tell you what PERT is useful for. It helps you *organize, schedule, budget,* and *monitor* any project that's got a definite goal or objective.

"If you're organizing a conference, a set of public hearings, or just putting together a booklet of information, PERT helps you organize the activity by identifying the tasks that need to be done and the number of people required to do them. It forces you to schedule their activities over a period of time. Say it's early September and you want your conference to start on December 1. Well, you've got 11 weeks to put it together. While the final event is the conference, a lot of preliminary events must precede it, such as press releases; mail publicity, recruiting speakers, experts, and outside consultants; clearance with public officials; and so on.

"Your staff has to do a number of things to accomplish each of these events. By laying out a PERT chart, you can assign a number of days to each activity leading to an event, and determine how many people you want to assign to each activity or group of activities. By scheduling your project this way, you can more accurately relate the actual program costs to out-of-pocket expenses and the cost of allocated manpower.

"Before I started using PERT, I never knew how much a project cost. Oh, I'd figure out what I needed for travel, telephone, office supplies, facilities, rental, consultation, and so on. Then I'd add some big vague figure for overhead. Most of the time, I underestimated. As a result, if we had more than one project going simultaneously we'd find ourselves working like dogs 15 hours a day some weeks, with nothing to do during others. Now, I use PERT charts to identify peak work loads. If I'm running several projects, I use PERT charts to scatter peak times around.

"I guess you could say PERT is a management tool that helps you to define and integrate those events which have to be accomplished over a period of time. It helps assure completion of tasks on schedule. Because all activities and events are reflected on the chart, a planner can make some intelligent decisions on tradeoffs in terms of time, resources, and skills necessary to meet the scheduled dates.

"I'll tell you what else it does. It helps you monitor your activities and impose necessary correctives or controls. You can control things because PERT enables you to chart actual scheduled progress. You can make changes in the work load of your staff. If you've got the wrong person in a job, that becomes obvious right away and you can switch that employee. And by comparing actual costs to planned costs, PERT can help you update your estimates of expenditures versus income.

"Now don't get me wrong. I don't use PERT for everything. I don't use it for simple routine events. A routine is a routine. Everybody knows what they're expected to do and when. And I don't bother with anything as elaborate as a PERT chart when I've got only one or two people working on something. PERT is most important when you have to integrate the activities of a large number of people, or when you have to complete a complex set of tasks in order to reach your specific objective. Of course, PERT's utterly useless when you haven't got a specific objective. That would be like trying to create an assembly line process without knowing what you want to manufacture or by when.

HOW IT WORKS

"If you want to find out how to build a PERT chart there are a number of elementary books and instructional manuals that can help you.

"The basic principles are very simple. A PERT network is nothing more than a visual representation showing a logical and temporal sequence of activities and the relationships among them and to events and sub-events in a project. Events are usually represented by circles on the chart. Each event is preceded by another event with a line leading from one circle to another. That line indicates the activities that need to be performed prior to a particular event. These are called leader activities.

"For example, the activities which might precede mailing out a brochure include designing the brochure, compiling a mailing list, putting addresses on the printed brochure, and carrying them to the Post Office. Different people might be involved in different activities. Sometimes one person's activities need to be completed before the next person can do his. You can't do the finished design on the brochure until you have all the program content; by the same token, the person addressing the envelopes must wait until the mailing list has been compiled, and so on.

"The event-activity relationship is probably the fundamental component of a PERT network. Most users of PERT work backward in designing a network of events and activities, starting with the final objective or event. It's a process called "backward chaining." It's just a technique to help you avoid omission of necessary steps. Some people aren't comfortable with backward chaining and prefer to start where they are working from—the present into the future. I find that perfectly OK, so long as you check on yourself as soon as you've completed the event on the chart.

"A sophisticated PERT chart can, of course, be tremendously complex. If you're springing a PERT chart for the first time on people who've never seen one, you'd do well to keep it simple. One time, I had to plan an inter-agency conference and wanted to make sure that each agency representative knew what his organization was to do and when. I wanted to impress on the planning committee that each organization's activities were significant in terms of the final objective—that succeeding events, and thus the final objective, would be delayed if activities weren't performed on schedule. So I drew up a PERT chart. (Of course, I built in some extra days of slack.)

"Boy, were they impressed! Each agency could really see how it fit into the big picture. And since all the leaders had a copy of the big PERT chart to take back to their own agencies, it was clear to everyone that pinpointing omissions and mistakes wasn't going to be terribly difficult. You put a PERT chart together, and it's not going to be easy for anyone to say, 'I didn't know it was my responsibility' or 'I'm too busy; let Joe do it.' "

PERT: What it is and How it's Used

PERT, the Program Evaluation and Review Technique, first received national attention when it was used to schedule and monitor events leading to the building and launching of the first Polaris submarine. Before that it was frequently used by the Allied Command during World War II for the planning of large military operations that required massive movements of men and equipment.

PERT is a management technique. It can be used by the planner to increase administrative control over the use of time, staff, and other resources. Used properly, it can provide the social planner with a guide—a map through time—that specifies what is expected by whom and permits the planner to monitor progress as it is being made. It can also be used to identify areas where shifts in personnel or in emphasis can lead to more efficiency or a greater likelihood of success.

While PERT cannot be used in defining objectives (since these must be defined in advance), it can be used to

1. chart the activities that are required in order to accomplish those objectives
2. coordinate those activities in an effective and efficient manner
3. estimate the time necessary to perform those activities and to accomplish a project's overall objectives (in some cases actually to minimize the time required)
4. communicate in a precise and visual manner the activities that must be performed in successive steps so that all those who are engaged in the planning activity can see where their contributions fit in

By using a flow diagram, sometimes known as a time-logic chart, the activities to be performed and the events to be managed can be presented in a more comprehensible manner than when the same material is written in narrative form. It helps the planner think systematically about the things that need to be done in order to accomplish specified objectives. It does so by specifying the events that must be completed, the activities required in order to complete those events, and the tasks necessary to perform those activities. The resulting network shows that events and activities have to be linked in a sequential order. No activity can be started until the event prior to it is complete.

In order to understand this better, let us look at Figure 9.1 and definitions.

Events on the schematic diagram have been numbered 1 through 4. An event represents the start or completion of a task. Examples of events include the following: a piece of legislation has been passed, a public hearing has been held, the first in a series of task force meetings has been scheduled. The event is not the actual performance of a task. It can be thought of as a significant step along the way toward achieving an objective. In PERT terms, some events may be identified as "milestones," particularly significant events which must be encountered, but which themselves do not consume time or resources.

Both time and resources are consumed in *activities*. An activity is the actual performance of a series of tasks required to move from one event to another. On the chart, activities are represented by the lines A, B, C, and D.

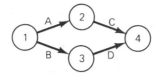

FIGURE 9.1.

They can just as easily be designated 1–2 (A), 1–3 (B), 2–4 (C), and 3–4 (D). In order to occur, activities may require manpower, materials, space, and personnel. In order for an activity to be completed, personnel must perform certain *tasks,* jobs that require time.

Events are connected by activities in the design of a PERT network. The event(s) that *immediately* follow another event are called successor events. Thus 2 is a successor event to 1 and 4 is a successor to 2. Predecessor events come immediately before another event. Thus 2 and 3 are both predecessors of 4 and 1 is a predecessor of both 2 and 3.

Estimating the Time Required to Complete a Project

Once events and activities have been charted on a PERT network, it may be possible to estimate the amount of time required to perform each of these activities that lead from event to event. This would give the planner some notion of how much time it might take to complete an entire project. In the illustrations that follow, the letters t_e designate the estimated time required to complete an activity. In a complex PERT chart, t_e may actually be a composite figure that includes estimates of "optimistic time," "most likely time," and "most pessimistic time." In order to simplify the discussion that follows, reference will be made only to t_e.

Having designed a PERT network to indicate the interrelationships between events and activities, the planner now makes a time estimate for each activity and enters that value on the PERT chart near the appropriate activity line. (See Figure 9.2)

Using this above network as a guide, a tabular summary can be made as follows:

Event Titles	Predecessor Event	Successor Event	t_e (weeks)
Begin planning for legislative hearing	1	2	6
Meeting of legislative committee held	1	3	12
Begin organization of coalition	1	4	6
Final meeting of legislative committee held	2	5	2
Begin arrangements for presentation to legislators	3	5	8
Hearing in state capitol held	4	5	10

The time required to reach event 1 (initiation of planning for a legislative hearing) is 0. However, the time required to reach event 2 is six weeks. It takes 12 weeks to reach event 3. It also takes 6 weeks to reach event 4. Activity paths 1–2, 1–3, and 1–4 can proceed simultaneously. Note, however, that it takes twice as long to complete the activities leading to event 3.

Totaling up the time required to move along each path from event 1 to event 5 will be instructive. It takes only 8 weeks to move along the path identified as 1–2–5, but it takes 16 weeks to move along the path identified as 1–4–5, and 20 weeks to move along the path 1–3–5. It is therefore logically impossible to complete the overall project in less than 20 weeks. The longest path (in terms of estimated time) on the chain is known as the "critical path," since it always represents the earliest possible time that a planner can expect to reach a final event.

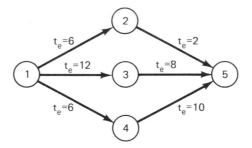

FIGURE 9.2.

Having gone this far, the planner is now ready to identify the latest acceptable completion date for a project. By definition, t_L is the latest time by which a single event must be completed in order to keep the project on schedule. t_L is arrived at within the framework of a previously established completion time or contractual obligation date. This final completion, or contractual obligation, date is given the symbol t_s. If the conference is scheduled for June 15, for example, and it is now March 15, the t_s is exactly 3 months.

The values for the t_L's are computed for each event and inserted between the events on the PERT network.

The t_L's are computed in exactly the opposite manner from that used for deriving the t_e's:

1. The planner starts from the last event and works back toward the first one.
2. To compute the t_L for an event, the value of the t_e must be subtracted from the value of the t_L for the successor Event.

3. If more than one value of t_L is obtained, the smallest value is selected.

The following example may help clarify this point:

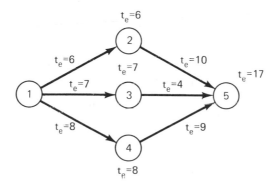

FIGURE 9.3.

1. The t_e for the activity connecting event 5 and event 2 (activity 2–5) is 10 weeks. Subtracting 10 weeks from the t_L of 17 weeks for event 5 gives a t_L for event 2 of 7 weeks.
2. The t_e for activity 3–5 is 4 weeks. Subtracting 4 weeks from the t_L of 17 weeks for event 5 gives a t_L for event 3 of 13 weeks.
3. The t_e for activity 4–5 is 9 weeks. Subtracting 9 weeks from the t_L of 17 weeks for event 5 gives a t_L for event 4 of 8 weeks.
4. In a similar manner, the t_L for event 1 is computed via three different paths:
   a. From event 1 to event 2, $t_L = 1$ week
   b. From event 1 to event 3, $t_L = 6$ weeks
   c. From event 1 to event 4, $t_L = 0$ weeks
5. The smallest value of 0 weeks is selected as the t_L for event 1. Our final PERT network looks like this:

Having derived the latest allowable time (t_L) and the expected time (t_e) for each event, the planner can now calculate how much "slack" exists. The slack of an event is $t_L - t_e$. In other words, if a project is allowed 25 weeks for completion and it can in fact be performed in 20 weeks, there is a 5-week grace period. Designated by PERT as slack, this plays a crucial role in analyzing the activities needed to complete a project.

The value of slack can be either positive, negative, or zero, depending upon the relationship between t_L and t_e. However, since there is no margin of safety—that is, no excess time or money to spend on any task—all the events that have zero or minimum slack form a critical path to the final event(s).

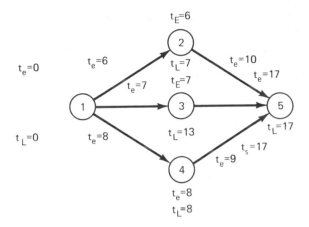

FIGURE 9.4.

Finding the Critical Path: Backward or Forward Chaining

The critical path is the most important one on the PERT chart. It indicates which part of a project requires the most time to get from the initial event to the final event. Any event on the critical path that consumes extra time will cause the final event(s) to fall behind by the same amount.

To decide how much time to allot to a project, the planner can choose to find the critical path by "backward chaining" or by "forward chaining." The choice between the two methods depends, in the final analysis, on whether or not a fixed date for the final event is established. In some complex situations, one might combine both approaches. An example of this technique will be given shortly.

It is always difficult to produce order from disorder. The PERT network designer can simplify this task and get better results if certain simple rules are followed.

1. Define the end objective precisely. This is frequently difficult, but a definitive statement is fundamental to a complete plan.

```
Event 1
Completion of network
End Objective
```

FIGURE 9.5.

2. Define all significant events that are precedent to the end objective. Do not start on any "chain" until this is done. The purpose is, of course, to make sure that no elements are inadvertently left out.

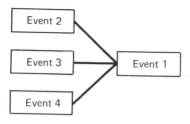

FIGURE 9.6.

3. Define all significant events precedent to event 2. This is a continuation of the strategy in the second step. Again, the purpose is to assure that nothing significant is omitted.

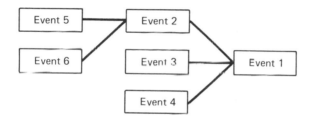

FIGURE 9.7.

4. Define all significant events precedent to event 3. If it is found that some event already shown is precedent to the event being worked on, interconnecting lines must be drawn (see asterisks).

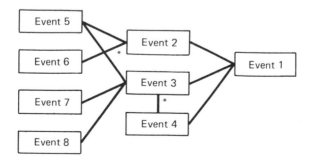

FIGURE 9.8.

5. Continue in a similar manner with other events. Work back one level at a time, making sure that all significant precedent events have been established.

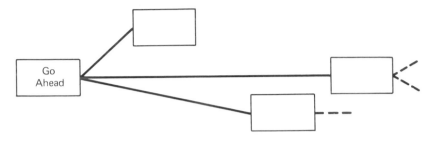

FIGURE 9.9.

6. Make sure that all events except the initial and final ones have at least one connection at each end. Recheck for omissions. If the omitted event is really important, find out whether it is covered by the scope of the work or related to it.

In developing the network, it is important to discard irrelevant matters from consideration. There is a tendency to over-elaborate a chart by including minor events which are inconsequential in the planning schedule. Although these events may be written down somewhere for reference and follow-up, they should be kept out of the network. The network should include only those events with time significance.

An Example: Policy Approval by a Council on Aging

Figure 9.10 is an example of how the PERT approach would be applied to a protective services program for the aging. The final event is an operational extension policy approved by the Board of Directors of a Council on Aging.

Reference No.	Event	Predecessor Event
1.	Board member requests consideration of special program for aged	0
2.	Tests completed regarding validity of request	1
3.	Authorization given by Board of Directors to conduct broad community survey	2
4.	Survey Committee appointed	3
5.	Report presented to Survey Committee of existing services in community	4
6.	Report presented to Survey Committee regarding similar studies in the U.S.	4
7.	Report presented to Survey Committee on other needs of older citizens	4

8.	Priorities determined regarding kind of services	5, 6, 7, 14
9.	Method of financing services determined	10
10.	Method of implementing services determined	8, 15
11.	Extension policy draft approved by Committee	9
12.	Extension policy accepted by Board of Directors (final event)	11
13.	Cooperating agencies and individuals (governmental and voluntary) notified	3
14.	Reactions received from other agencies	13
15.	Facilities available for use in new program determined	6

Between Events	Activity	t_e (weeks)
1 and 2	A. Ad hoc committee of Board and staff appointed to examine request	4
2 and 3	B. Recommendations sent to Board and staff	3
3 and 4	C. Resource people and community representatives recruited for committee staff assigned to committee	3
4 and 5	D. Staff prepares report of existing programs; secure cooperation between the agencies offering special services; determine types of services available.	1
4 and 6	E. Contact national agencies, e.g., Institute of Gerontology, for similar studies; follow-up on model local community programs cited by several national agencies	4
4 and 7	F. Study of needs by resource people and community representatives; locate and identify those needing protective services	4
5 and 8	G. Report examined and integrated with others	3
6 and 8	H. Report examined and integrated with others	3
7 and 8	I. Report examined and integrated with others	3
8 and 10	J. Best methods for meeting needs reviewed	3
10 and 9	K. Financial resources explored	4
9 and 11	L. Decisions to date collated; Draft policy written and sent to Committee	2
11 and 12	M. Draft policy distributed to Board of Directors; special meeting of Board called	3
4 and 15	N. Agencies and others contacted; Workers in selected social agencies trained in services of other agencies	7
15 and 10	O. Schedules and kinds of use discussed	3
3 and 13	P. Letters sent to national agencies	1
13 and 14	Q. Non-respondents contacted by phone	6
14 and 8	R. Priorities from others rank-ordered	3

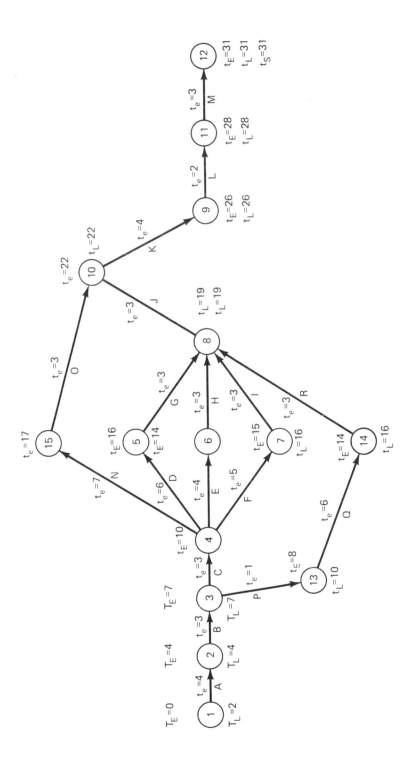

FIGURE 9.10.   PERT/Time Network—Coordinated Approach to Protective Services to the Aged

A Second Example

There are many ways to draw a PERT chart. In Figure 9.11 drawn from the Michigan Heart Association, the chart specifies the times of the year in which the events are to be completed by listing the months at the top of the page. A similar PERT chart might be drawn up and tacked on to a bulletin board, permitting all agency staff periodically to review completion times or target dates. It can be used by the planner to monitor progress, and to make adjustments when these are necessary or possible.

Other Scheduling Techniques

Scheduling techniques are of course not new to planning and program management. Two techniques, neither of which are as comprehensive as PERT, but both of which are quite extensively used in social planning will be described. The first was developed by Henry Gantt more than fifty years ago. It involves the use of bar charts to reflect purposive activities conducted over a period of time in order to complete a project.

Horizontal lines are drawn under calendar dates. Their lengths are proportional to the duration of the activity. Progress on the completion of these activities can be monitored by the drawing of parallel lines adjacent to the activity lines themselves. An example of the Gantt chart is found in Figure 9.12.

The Gantt chart only describes activities. It does not indicate events as in the PERT network, nor does it graphically describe the interconnections between activities and events. The Gantt technique is used only in the forward direction; backward chaining, which is often employed in the PERT technique is not possible. Weaknesses of the Gantt technique are obvious: It is almost impossible to reflect slack; neither can interrelationships among activities be illustrated nor coordinating functions or precedent relationships adequately shown. On the other hand, it is a relatively simple method that can prove invaluable in planning less complex projects.

Another instrument, called the "Sched-U-Graph," was designed by Remington-Rand and is similar to the Gantt chart. In its original form it was designed on a 24" X 42" chart containing pockets in which to insert 3 X 5 cards. The horizontal portion of the chart is labelled by months near the top. Specific activities or tasks to be performed are typed on 3 X 5 cards and inserted in appropriate slots on the chart. For example, if a planner were preparing a

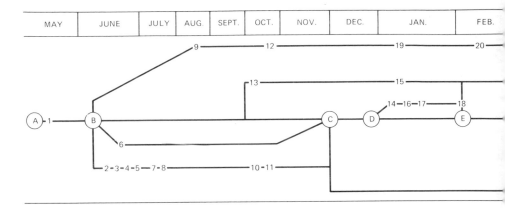

Events

A. Date and place selection
B. Program committees meet: scientific sessions, nursing, stroke, cardiopulmonary resuscitation, screening and detection, delegate meetings, physician education committees
C. Executive committee and board of trustees review
D. Final program committee review and approval of program format, content and speakers. Nursing, stroke, cardiopulmonary resuscitation, screening and detection, delegate meetings, physician education committees
E. Preliminary program announcement mailed

Activities

1. Confirmation of date and location
2. Determine program format and content
3. Select speakers
4. Set honorariums
5. Assign responsibilities to committee members and staff
6. Determine admission policy and fees
7. Calls to speakers
8. Letters to speakers
9. First letter to exhibitors
10. Programs, speakers, and topics confirmed
11. Letter to speakers regarding audio-visual equipment and other information
12. Second letter to exhibitors
13. Outside mailing lists requested
14. Develop first program announcement
15. Outside mailing lists received
16. Plate making
17. Printing
18. Addressing
19. Third letter to exhibitors
20. Final exhibitor list compiled

FIGURE 9.11A. Michigan Heart Association Annual Heart Days Planning PERT
Part I

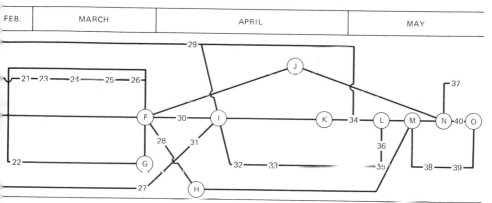

Events

. Final program mailed
. Special mailings mailed
I. Pre-registration
. Program guide book completed and distributed
. Annual meeting notice mailed
K. Final meeting with hotel
.. Set-up
M. Heart days programs, annual meeting and
   registration
N. Tear down
). Evaluation

Activities

21. Order emergency phone
22. Develop special promotion materials
23. Final space allocations made
24. Final program copy developed
25. Program printed
26. Addressing
27. Speakers' audio-visual needs set
28. Order badges, tickets, and awards
29. Floor plan to exhibitors
30. Finalize staff assignments
31. Complete room arrangement forms
32. Check audio-visual equipment and exhibits
33. Order outside services and equipment: labor,
    moving, projection, security, audio-visual
    equipment
34. Commercial and MHA exhibits delivered
    and set up
35. Check and set up individual rooms
36. Emergency phone installed
37. Return equipment and exhibits
38. Evaluation sheets analyzed
39. Registration counts

FIGURE 9.11B.   Michigan Heart Association Annual Heart Days Planning PERT
Part II

THE RUFUS FOUNDATION

ACTIVITY SCHEDULE AS OF Sept. 23, 1977

ORGANIZATION Kamp Steel

PROJECT TITLE Salesmanship

GRANT START DATE February 1, 1977

MAJOR OBJECTIVES		ACTIVITIES		DURATION											EXPECTED RESULTS	GRANTEE COMMENTS ON STATUS	EMCF USE ONLY
				1st QTR.	2nd QTR.	3rd QTR.	4th QTR.	5th QTR.	6th QTR.	7th QTR.	8th QTR.	3rd YEAR 1 2 3 4					
1.0		Certificate Program II	Plan / Status														
	1.1	Selection of trainees	Plan / Status														
	1.2	Curriculum/materials prep.	Plan / Status														
	1.3	Conduct training	Plan / Status											Cohort of 30 trained			
	1.4	Evaluation/follow-up	Plan / Status														
2.0		Certificate Program III	Plan / Status														
	2.1	Selection of trainees	Plan / Status														
	2.2	Curriculum/materials prep.	Plan / Status														
	2.3	Conduct training	Plan / Status											Cohort of 30 trained			
	2.4	Evaluation/follow-up	Plan / Status														
3.0		Social Work Education	Plan / Status														
	3.1	Workshop # 1	Plan / Status														
	3.11	Recruitment/selection	Plan / Status														
	3.12	Develop overall strategy	Plan / Status														
	3.13	Develop workshop plan	Plan / Status														
	3.14	Complete materials	Plan / Status											Cohort of 20 trained & curriculum/course plans developed			
	3.15	Conduct workshop	Plan / Status														
	3.16	Evaluation/follow-up	Plan / Status														

NOTE:
• Planned duration indicated with horizontal line covering respective time periods.
• Actual status indicated below planned duration with 'horizontal line. (up-dated for each reporting period).
• The original plan is duplicated by the Foundation in quantity needed for all quarterly progress reports.

178

THE RUFUS FOUNDATION

ACTIVITY SCHEDULE AS OF _____

ORGANIZATION _____   PROJECT TITLE _____   GRANT START DATE _____

MAJOR OBJECTIVES			DURATION										EXPECTED RESULTS	GRANTEE COMMENTS ON STATUS	EMCF USE ONLY
	ACTIVITIES		1st QTR.	2nd QTR.	3rd QTR.	4th QTR.	5th QTR.	6th QTR.	7th QTR.	8th QTR.	3rd YEAR 1 2 3 4				
3.2	Workshop # 2	Plan / Status												
3.21	Recruitment/selection	Plan / Status												
3.22	Develop workshop plan	Plan / Status												
3.23	Prepare materials	Plan / Status												
3.24	Conduct workshop	Plan / Status									Cohort of 20 trained & curriculum/course plans developed		
3.25	Evaluation/follow-up	Plan / Status												
3.3	Sch. of Social Work Graduate Course	Plan / Status												
3.310	Course offered, term 3A '77	Plan / Status												
3.311	Develop course plan	Plan / Status												
3.312	Include curriculum course	Plan / Status												
3.313	Develop course outline	Plan / Status												
3.314	Teach course	Plan / Status												
3.315	Evaluate	Plan / Status												
3.320	Course offered, Winter '78	Plan / Status									Course developed, established & included in SSW curriculum		
3.321	Modify above plan based on evaluation	Plan / Status												
3.322	Teach course	Plan / Status												
3.323	Evaluate/plan continuation	Plan / Status												
3.4	Spring/Summer Symposium Workshop	Plan / Status												
3.41	Develop workshop plan	Plan / Status												
3.42	Conduct workshop	Plan / Status									Cohort of 35 trained		
3.43	Evaluate workshop	Plan / Status												

NOTE:
• Planned duration indicated with horizontal line covering respective time periods.
• Actual status indicated below planned duration with horizontal line. (updated for each reporting period)
• The original plan is duplicated by the Foundation in quantity needed for all quarterly progress reports.

179

THE RUFUS FOUNDATION

ACTIVITY SCHEDULE AS OF _____

ORGANIZATION _____ PROJECT TITLE _____ GRANT START DATE _____ END DATE _____

MAJOR OBJECTIVES	ACTIVITIES		DURATION													EXPECTED RESULTS	GRANTEE COMMENTS ON STATUS	EMCF USE ONLY
			1st QTR.	2nd QTR.	3rd QTR.	4th QTR.	5th QTR.	6th QTR.	7th QTR.	8th QTR.	3rd YEAR 1	2	3	4			
4.0	Training of Trainers	Plan Status																
4.1	Recruit/select participants	Plan Status																
4.2	Develop workshop plan	Plan Status														Cohort to 40 trained & provided with supportive materials.		
4.3	Conduct workshop	Plan Status																
4.4	Evaluation	Plan Status																
		Plan Status																
5.0	Materials Development	Plan Status																
5.1	Complete materials development plan	Plan Status																
5.2	Complete first cluster	Plan Status																
5.3	Complete second cluster	Plan Status																
5.4	Complete third cluster	Plan Status																
5.5	Complete fourth cluster	Plan Status																
5.6	Complete sixth cluster	Plan Status																
5.7	Arrange publication	Plan Status														Five clusters of training materials relating to child placement available in pre-publication form		
		Plan Status																
		Plan Status																
		Plan Status																
		Plan Status																
		Plan Status																
		Plan Status																
		Plan Status																
		Plan Status																

NOTE:
• Planned duration indicated with horizontal line covering respective time periods.
• Actual status indicated below planned duration with horizontal line. (up-dated for each reporting period)
• The original plan is duplicated by the Foundation in quantity needed for all quarterly progress reports.

budget for presentation to an agency's board of directors, the preceding activities might be identified as in Figure 9.13.

July	August	September	October	November
Budget Sheets Duplicated	Preliminary by staff completed	Tentative Budget completed, Mail budget to treasurer	Final Draft approved by Treasurer, Mail to Board of Directors	Approval by Board of Directors

FIGURE 9.13.

There are similar weaknesses in the Sched-U-Graph as those described for the Gantt chart. It is difficult to determine the time needed to complete the required tasks; since more than one task is generally scheduled for a particular day, week, or month, it becomes increasingly difficult to show the relationships between these tasks and completed events.

Review

Social planners are often required to manage complex, long-term projects. In order to plan for the efficient and effective utilization of personnel and materials it is necessary to consider both the events that need to be accomplished and the activities required to reach those events.

PERT is described as a method that permits the planner to devise a comprehensive chart or flow diagram which may be easier to understand than attempts to communicate the same material in narrative form. It enforces a certain discipline that can help the planner avoid gaps in the overall logic of a plan. By designing a network that outlines the activities that must be undertaken prior to each event, it is possible to schedule these activities over time so that final outcome of the project can be achieved within the time allowable. A PERT chart can be used not only to plan activities, but to monitor the extent to which activities are on schedule and events are on target.

It is especially helpful in providing a clear and visual map of the inter-relatedness of the various aspects of a project, and in identifying those activities that are more likely to cause delays. Two other scheduling devices, Gantt Charts and Sched-U-Graphs, are useful in the design of less complex projects. Their limitations were identified.

1976 SPRING-SUMMER SYMPOSIUM

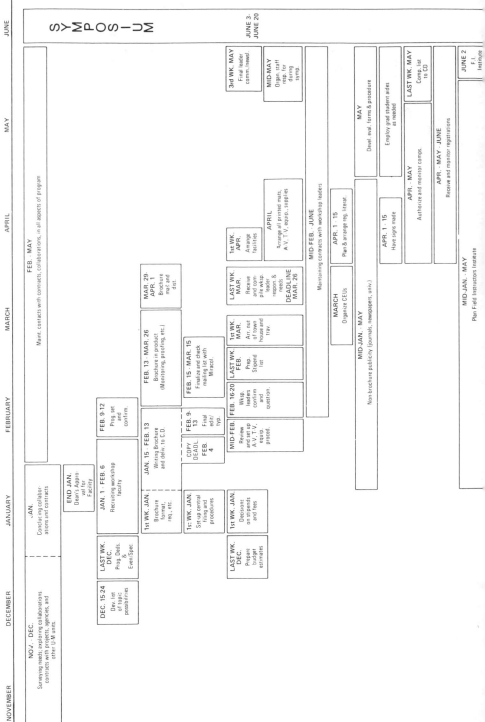

1. Select a project with a clear-cut objective and a specific time limit. Design a PERT chart and follow it as you complete each activity.
   a. Begin by listing all the events that you can think of. Be sure that these are actually events and not activities.
   b. Examine your list of events for completeness. Are there others you would add?
   c. Try to arrange the list in a reasonable chronological order. Determine the predecessor events for each event.
   d. Beginning with the last event, place its immediate predecessor events before it. Follow this procedure until you have reached the first event. Feel free to use several branches or paths if you find them necessary.
   e. Now chain the events together with lines showing the relationship of each event to its predecessor. You are designing a network.
   f. Estimate the time needed to move from each event to its successor. Note this along each line.
   g. Finally, determine the critical path by adding the times required to move from the first to last event along each conceivable path.
2. Identify at least two projects each in which PERT, a Gantt Chart, or a Sched-U-Graph could be used. Which method would you prefer using and why?
3. Can you anticipate resistance to using one of these techniques in an agency you are familiar with? How would you overcome this resistance?

Recommended Readings

COOK, DESMOND L. *Program Evaluation and Review Technique—Applications in Education.* Washington, D.C.: Office of Education, Department of Health, Education and Welfare, 1966.
The basic concepts and principles of PERT as they apply to either large or small projects are presented. The following steps are discussed: work structure, network development, activity time estimation, network time calculation, scheduling, probability aspects of PERT, replanning the project, and PERT-cost. Several illustrations in which PERT can be applied to research and development models are given.

HOFFER, JOE R. *A Programmed Introduction to PERT-Program Evaluation and Review Technique for Planning Large Projects in Social Welfare.* Columbus, Ohio: National Conference on Social Welfare, 1971
An excellent programmed instructional text by the former director of the National Conference on Social Welfare. It takes the reader on a step-by-step walk through a PERT network.

Suggestions for Further Reading

BLOOD, J. W. (Ed.). *PERT: A New Management Planning and Control Technique.* New York: American Management Association, 1962.

BUCKLEY, CLAIR A. "PERT" and Its Possible Uses in Planning YMCA Programs." New York: National Council YMCA *Forum,* April 1970, pp. 11–14.

CATANESE, ANTHONY J. "Programming for Government Operations: The Critical Path Approach." *Public Administration Review,* March/April, 1968.

FOURRE, JAMES P. *Critical Path Scheduling—A Practical Appraisal of PERT.* New York: American Management Association, 1968.

HOFFER, JOE R. "PERT: A Tool for Managers of Human Service Programs," in *Tactics and Techniques of Community Practice,* Fred M. Cox, John L. Erlish, Jack Rothman, and John E. Tropman (Eds.). Itasca, Illinois: F. Peacock Publishing Co., 1977.

III

The Coordination
of Services
at the Local Level

Planners spend a great deal of time attempting either to coordinate the services of many providers or to improve the social mechanisms that can facilitate such coordination. Chapter 10 presents an overview of the potentially available inter-agency exchanges and linking mechanisms that improve the availability, accessibility, effectiveness, efficiency, and accountability of services. More than thirty such mechanisms are enumerated, ranging from ad hoc coordination through the creation of joint projects and the use of information and referral systems.

Linking mechanisms that result in new relationships between professional service providers and elements in the extra-professional service system are discussed. These include volunteer bureaus, ombudsmen and social brokerage services, grievance machinery, and staff training and community education. The planner's decision about the kinds of coordinating structures to be employed is analyzed in terms of the kinds of resources that are available.

The next chapter examines seven variables that are crucial to the establishment and maintenance of effective linking mechanisms. Each is discussed in relation to increasing the accessibility, effectiveness, efficiency, availability, and accountability of needed services.

Chapter 12 explores the pros and cons of more comprehensive planning at the local level. Three national trends that affect coordination and planning at the community level are discussed in some detail: the progressive transfer of policy and planning responsibilities from the federal government to state and local authorities; functional consolidation of both special district and general-purpose local governments; and the creation of a number of administrative mechanisms intended to catalyze planning efforts. These include A-95 and other review and comment mechanisms, the creation of planning and allocating agencies, permanent federations of service providers, and ad hoc coalitions.

10

Inter-Agency Linkages: Coordination at the Operational Level

Linking Mechanisms Between Service Providers

Many social planners at the community level assume that human service agencies and their staffs have a "natural" tendency voluntarily to coordinate their activities. This assumption stems from the premise that it is both economical and "in the community's interest" for a variety of service agencies to rationalize and integrate their separate programs so as to complement each other. While community interest is often the raison d'être of these agencies, nonetheless it does not always coincide with agency interests. Instead of naturally gravitating toward each other, agencies are more apt to be governed by self-interests that work against certain forms of coordination while encouraging others. Coordination involves certain costs, some of them substantial. These costs are reckoned in loss of autonomy; expenditure of manpower and other resources; pressure to respond to new expectations or new service demands, and so forth. For these reasons, coordination among community agencies has always been a strong desire, but never a great reality.

Nevertheless, more effective coordination and pooling are not only desirable, but feasible. This is particularly true when planners limit their coordinating activities to the establishment and maintenance of inter-organizational "linking mechanisms" at the "operational" level. A *linking mechanism* is defined as an exchange relationship that facilitates the coordination of two or more organizations. An agency's *operational level* refers to its administrative or programmatic activities. More than thirty such linking mechanisms will be described in this chapter. Several of these mechanisms are in fact linking "services."

RATIONALE FOR LINKING SERVICES AT THE OPERATIONAL LEVEL

The fragmentation of services at the area level results in many problems. These include the duplication of some services; the underuse of others; the unavailability of continuous care. Some services reach only those populations which have little need for them, leaving large segments of the poor and minority populations unserved. Moreover, the uncoordinated nature of the service system makes it all the more difficult to spot gaps in services. Even for those clients who do not "fall between the cracks," services are often inadequate because they are not complemented by the necessary supportive services.

Social planners promote the development of inter-agency linkages and other coordinating mechanisms in order to increase: (1) the availability of services; (2) their accessibility; (3) the effectiveness of those services; (4) their efficiency; and (5) their responsiveness and accountability. Linking mechanisms that promote one of these objectives frequently lead to mechanisms that promote others.

LINKING MECHANISMS CATEGORIZED

Linking mechanisms can be categorized as *administrative* and *programmatic*. Administrative linkages can be further subdivided into *fiscal, managerial,* or *supportive linkages.* Programmatic linkages involve the use of *centralized services* and *service integration.* Linkages involving *agency personnel* can be categorized as both administrative and programmatic. In general, successful linking mechanisms in one category increase the chances of developing additional mechanisms in another category.

Administrative Approaches: Fiscal Integration

Agencies can be linked administratively through one or more of the following fiscal mechanisms: (1) purchase of service, (2) joint budgeting, or (3) joint funding.

Purchase-of-service agreements generally require contractual arrangements between one agency with funds and another equally autonomous agency that can provide needed services. Vocational rehabilitation counselors, for example, have traditionally purchased such services as the fitting of a prosthesis and job training for their clients. Community mental health centers or state mental hospitals purchase supportive and residential services which permit the discharge of hospital patients into the community. Such arrangements permit "purchasers" to extend services to their clientele that they could not as effectively or efficiently provide on their own. Contracting agencies find these arrangements beneficial, because they are able both to increase their operating budgets and to extend their services to a client population they might not otherwise be able to serve.

Although social planners themselves may not always be in a position to purchase services, their vantage point for brokering relationships between purchasers and providers of service—and with the consumers of those services—is excellent. Planners often have data on the needs of target populations, know which populations are in greatest need, and have access to those populations. They also know which agencies have the capability to provide needed services, which have the financial resources to purchase them, and they may be in the position of being honest brokers between those agencies.

"The Social Security Administration, the Department of Public Welfare, and the mental health hospital were all interested in community placements," reports a social planner. "They knew what they wanted, and they had the money to pay for it, but they didn't have any idea of how to build a network of supportive services that would have permitted mildly disabled older persons to remain in the community. Well, I'm on good terms with the people from the Homemaker Service, as well as the directors of the Family Agency and the settlement house. It wasn't particularly difficult, although it was time-consuming, for me to broker a set of relationships between the parties concerned. A by-product of the arrangement was the expansion of the Homemaker Service to include friendly visiting and a home handyman program. The purchase-of-service business actually helped me get into a number of other cooperative arrangements with agencies in the community."

In addition to brokering relationships, planners may also be involved in monitoring the efficiency and effectiveness of these arrangements, and in the development of standards. The funneling of money to participating agencies can, for example, be made contingent on their agreements to participate in other joint programming efforts. Continuation of contracts can be made contingent on adherence to performance standards, especially when the sources of funds for the purchase of service is open ended and can be expected to remain available over a relatively long period.

JOINT BUDGETING

When several providers agree to share decisions regarding the financing of existing or new services, they are involved in a *joint budgeting* process. The most powerful incentive for joint budgeting is the availability of additional money. "I knew we could get new money to purchase special mini-buses for use by senior citizens," explains an area planner, "but we needed local matching funds. And we had to show the involvement of a number of service providers. It took four months, but I was able to get the local transportation authority, the Model Cities agency, the Board of Education and the Community Mental Health Services Board each to kick in their share of matching funds. We were then able to get 70 percent additional monies from the federal government."

"Our experience at joint budgeting had some additional payoffs as well. First of all, it gave us an experience at working together. Secondly, it led to other joint budgeting agreements that put us in a more powerful position to compete for revenue sharing dollars. It also made it possible for me to introduce agency staff to some new budgetary procedures based on performance objectives. Once they accepted my expertise in this area, they began using me as a consultant. Once my foot was in the door, I found I could use the budgetary process to help them create new agency performance objectives."

JOINT FUNDING

Joint funding arrangements refer to a process by which two or more service providers collaboratively finance a service program or project. Such arrangements are particularly appropriate when federal regulations allow the use of "in-kind" contributions as local share requirements for a project or service program. Combining funds or in-kind contributions from different agencies makes it possible to realize shared objectives by making available new or extended services that were previously beyond the financial capability of any of the contributing providers. An outreach service, for example, might be too costly for a single agency, but within reason when collaborating agencies pool their funds. The planner's leverage over joint funding arrangements is strong when he is in a position to influence the flow of funds to independent service providers; the flow can then be made contingent on a cooperative agreement in which funds are pooled with other providers.

Joint funding, joint budgeting, and purchase of service agreements have been used to standardize or centralize intake and other agency procedures. They frequently result in making new services available or in extending existing services. Such arrangements may also provide the local planner with opportunities for involving providers in other linkages or exchange relationships.

Administrative Support Services

Supportive services that make agency operations more effective and more efficient are found in many locales. These services include (1) the conduct of studies; (2) information processing, dissemination, and exchange; (3) record keeping; (4) grants management and technical assistance; (5) publicity and public relations; (6) procedural integration; (7) joint project evaluation; (8) central project or program evaluation; and finally, (9) centralized standards and guidelines.

CONDUCTING STUDIES

Effective planning or program development often depends on obtaining accurate, useful information about client populations, their needs and their expectations as well as on the resources available to serve them. Studies are often used to describe a social problem or to describe the attitudes, opinions, or changes in an agency's actual or potential consumer population. They can be used to help determine the need for an agency's program or services; to describe the effectiveness of that program; and when combined with cost analytic and time and motion studies, to form estimates of a service program's efficiency.

Because most service providers do not have the capacities to conduct extensive surveys or other types of studies, planners sometimes conduct them in response to agency requests. At other times, they conduct or use studies to support or further their planning objectives.

"I use *surveys* not only to get needed information," explains a welfare council executive, "but also to highlight service deficiencies, to identify gaps. To me, surveys are not only technical tools, but political ones as well. I don't use my findings to clobber people with. Instead, I often involve agency people in evaluating the meanings of survey findings, hoping that in the process I can get them to identify needs that their agencies can address. I often use volunteers in my surveys."

In addition to surveys, planners use case studies; experimental or demonstration studies; accountability or administrative audits; and program assessment and evaluation techniques (items 7 and 8, to be discussed shortly). *Case studies* focus on detailed descriptions of the processes by which services are provided or coordinated, and of the administrative support functions that complement them. They generally require such techniques as participant observation, informal interviews, and content analyses of written documents. While case studies take time, they are relatively easy to do and can be conducted by trained volunteers. They are particularly useful for assessing programs for which objectives may be blurred or for selecting strategies to accomplish those objectives. They are also helpful in trouble shooting potential problems in program operations and for uncovering the reasons for program ineffectiveness or inefficiency.

Experimental or demonstration projects sometimes include case studies as a way to determine whether certain forms of service intervention have any effect upon the accomplishment of formally prescribed objectives. In such projects, alternative strategies may be attempted and the impact of each assessed. While local planners are rarely involved in the conduct of experimental studies, they can be influential in assisting service providers to be more rigorous in their examination of their own practices. In a case where several agencies are involved in providing similar or complementary services (especially where the value of one or another service approach is unclear), the use of demonstration or experimental approaches may be of particular value.

Accountability audits are used to review the consistency, dependability, and accuracy of records pertaining to program expenditures, allocation of resources, and related operations. Although social planners do not generally have the authority to demand the use of audit techniques (a prerogative usually reserved for the organization lending its auspices or providing funds), they can provide technical assistance to agency administrators in the conduct of their own audits.

"I got into the business of helping agencies do accountability audits," an Illinois planner explains, "when I was helping an administrator of a mental health center describe the services his staff provided for kids in trouble with school authorities. I was helping him determine whether or not his staff actually performed functions related to the agency's objectives. I had done a lot of administrative audits before coming to this town. It was easy for me to transfer skills developed in another capacity to my work as a social planner. I also found it easy to use these skills to help agencies study their own effectiveness. Accountability auditing has become a major tool in my technical assistance kit."

INFORMATION PROCESSING, DISSEMINATION, AND EXCHANGE

Sometimes the problem is not in the inadequacy of data or their unavailability. The problem may lie rather in the inaccessibility of data. Information on a particular ethnic population, for example, may be available in reports by the U.S. Census Bureau, state and local studies, monthly bulletins of the Social Security Administration, Department of Labor statistics, county and city health department statistics on mortality, morbidity, and infectious or communicable diseases, and reports by public recreation departments.

It may be difficult, however, for the staffs of service agencies to avail themselves of these data. Daily pressures may leave little time to go to the library. Published reports may look foreboding to the inexperienced and untrained. Statistics may be overabundant, so that most service providers are unable to determine what information is useful or how to use it. In many other instances, information may be locked in service agency files, or in the personal experiences of their staffs.

For these reasons, planners frequently assume responsibility for culling out useful and significant information and making it readily available through newsletters, digests, presentations in the public media, and so on. Planners also provide opportunities for service agency personnel to *exchange information* with each other through conferences, dialogues, inter-agency visits, published reports, continuing education, and staff development activities.

RECORD KEEPING

Planning and coordinating agencies sometimes assume responsibility for *centralized record keeping* which includes gathering, storing, and disseminating information about clients. A centralized client data system with standardized procedures for the flow of information can be useful in planning and evaluation, in grants management, and in the coordination of client services. Few service agencies, however, have the funds to establish centralized data banks. Attempts by service agencies to exchange records directly are at best inefficient, even when the issue of confidentiality is not a barrier.

A central client data processing system, on the other hand, is generally of sufficient scale to permit the use of electronic data processing systems. While many planners do not have control over such systems in their own right, they can and do work with colleagues in Councils on Government, metropolitan health planning agencies, departments of public welfare, which do have such capacities.

GRANTS MANAGEMENT AND TECHNICAL ASSISTANCE

Most service providers have their own procedures for grants management. Many, however, are unaware of the technical requirements for proposal writing and submission and may be even less aware of the potential availability of funds through various federal and state categorical programs, through local revenue sharing, or from private and voluntary sources. Social planners are in the position to share relevant information, and to help service providers seek new funds to expand their services. Their technical assistance can be used to encourage the establishment of complementary and coordinated service programs.

PUBLICITY AND PUBLIC RELATIONS

Many observers feel that human service agencies enjoy a low degree of public support, in part because they have been indifferent to or inexpert in the use of public relations techniques. Although many service providers are capable of designing publicity programs, issuing press releases, or even creating and disseminating information about newsworthy events, most do not have staff who are competent in the more subtle aspects of public relations.

Social planners, on the other hand, can play a significant role in the development of public relations strategies. The objectives of such strategies include (a) maintenance of a favorable climate of public opinion leading to support of services to a population in need; (b) encouragement of public confidence in the providers of services; (c) persuasion of contributors or taxpayers that these services are worthy of their financial support; (d) dissemination of information on the availability of services and how they may be attained; (e) recruitment of potential staff and volunteers for the provision of those services; and finally (f) legitimation for efforts to plan and coordinate those services.

PROCEDURAL INTEGRATION

Procedural integration is sometimes built around the provision of centralized supportive services such as auditing, purchasing, the exchange of material and equipment, and so on. It may include the development of uniform recording and reporting forms, routing procedures, or payment and fee schedules. These procedures may be used to increase the efficiency of agency operations; make possible case monitoring and case coordination; and to facilitate inter-agency exchanges and collaborations through other means.

JOINT PROGRAM OR PROJECT EVALUATION

Evaluation is generally aimed at determining the effects of a service program, measuring its effectiveness, and tabulating its efficiency. Where two or more service providers are involved in some form of collaborative effort on behalf of a particular consumer population, or where benefits to the consumer depend on inputs from two or more providers of service, *joint evaluation* may be the only feasible assessment method.

"The hospital staff was doing a terrific job of rehabilitating retarded patients and getting them ready for placement in the community. If we were to evaluate their services alone, we would have had to give them an "A" rating.

Yet, three-quarters of the discharged patients wound up back in the hospital or in another intensive care facility. Why?" continues a local planner, "because the community's supportive services were inadequate. You can't evaluate the impact of a rehabilitation program without evaluating the impact of its supportive services as well. If we had participated in an evaluation with the hospital staff alone, they probably would have continued doing what they were doing, feeling quite satisfied in performing services that met a high professional standard. They would have blamed the problem of recidivism on others. But by involving them in a joint evaluative effort with those organizations that should have been providing services in the community, we were able to help all the agencies involved identify the deficiencies in their own programs, and to create better mechanisms for placement and follow-up."

CENTRAL PROGRAM EVALUATION

It is not always possible, however, to perform an evaluation on a joint basis. Often planners involved in evaluating the effects, effectiveness, or efficiency of services do so on a *central* basis. This can be particularly difficult if service providers are suspicious or defensive. They may view the evaluator and the evaluation procedures as potentially destructive, aimed only at pointing out their (the providers!) weaknesses, and as threats to their autonomy. In such cases, it may pay to use a "third-party" evaluation procedure, in which the planning or coordinating agency employs an outside evaluator, thereby disassociating itself from the process or the outcome. Because the decisions about what and whom to evaluate are made centrally, however, these procedures can be used to point out deficiencies inherent in the fragmented nature of most service systems.

STANDARDS AND GUIDELINES

By themselves, standards and guidelines may have little impact on the development or delivery of services. They are effective only when they are backed by the force of moral opinion or by control over an agency's resources. Any element in a service agency's task environment can exert pressure on that agency. A funding agency, for example, can make eligibility dependent on a recipient agency's following certain guidelines. A regulatory agency or a body lending its auspices may require that the service agency accept certain standards for hiring personnel or for treating and recruiting clients.

For these reasons, planners often use "oblique" approaches, using their leverage to influence the standards by which others judge the performance of service providers. Such leverage may be complemented by strategies aimed at moving agencies toward voluntary compliance with a community-wide standard. Community-wide standards are often promoted by a policy-coordinating body such as a welfare council or hospital federation. At other times they may arise from the planner's work with task forces and advisory groups.

Administrative and Programmatic Linkages Involving Agency Personnel

Inter-agency linkages can also be promoted through staff exchanges and through centralized screening and training services. Staff exchanges include (1) the use of loaner staff and staff transfers; (2) the out-stationing of staff; (3) the establishment of liaison teams and other joint staff arrangements; (4) centralized staff training and development, which is often complemented by (5) centralized screening, employment counseling, and placement, and the use of (6) volunteer bureaus; or (7) ombudsmen.

LOANER STAFF

Later in this chapter, the location of a rehabilitation staff person on a loaner basis in a manpower agency will be described. Area planners have also facilitated the relocation of city recreation workers in hospitals, multi-purpose centers, and nursing homes. Loaner staff are employed by one agency, but operate as if they were in fact administrative and programmatic members of their host agency.

Such arrangements, however, may strike at the very heart of agency authority and autonomy. Success is based on the mutual interests of collaborators to reach more clients, or to provide more comprehensive services to those clients. Staff transfers require clear understanding and closely monitored contractual agreements between collaborating parties. Tensions and misunderstandings frequently arise. Local planners can be helpful in mediating conflicts, in anticipating them or heading them off, and in helping the parties involved clarify and update their expectations of each other.

OUT-STATIONING

Similar to the loaner staff concept, out-stationing also involves situations where one agency places its personnel at the disposal of another. The first agency, however, maintains administrative and programmatic control over its own employees. For example, an outreach worker may be located "in the community," touching base with a number of agencies. This worker may be available every Tuesday afternoon in the public library, on Mondays and Wednesdays in recreation department facilities, on Thursday in a settlement house or a multi-service center, and so on. Out-stationing is a way of providing services where they might not otherwise be available, or of passing on information about services to potential client populations. Because it requires a clear specification of objectives, it is sometimes inhibited by the defensiveness of those agencies trying to maintain control over "their turf" or fearful of having their deficiencies uncovered.

LIAISON TEAMS AND JOINT USE OF STAFF

The joint use of staff requires agreements by two or more agencies to deliver a particular service or complement of services with staff employed by the collaborating organizations. It may be promoted by a desire to reduce waste and duplication or to provide a service that requires multiple technolo gies. Liaison teams, for example, are generally multidisciplinary in nature. While each team member is paid by his own agency, he or she operates as if professional allegiance to the team were primary. Supervision is generally provided by one person delegated to perform that function, but acceptable to all the cooperating agencies.

Inter-agency liaison "review committees" are used to oversee team efforts; to mediate any jurisdictional disputes that might arise; and to review the efficacy of the structure and the processes involved. Liaison teams are rarely self-generated. They may be initiated by a funder who offers a monetary inducement, or by a planner who serves as both a stimulus and broker of inter-agency agreements. The underlying strategy is often to "convince" service providers of the mutual benefit of such arrangements.

STAFF TRAINING AND DEVELOPMENT

Because education is frequently viewed as "neutral," social planners use *training activities* as vehicles for effecting organizational change and interorganizational exchange. Most service providers do not have the resources to do an effective job of staff training and development without outside help.

Centralized *staff development programs* can be used to emphasize new or different skills leading to improved service provision; new knowledge about the causes or consequences of individual and social problems; or newer and different approaches to dealing with clients and their problems. By bringing together two or more agencies whose agency representatives share common problems and concerns, the exchange of ideas on successful intervention strategies can be promoted. Social planners frequently assume responsibility for the conduct of such training programs or they may arrange for the training to be conducted by an outside contractor.

"Of course, we'll never be in a position to determine what staff each agency should hire," confides a planner, "but I have devoted a great deal of time to establishing criteria for the employment of staff. I am thoroughly familiar with the state civil service commission, and have also provided technical assistance to agencies. Essentially what that assistance consists of, is helping agency administrators identify those staff skills required in order to accomplish the objectives inherent in our three-year plan. I have found the application of functional job analysis, and the use of task banks developed by Sydney Fine for SRS, of immeasurable benefit.

"I have also made certain that I am known to the community college and university personnel. This almost puts me in a position of being able to do some effective screening. I talk to students and counsel them to apply for one or another of the jobs I know are available in my area. I don't do job placement per se, but I do work very closely with the placement personnel at the university, with the state employment commission, and in our local volunteer bureau. It is a far cry from being in full control, but I do have considerable influence."

The planner went on to explain that she was sensitive to the potential of agency "paranoia" about her activities, but had been on sufficiently good terms with agency administrators to deal with any incipient anxiety. "In fact," she confides, "they have appreciated my efforts and view my work as upgrading standards and increasing the supply of capable manpower."

VOLUNTEER BUREAUS

The work of professional service providers is frequently supplemented by the work of volunteers. Many social planners work with or promote the development of volunteer bureaus. As centralized services, volunteer bureaus recruit, train, and assign volunteers, often to more than a single agency. In many cases, volunteers work in more than one agency, helping to interpret the services of one to the other. Information is sometimes passed on from a volunteer in one agency to a volunteer in another.

Volunteers can be assigned to a large variety of tasks, enabling the agency to expand its services and often to reach previously underserviced populations. They perform clerical, programmatic, promotional, resource development, and policy functions. Examples of clerical functions include typing, answering the telephone, filing. Programmatic activities may include working with groups of preschool children, friendly visiting, escorting or driving the disabled or elderly, preparation of meals, counseling, tutoring children with reading difficulties.

Promotional activities include developing informative booklets, speaking to area associations, preparing news releases. Resource development may include fund raising or arranging for resource exchanges between two or more agencies. Policy making may include participation in advisory councils, boards, and task forces.

OMBUDSMEN

Few individual clients possess complete or adequate knowledge about the service system. They may be unaware of the procedures for obtaining service, ignorant of the services to which they are entitled, unfamiliar with government regulations. To deal with these problems, a number of communities have adapted the Scandinavian *ombudsman* approach to local conditions. An ombudsman is generally employed by a government agency to guide individual citizens through what may seem like a maze of services and regulations. The ombudsman's function is to inform the client of the current procedures to use, to tell clients about their rights, and to counsel them in securing those rights. Social planners sometimes arrange for the funding or development of ombudsman services.

The ombudsman sometimes works in connection with an information and referral agency or volunteer bureau. Because few agencies employ staff who perform only ombudsman functions, the ombudsman may perform other tasks as well. Most of these tasks, however, relate to representation of the client in his relationships with the bureaucracy. The ombudsman role is particularly important when the client has been mistreated, mishandled, or lost in the shuffle.

Programmatic Linkages Through Development of Centralized Services

Centralized services may include (1) information and outreach, (2) intake, (3) diagnosis, (4) referral, (5) transportation, (6) follow-up, and (7) grievance machinery. These are sometimes described as "linking services" because they link consumers to providers.

INFORMATION AND OUTREACH

Outreach refers to systematic efforts to "recruit clients" so as to narrow the gap between actual and potential client populations. Outreach may require mounting effective information programs, including intensive door to door campaigns; TV spot announcements; speaking engagements at meetings of fraternal and civic organizations; communication with persons in the lay or ad hoc service system, and so forth. Effective outreach efforts may require face-to-face contacts with potential clients before they actually make use of a service.

Information services may also include centralized data banks where public or private agencies can maintain current and up-to-date information with respect to opportunities and services available. Moreover, this information may be matched with lists of persons in need of such services and opportunities. Specially trained staff, including bilingual individuals, may be employed to inform people of those opportunities and services available, and to assist them in taking advantage of them.

INTAKE

Although the acceptance of clients is a prerogative that few service providers are willing to abrogate, *centralized intake* procedures are nevertheless available in many areas. Centralized intake may go no further than "interception screening" which is, in effect, a pre-intake procedure. It includes only the grossest screening of telephone or walk-in inquiries and some assessment of which service sectors (housing, health care, employment, assistance for the elderly) might be involved.

More detailed screening may subsequently take place at the level of "sectorial intake." Clients with health problems, for example, may then be referred to the health intake worker. Another worker would be responsible for intake of clients requiring educational or recreational services; another for mental health services; still another for counseling and socialization services; ad infinitum.

In some communities, all intake procedures are under a single worker or under intake "generalists." But in larger metropolitan areas, where the service system is diffuse and where services may be extensive, it is often necessary to provide intake on a "two-step" basis as has already been described. In addition, some intake workers may operate on an out-stationed or loaner basis.

DIAGNOSIS

Diagnosis generally follows intake and screening. It includes the assessment of total client needs and frequently results in the development of a comprehensive plan for service. Although it may occasionally happen that clients appear directly at a service provider's door (and are diagnosed by the intake worker in a family agency or a community-based medical clinic), categorical service providers are rarely capable of diagnosing a client's problems from a "total person" or "holistic" perspective. This makes it unlikely that other service providers will accept the diagnosis made outside their own agency boundaries. Many autonomous service providers, in fact, will be reluctant to abide by the diagnosis of a *central* intake and referral staff person if they do not have confidence in that staff's diagnostic capability. This is why it is often necessary for intake and referral services to be divided along sectoral lines.

REFERRAL

Diagnosis often leads to referral. Referral is a process by which a client is directed to another provider for services. At the simplest level, the intake worker will inform a client of where and how to go about getting a service; in other instances he may contact the service provider to facilitate entry by relaying information, setting up appointments, or even modifying the procedures by which clients may enter such services. Standardized forms are generally used to introduce the client and to relay information regarding his needs or interests.

Effective referral often requires contractual agreements between the intake and referral service and the provider of services. Without such agreements, rejection of clients is common. The very existence of a centralized intake and referral system can serve to cut down instances of rejection. If clients are appropriately screened, service agencies need not reject clients outright if they cannot provide the requested service. They need only refer the client back to the referral source, or they themselves may request information from the central intake worker about where to refer the applicant.

TRANSPORTATION

The development and promotion of transportation services that put isolated persons in touch with community facilities and resources is of central concern to some planners. In addition to linking consumers to providers, transportation services can be used to reduce isolation, open up access and opportunity, and assure that untapped services become utilized.

"If we can't get people to the services, or services to the people, all the rest of our efforts are worthless," explains a planner. "I put a great deal of my energy into trying to influence our area's transportation plan right from the start. Obviously I was never going to get enough funds to buy transportation for all the older folks in this area, so I figured to influence the transportation authority in county government to recognize the needs of the elderly. I used some well placed news stories, and had older persons attend transportation authority meetings. Then I got myself invited to attend a meeting and testify on needs. I did more than that!

"Had a whole lot of data available. Handed out maps on which I had concentrations of older persons identified by sections of the county. Showed them where service centers were and how impossible it was for older persons to get there via public transportation. Made my point, too. Later, I was able to supplement public transportation with pools of volunteer drivers. Now the energy crisis has hit, and I've got to find some way of dealing with that too."

FOLLOW-UP

Transportation services, combined with a well-staffed, centralized outreach, intake, diagnosis, and referral system, however, provide no assurance that clients will actually get to those services to which they are referred. *Follow-up services* are frequently needed to help clients to negotiate a particular service delivery system; to make certain that they actually get services; and to ascertain what additional needs may arise. Although follow-up activities may be extremely time-consuming, they are often the crucial variable in assuring that clients do get served.

Follow-up may be informal, consisting of telephone contacts between the intake worker and the service provider to which a client has been referred. Or it may consist of formal routing procedures, with standardized referral forms and return slips routed back to the referral worker once the client has reached his destination. Centralized record keeping makes continued tracking of clients through the system possible.

Follow-up procedures may also require *escort* services in which the client is literally escorted to a service provider. Escort services are frequently managed by volunteers and are especially useful when clients are physically, socially, or emotionally incapable of negotiating their own way to a service provider.

GRIEVANCE MACHINERY

While most funding or planning agencies may not be in a position to establish community-wide grievance machinery, they can insist that grievance procedures be established in all projects or agencies they support or to which they channel funds from other sources. Local service plans can be written to include reference to the establishment of grievance machineries. Social planners also use public opinion and their work with task forces to induce agencies to develop such grievance procedures voluntarily.

Programmatic Coordination Through Service Integration

Centralized services frequently lead to other forms of service coordination. Social planners have been effective in promoting procedures and action programs that lead to (1) case management; (2) ad hoc case coordination; (3) case conferences; (4) joint program development; (5) joint projects; and (6) the establishment of multi-service centers.

CASE MANAGEMENT

Case management should not be confused with casework. Case management refers to management of the client's progress through a network of services so as to assure that he receives those services he is due. In some communities, case coordinators are assigned by service agencies; in others by an information and referral service. In still other communities, case coordination is performed on an ad hoc basis or an occasional basis by an ombudsman or by a member of a volunteer bureau.

AD HOC CASE COORDINATION

Ad hoc case coordination may involve no more than a decision by a worker in one agency to contact a worker in another agency concerning a common client. Although agency policy may permit such cooperation, there may be considerable cost to the workers in communications time and additional activities undertaken. Unfortunately, although agencies may encourage workers to engage in such activities, they do not sufficiently reward them for such efforts.

"One of the facts discovered in our survey of community facilities," says a member of a task force on "Alternatives to Institutionalization," "is that once an agency delivers its rather specialized service, no one bothers to see to it that a client receives the supportive services he needs from another agency. When a medical social worker spends time outside the hospital to arrange for coordinated home care services, she has got to do it on her own time. With the case load she's got, you won't find her volunteering much."

Efforts to answer this problem are often couched in terms of asking for "more money for more staff." Rarely do agencies decide to view their common clients as "shared" clientele, requiring shared or coordinated services. Doing so requires the regularization of ad hoc procedures and the provision of suitable supports or rewards to staff for assuming coordinating responsibilities.

CASE CONFERENCES

Case conferences are well-worn techniques, used for many years to regularize ad hoc procedures. Several agencies with clients in common may instruct line staff to attend regular or bimonthly meetings to discuss the progress of individual cases. The client may be tracked through the system, so as to identify the points where he was well served, where he may have been sidetracked, or where he may not have received any service. Members of the case conference committee, often representatives of different disciplines and professions, consult with each other on the development of treatment plans and the assignment of responsibilities for care.

Some critics of the case conference have noted that it works well only when participants are all equally supported in their efforts by their agency supervisors, or when a central authority has the clout to induce particular agencies to take on specific tasks on behalf of a client. Unfortunately, these conditions are rare. Critics also charge that case conferences are inordinately time-consuming; that they create situations in which there is staff "layering" —multiple layers of staff becoming involved in what should be a simple service.

Case conferences, critics argue further, permit some agencies to get off the hook by dumping a problem case, or by slowing down service. One United Fund executive charges that "they often result in inflated or duplicated service or client counts." For these reasons, planners may attempt to move from case conferences to more permanent and regularized case coordination or toward the development of liaison teams.

JOINT PROGRAM DEVELOPMENT

Joint program development refers to collaborative efforts by two or more service providers to devise programmatic solutions to specified problems. It may result in such mechanisms as liaison teams, joint intake or referral procedures, case management, or procedural integration. Providers can be brought together even when they do not fully subscribe to the same goals or objectives. All that is needed is an awareness that joint program development may be helpful in accomplishing each of the collaborator's objectives.

JOINT PROJECTS

The *joint administration of a common project* frequently flows from joint efforts at program development, from procedural integration, from the use of liaison teams, or from the allocation of loaner staff. Common projects usually require the allocation of new funds which permit the creation of a programmatic service unit on an independent or a semi-independent basis. The project itself may be sponsored by two or more agencies, and its staff composed of either loaners or personnel specially employed by the project. The administrator of a joint project may be responsible to an advisory panel or to a committee made up of representatives of the co-sponsoring agencies.

During the past decade, joint administration frequently led to the establishment of multi-purpose neighborhood centers under the auspices of a local anti-poverty organization or Model Cities agency. Many of these continue to serve as models for the coordination and, ultimately, the full integration of services.

Multi-service centers are generally geared to serving clients in a given geographic area, for example, a neighborhood or a rural county. The desire to provide the variety of services required to meet the needs of a particular population may result in the location of services of separate agencies within a common facility. These services need not be functionally related, nor need all staff be employed by the center.

Direct services may be provided by out-stationed staff from a variety of independent agencies. In some cases they cooperate on a multi-disciplinary basis to work on common problems (similar to liaison teams). In others, they function entirely independently. Frequently they include common core services (outreach, intake, diagnosis, referral, and follow-up). Almost always, they require some form of joint budgeting, and frequently joint funding (as is the case with in-kind services that demand new funding from outside sources).

Occasionally, multi-service centers develop along completely independent paths, absorbing the staff in a common goal and assuming administrative, fiscal, and programmatic responsibilities. In such cases, at least segments of the participating agencies have merged, in a sort of logical conclusion of the application of various linking mechanisms.

In general, *mergers* result when two or more agencies decide to fully integrate their administrative procedures and service programs. Either a new agency is created, or the less dominant agency becomes absorbed into the structure of the other. When several agencies merge their services, or agree to become a specialized department of a larger organization, the result may be the creation of *super agencies*—such as metropolitan human resource administrations. Information and referral agencies are examples of mergers that include only certain functions of otherwise independent service agencies.

These arrangements may permit greater coordination and integration and thus result in services that are more available, accessible, and adequate. At other times, however, super agencies, multi-service centers, and centralized information systems may only increase certain services while fostering other inefficiencies inherent in bureaucratic organization.

Illustration From Practice: Service Integration as a Form of Advocacy

The following example from practice may help illustrate how social planners engage the development and management of various linking mechanisms. It is drawn from the activities of the Community Mental Health board staff introduced in Illustration III of Chapter 1. In some ways the approach is remarkably similar to the protagonist role assumed by the planner we first encountered in that chapter.

"Soon after we compiled our 'laundry list' of institutional abuses," reported the assistant director for planning of the CMH board, "we decided that the creation of client grievance procedures was going to be one of our highest priorities. Remember, we'd found that price schedules were unfair, many clients were being put off, and others had to endure unconscionable delays. Many agencies refused to respond to real emergencies. Some clients fell between the cracks—not because services weren't available, but because agencies had created administrative procedures which screened clients out instead of in.

"It was obvious that we were a long way from accomplishing our major objectives—the creation of a coordinated network of services accessible and available to people in need of mental health services. We felt a massive and comprehensive attack on the problems we saw was unfeasible. So we decided to pick at the vulnerable spots in the system—the places where it was obviously not working correctly. The absence of a grievance machinery through which clients could get redress when their rights were trampled on seemed to be one major gap we could try to plug.

"With the documentation provided by our two-week survey, we got the mayor to appoint a blue-ribbon committee to look into client rights. The committee did a damned good job. More important, it took us off the hook. If we'd done all the work alone, the agencies would have seen us as hatchet men. It would have been a long time before we could develop other kinds of relationships with them.

"But the committee was made up of agency people, with a sprinkling of influential citizens. With staff help, they first drew up a statement on clients' rights; then recommended the creation of a complaint bureau as part of the CMH board's soon-to-be-established information and referral service. The committee then reconstituted itself as an advisory panel to the complaint bureau so as to give the bureau more clout. It also suggested that the board establish standards of practice for all agencies and withhold funds under its jurisdiction from those agencies which did not comply.

"These last recommendations are a bit premature. We do have a plan in mind for establishing standards, but this is way off into the future. It will require many self-study groups and the input of various professional and accrediting associations. As for putting the squeeze on agencies through the funds we control . . . well, we just don't control enough of the dollar flow to make any significant difference.

"Now if our complaint bureau was to have any impact, it could not depend on coercive means alone. We wanted agencies to agree with our values about clients' rights. First off, the blue-ribbon committee sponsored a number of meetings on the topic through such professional associations as the local medical society, the social workers association, and the nursing home and hospital association. We figured the professional groups had as much of a stake and a commitment to the issue as we did. Then we began publicizing good practice and getting the word out on who we felt were the worst offenders.

"We started a column called 'Complaints Bureau' in the CMH board's newsletter, which described how agencies changed their procedures. We leaked stuff to the newspapers about agencies that were particularly bad offenders and we arranged for others to write letters to the editor. Some change became evident."

The board's other approaches included staff visits with agency administrators, a kind of technical assistance or consultation function; social brokerage; the eventual creation of a procedure for establishing standards and guidelines.

Review

Coordination at the operational level is made possible through the utilization of a variety of linking mechanisms. Fiscal mechanisms include the purchase of services, joint budgeting, and joint funding. Providers may also be linked through administrative support services such as the conduct of studies, central record-keeping, central information processing, dissemination of information, grants management, the provision of technical assistance, publicity and public relations, procedural integration, joint project evaluation, and central project or program evaluation.

In other instances, agencies can link their services through a variety of exchanges involving personnel. These include the use of loaner staff and other staff transfers, out-stationing, and the co-location of staff or the use of liaison teams. Area planners can also increase the likelihood of staff collaboration through staff training and staff development; screening; employment counseling and placement; management of volunteer bureaus and assignment of volunteers to agencies; or the provision of ombudsman services.

In a number of communities, local planners have been responsible for the establishment of centralized information and outreach, intake, diagnostic, referral, transportation, and follow-up services. In some cases these are complemented by grievance machinery. Other examples of inter-agency exchanges leading to service integration include case management, ad hoc case coordination, and case conferences. Success in these ventures sometimes leads to joint program development, or collaborative projects. Occasionally collaboration results in the establishment of multi-service centers or super agencies.

1. Think about an agency you are familiar with, or interview staff at an agency you want to know more about. Identify the inter-agency linkages discussed in this chapter that already exist between it and other providers of service. Do these providers coordinate their efforts around a functional or sectorial concern (for example, health care, nutrition, or transportation)? Or are they clustered around a specific geographic area? Do they cater to the needs of a particular population, such as retarded children, people whose incomes fall below the poverty line, the aging with cardiac problems, a minority population? Exercises 1 and 2, which follow, may help you organize your thoughts.

2. Review the sections on resources, pathways, and leverage in Chapter 5. What kind of resources do you or a planner with whom you are acquainted have at your (his or her) disposal? Are you or the planner in a position to direct any agencies to engage in exchange relationships? Is it more appropriate for you (the planner) to assume a broker or mediator role? What leverage techniques are open—coercion; inducement; persuasion; selling; friendship; obligation?

3. If you were to expand the range and scope of exchange relationships or coordinating linkages between agencies in your area, which service providers would you involve? What kind of linking mechanisms would you employ this year; next year; the year after? Why?

4. In your area, what are the major facilitators to interorganizational exchange and to the development of a more comprehensive and integrated service delivery system? What are the inhibitors?

EXERCISE 1: BUILDING AN INTER-AGENCY LINKAGE DIAGRAM

1. Use the diagram that follows or blow it up on a piece of newsprint. Put your agency or a service agency in the center.
2. Now fill in the spaces along the periphery with the names of service providers in its task environment. Refer to the Program Resources Matrix you designed (pp. 57–59).
3. Along the connecting lines, indicate which of the linking mechanisms discussed in this chapter are employed by one or the other partner to the exchange. You might develop letters and numbers to code each type of linking mechanism (for example, A.1 = case conference). Also indicate the direction of the exchange by an arrow (→ , ←) or double arrow (⇆).

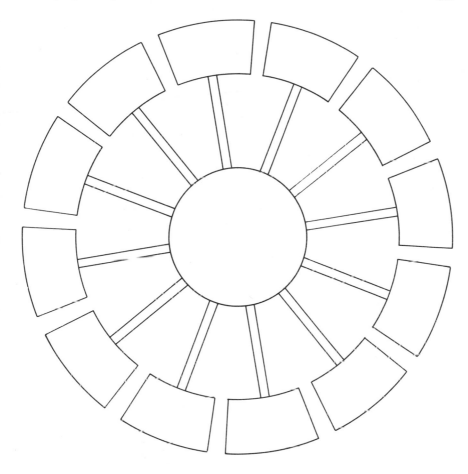

EXERCISE 2: LINKING MECHANISM—PROVIDER ANALYSIS

1. Select a service provider with whom the central agency on your diagram interacts on a number of linking mechanisms.
2. Using the Linking Form provided, indicate in *black* ink which linking mechanisms are in effect and which direction they take. If you feel the mechanism is not working properly, indicate it in *red*.
3. Now indicate in *red ink* those mechanisms not currently utilized but that you think potentially useful. (i.e. add new and needed mechanisms).
4. What strategic resources are necessary to modify existing linkages or set up new ones?
5. Complete steps 2, 3, and 4 for other agencies on your diagram

Linking Form for Exercise 2:

Service Provider _____

Linking Mechanisms* _____ _____

                     _____ _____

                     _____ _____

                     _____ _____

                     _____ _____

                     _____ _____

Notes _____

* ↑indicates that the linking mechanism │indicates that it flows ↑│linkage
   ↓is in the direction of your agency. │from your agency to   ↑│↓is mutual.
                               ↓another.

Service Provider _____

Linking Mechanisms* _____ _____

                     _____ _____

                     _____ _____

                     _____ _____

                     _____ _____

                     _____ _____

                     _____ _____

Notes _____

* ↑indicates that the linking mechanism │indicates that it flows ↑│linkage
   ↓is in the direction of your agency. │from your agency to   ↑│↓is mutual.
                               ↓another.

Recommended Readings

LITWAK, EUGENE, and JACK ROTHMAN. "Toward the Theory and Practice of Coordination Between Formal Organizations," in *Organizations and Clients: Essays on the Sociology of Service,* William R. Rosengren and Mark Lifton (Eds.). Columbus, Ohio: Bobbs Merrill, 1970.
Litwak and Rothman begin this chapter with a discussion of the nature of interorganizational relations and the types of formal linkages which effectively join organizations to each other. Factors that appear to contribute to the effectiveness of interorganizational linkages (for instance, the amount of interdependence between systems) are then identified. It is suggested that relations between organizations might also be affected by the structure of their relational network. The authors conclude by pointing out some yet unresolved problems in maintaining appropriate relations between formal systems.

MUNRO, JOSEPH. "Intersystem Action Planning: Criminal and Noncriminal Justice Agencies." *Public Administration Review,* 1976, *36*; 390–397.
Inter-agency planning may be a satisfactory alternative to fragmented and isolated service delivery. It is clear, however, that its implementation is fraught with problems. Munro contends that inter-agency or inter-system planning is frequently doomed to little more than "pseudo-scientific ceremony," because political, organizational, and personal career imperatives have either not been met, or are highly threatened by this type of planning. These imperatives, the author asserts, must be met within the context of existing legal, economic, and psychological constraints. Munro concludes that it is only through adequate political and administrative effort that inter-system planning can effectively overcome these constraints.

PEARL, G., and D. H. BAR. "Agencies Advocating Together." *Social Casework,* 1976, *57*, 611–618.
The Metro Agencies Action Committee (MAAC) is a coalition of eleven social service agencies in metropolitan Toronto. For several years, MAAC affiliates have worked together to change social policies and legislation affecting the Toronto community. This article chronicles the formation and development of MAAC and discusses some of the major activities in which the coalition has engaged. The authors also attempt to describe some of the benefits gained and the lessons learned from this inter-agency experience.

THOMPSON, JAMES D., and WILLIAM J. MCEWEN. "Organizational Goals and Environment: Goal-setting and an Interaction Process." *American Sociological Review,* February, 1958. (Reprinted in Mayer Zald, *Social Welfare Institutions.* New York: John Wiley and Sons, 1957.)
According to the authors, the relations among organizations are mediated by (1) the role-sets of boundary personnel, (2) the flow of information among them, and (3) the flow of personnel. The article identifies and discusses basic attributes of the interorganizational relationship, including overlap in goals and boundary personnel. Some of the problems involved in establishing and maintaining these relations are explored, and hypotheses are developed regarding the nature of interactions among organizations.

Suggestions for Further Readings

AIKEN, MICHAEL, et al. *Coordination of Services for the Mentally Retarded*. Madison, Wisc.: The University of Wisconsin, 1972. Available from Project Share, Department of Health, Education and Welfare, Washington, D.C.

Census of Local Services Integration, 1975 (A Working Note). Santa Monica, Calif.: The Rand Corporation, 1975.

EVAN, WILLIAM. "The Organization Set: Toward a Theory of Inter-Organizational Relations," in *Approaches to Organizational Design*, James D. Thompson (Ed.). Pittsburgh: The University of Pittsburgh Press, 1966.

HORN, GERALD T., VICTORIA M. E. CARR, and GEORGE J. CORCORAN. *Illustrating Services Integration from Categorical Bases*, Human Services Monograph Series, No. 3. Washington, D.C.: Project Share, Department of Health, Education and Welfare, 1976.

"Integrating a Housing Allowance with a Welfare System: Further Analysis of Program-Linking Strategies and Administration." Washington, D.C.: Urban Institute, November 1975.

Integration of Human Services in HEW: An Evaluation of Service Integration Projects, Vol. I. Washington, D.C.: Department of Health, Education and Welfare, Social Rehabilitation Services, 1972.

LEVINE, SOL, and PAUL WHITE. "Exchange as a Conceptual Framework for the Study of Inter-Organizational Relationships." *Administrative Science Quarterly*, March, 1961.

LITWAK, EUGENE. "An Approach to Linkage and Grassroots Community Organization," in *Strategies of Community Organization A Book of Readings*, Fred M. Cox, et al. (Eds.). Itasca, Ill.: F. Peacock Publishing Co., 1973.

MEYERSON, M. "Next Challenge for the Urban Planner: Linking Local and National Economic Planning." *Journal of the American Institute of Planners*, 1976, *42*, 371–376.

MIKULECKY, ROBERT (Ed.). *Human Services Integration*. Washington, D.C.: American Society for Public Administration, 1974.

Pooled Funding as a Method of Achieving Human Services Coordination. Hartford, Conn.: Community Life Association, 1975.

SAMPSON, BARBARA C. *Services Integration* (Parts I and II). Cambridge, Mass.: Abt Associates, 1975.

WARREN, ROLAND L., STEPHEN M. ROSE, and ANN F. BERGUNDER. *The Structure of Urban Reform*. Lexington, Mass.: D. C. Heath and Co., 1974, chap. 2, 3, 4 and 8.

11

Strengthening Operational Linkages
Between Providers

It is not enough for planners to know what linkages exist and which ones are possible among service providers at the local level. It is also important to know how to strengthen these linkages in the interest of more effective service delivery.

Factors Which Facilitate or Inhibit Linkages Between Service Providers

THE EXTENSIVENESS OF INTER-AGENCY LINKAGES

Unfortunately, many agencies are reluctant to engage in any more than the most perfunctory exchanges for fear of loss of autonomy or of exposure to outside examination. It is not enough that the planner establish clear-cut objectives specifying the nature and range of coordinating mechanisms to be developed over a specified period of time. It is not even sufficient for agency administrators to agree on the relevance of these linkages to the development of a comprehensive and coordinated service delivery system. Agreement does not lead directly to action.

The linking of service providers into a coordinated and comprehensive system takes time. It takes time to design a linking mechanism, to promote its adoption by providers, to mediate agreements between providers, and to evaluate the effectiveness or appropriateness of that mechanism. Most linking mechanisms are not quick to prove themselves. Comfortable working relationships are not easy to achieve. Even those linkages that seem to be fully operational need continued attention and support in order that the gains made are protected, and that further progress becomes possible.

OVERCOMING RESISTANCE

The planner's ability to either circumvent or overcome the resistance of some service providers to engage in exchanges with others is largely related to the planner's perceived leverage over those providers. The extent of that leverage is in turn dependent on his or her access to or control over the resources essential to service providers. These resources include money and credit, facilities, personnel, knowledge and expertise, and political influence. Perceived leverage is not sufficient in and of itself, however.

When the service provider views inter-agency exchanges as a threat to its autonomy, as unrelated to the accomplishment of its own objectives, or irrelevant to meeting the needs of its service clientele, it will not be motivated —even perhaps by the availability of new resources—to support inter-agency linkages.

In general, it is possible to group those factors which inhibit or facilitate inter-agency exchanges and operational linkages into seven categories: (1) the capability of the social planner; (2) the availability of fiscal and related resources; (3) public and environmental support; (4) complementarity with agency objectives; (5) complementarity with policies and procedures that govern the functions of service agencies; (6) the existence of a support system; and (7) a mixture of other variables.

THE SOCIAL PLANNER

When resources to compel agencies to engage in exchange relationships are lacking, the informal leadership provided by the social planner is often a critical factor. The esteem with which the planner is regarded and the trust he or she is able to engender are extremely valuable assets. These assets, however, must be supported by access to and contact with relevant community influentials, with other agency administrators, and with clients of the agencies involved. Such contacts make it possible for the planner to broker relationships that facilitate exchange.

The planner may not be successful, however, if, having promoted an inter-agency exchange process, he or she is not available to serve as a legitimating agent, particularly when breakdowns in that process require technical assistance or mediation. The planner's inaccessibility may be perceived as a lack of concern.

Social planners should approach the task of promoting and managing exchange relationships with some modesty. "I'm glad I was tempered by my experiences in a community mental health setting," explains a welfare council executive, "or I would have tried to accomplish too much all at once. You can't act like an eager beaver, or agencies will turn you off right away. The gangbuster's approach is not guaranteed to engender trust."

MONEY AND FACILITIES

Procedures for joint funding, joint budgeting, and the purchase of services were discussed earlier. In general, linkages are promoted when: (a) supportive funds are flexible and open ended; (b) funders specify exchange or cooperation as requirements of a grant or fiscal support; and (c) the local planner can be helpful in securing funds for service providers.

Probably few variables are more significant than the extent to which service providers are free to use their funds in a flexible manner. Unfortunately, dollars are too often earmarked so tightly as to make allocation to coordinating activities almost impossible. Few service providers are accorded the freedom of vocational rehabilitation counselors who have relatively open-ended budgets with which to purchase and to coordinate services to meet client needs.

Increasingly, however, federal support includes with it some requirement for the conduct of inter-agency exchanges. Federal guidelines are most helpful when they specify not only what can or ought to be done, but *how* it should be done. When regulations are not sufficiently specific, the social planner can be helpful by working directly with the agencies concerned or by recommending supplements to the guidelines offered by state and federal agencies. These activities also complement the planner's technical assistance to service providers; that is, the location of possible sources of grants or other funds, project design, proposal writing, elements of grants management, and so forth.

The availability of facilities can often serve as a substitute for funds. A central facility for record keeping, information processing, intake and referral, or staff training, for example, may be all that is needed to start an exchange process. Available office space in one agency's building may be sufficient to suggest the possibility of out-stationing or exchange of staff.

PUBLIC AND ENVIRONMENTAL SUPPORT

When government agencies and public funding sources support the integration of services or the establishment of inter-agency linkages, their chances of success are heightened considerably. Active support, however, requires more than mere funding. It may also require technical assistance beyond that given by the planner, and it requires agreed upon policies and procedures at the state, regional, or federal level. In the case of voluntary agencies, such support might come from national bodies, from influential citizens, and from board members. Both public and voluntary agencies are subject to political influence applied by various local influentials and, to a greater or lesser degree, by the users of their services.

AGENCY OBJECTIVES

Unless the local planner has compelling leverage, at least some shared or complementary goals between service providers are prerequisites to the development and maintenance of inter-agency linkages. *Service agencies need not have the same goals; it is only necessary that the exchange be perceived as mutually beneficial.* It does not matter if one agency is perceived as gaining more than another; its important that there be gains for all parties involved. Agency administrators perceive the exchange as a means of maintaining the organization, or even extending services to a larger number of clients and reaching a new clientele.

Exchange in which the participating agencies are willing to submerge some of their own prerogatives in support of integrated objectives occurs only when service providers consider themselves part of an overall service delivery system. Arrival at such a perception may require considerable "education" on the planner's part. It may be facilitated by involvement of agency staff in training programs, by promoting information exchanges through public relations and community education campaigns, and by a great deal of individual contact between the planner and agency personnel.

POLICIES AND PROCEDURES

Unfortunately, agency willingness to engage in interorganizational exchanges may be subverted by internal policies and procedures. Inflexible eligibility requirements and divergent sources of funding can easily subvert efforts at interorganizational cooperation. Some agencies, for example, are funded on the basis of numbers of clients served; others on the basis of staff size; still others on the number of cases closed or tasks accomplished. These differences may make it virtually impossible to engage in personnel exchanges or in any forms of joint budgeting and funding.

The internal administrative structures of the relevant agencies can also make exchange extremely difficult. An organization with a structure of formal hierarchical authority will find it very difficult to engage in collaborative efforts with an agency administered on the basis of collegial relationships. Since the agency run on a collegial basis views its entire staff as being on a similar level, and the hierarchical agency has staff on different levels, it becomes very difficult to decide who is to relate to whom.

The length of time needed to negotiate agreements up and down the line within bureaucratic organizations may preclude any possibility of involvement in horizontal exchanges with other organizations. Personnel turnover is another variable which sometimes destroys an emerging relationship before precise contracts delineating the responsibilities of each partner to the exchange can be developed. Poor administration or management in one agency may make it suspect in the eyes of a potential exchange partner.

SUPPORT SYSTEMS

A number of logistical factors can serve to support or inhibit interagency linkages. Standardized data collection processing and feedback systems, when available, do much to improve communication between service providers. Periodic studies on the needs of local populations can serve to highlight service gaps and other problems inherent in a noncoordinated system. Task forces and advisory committees composed of consumer populations, agency representatives, and community influentials are useful in maintaining open communication and in further highlighting problems in the overall service delivery system.

The physical proximity of certain agencies can be used to encourage exchanges. In other instances, the very fact of their distance from each other will suggest the need for out-stationing or loaner staff techniques. Sometimes supportive services like transportation (including escort services) and intake and referral procedures frequently lead to other forms of exchange.

OTHER VARIABLES

A number of other variables may affect the extent to which integrating or coordinating linkages are established. Frequently these are idiosyncratic to particular areas, communities, or neighborhoods. A one-time negative experience between two agencies may discourage willingness to risk a new exchange. On the other hand, positive experiences may encourage the development of new linkages and may make it possible to build on existing linkages.

The existence of structured consumer groups and self-help organizations advocating in their own behalf, or civic organizations and social action groups acting as spokesmen for a consumer population, may create a social environment in which providers perceive themselves under some pressure to coordinate or integrate aspects of their services. In some instances, providers may band together for mutual protection. In others, social planners may have to assume the role of "buffer" between the agency and a militant consumer population.

Other variables that may affect the potential for effective coordination include the extent to which staff in each of the agencies subscribes to similar professional values and standards; the expertise of that staff in negotiating and in cooperation; the extent to which the agencies involved hold a monopoly over access to clients, provision of certain services, facilities, or other necessary resources; or the trust or mistrust that may exist because of previous experiences.

The Question of Mandate

Under the best of circumstances, the social planner may be armed with a legislative or administrative mandate to reorganize and integrate services at the area level. This mandate sometimes derives from functional agreements inherent in such structures as metropolitan planning councils, councils on governments, or human resource commissions. These higher level organizations may themselves represent a similar reorganization at the state level, in which a number of human service departments are reorganized into a single agency. State regulations and guidelines then provide the area planner with sufficient authority to compel certain forms of service coordination and integration.

In these instances, the planner may be part of a multi-sector team, invested with both moral authority and some legal power. Such power may rest in "sign-off" authority on funds. Unfortunately, it is all too often the exceptional circumstances in which social planners have such a clear mandate at the community level.

Gains to Clients from Increasing Inter-Agency Linkages

Several gains to clients from the integration and coordination of services were identified earlier in the chapter. These include increases in the availability, accessibility, effectiveness, efficiency, and responsiveness of services.

AVAILABILITY

Purchase-of-service agreements in which one agency contracts with another to provide a service to a designated clientele can be used to increase the availability of services, as can joint budgeting and joint funding arrangements between agencies. Such arrangements frequently lead to joint program development or the sharing of information. Information exchanges and centralized referral projects increase the extent to which knowledge about alternative and complementary services are available. The mere fact that a service exists does not make it available if the persons to be served are unaware of that service.

ACCESSIBILITY

Such mechanisms as stationing staff members from one agency on the premises of another (as when a public health nurse regularly makes visits to public libraries and senior citizen centers) brings a service directly to a population in need. Staff transfers between agencies or the establishment of loaner staff and liaison team arrangements increase accessibility on a structured and sustained basis. The development of intake and referral projects that include both outreach and follow-up activities can also be used to increase accessibility of services, first by reaching the people in need and then bringing them to the service providers. Transportation services can make other services both accessible and available.

EFFECTIVENESS

Even the most qualitatively sound service can be ineffective if it is discontinuous with other needed services or if it treats one element of a client's problem without regard to other aspects of a total condition. Continuity refers to client movement within a system of services. In many cases, client flow is aborted because of the lack of integrating linkages between agencies.

Effective medical treatment and physical therapy, as noted, are rendered ineffective if the patient cannot be discharged into the community because of the unavailability of supportive services, or because cooperative agreements do not exist between community-based service agencies and the hospital staff involved. Job training and job counseling are ineffective without job placement and—in those situations in which jobs are not readily available—job development.

Client populations may also require supportive counseling services for other members of the family, supplementary income, child care (as in the case of parents or grandparents responsible for young children), transportation services, and so on. Too often, the client is left to do the integrating, and to assume the burden of orchestrating what the professionals have left a fragmented and gap-ridden system.

Joint program development, collaborative projects, case management procedures, the use of loaner staff, the development of centralized record-keeping procedures, and information processing are all useful in promoting continuity.

The development of linking mechanisms cannot always be justified in terms of dollar savings. To the extent, however, that they contribute to effectiveness and accessibility, they may represent a saving in terms of a coordinated flow of services applied to the total resolution of a client's problem(s).

Economy of scale, made possible by collaborative arrangements between service providers, does often save dollars through elimination of wasteful duplication. Certain administrative support services such as the conduct of studies, joint record keeping, information processing and client tracking are tasks that cannot be performed independently by most service providers with any degree of efficiency. Procedural integration and the development of central services such as outreach, intake, diagnosis, referral, and follow-up make the entire service system more efficient by increasing the likelihood that clients actually reach their destination and receive the needed services.

RESPONSIVENESS AND ACCOUNTABILITY

By bringing two or more agencies together, linking mechanisms increase the extent to which agency services are open to scrutiny by outsiders. Effective collaborative relationships require that an agency spell out its share of the agreement and its expectations of collaborators. Successful collaboration thus requires formal or informal contractual agreements that can be monitored and evaluated periodically to ascertain whether each partner is living up to his obligation, and whether the purposes of the agreement (perhaps better service to a client population, service to a new client population, or more efficient services) are being met.

Agencies, therefore, become accountable to each other, just as they may also be accountable to an outside funder who may impose certain standards and obligations. The creation of ombudsman services, the use of volunteers, the establishment of grievance machinery, and other linking mechanisms further ensure that service providers will be made more responsive to their clientele.

A Case Illustration and Some Discussion

PUTTING THE SCREWS ON THE NURSING HOMES

"The nursing homes on the northwest side of town had elaborate rehabilitation facilities which were financed under Hill-Burton," a planner recalls. "They never used them. We approached the rehab agency with an offer to fund a project if they could locate it in these nursing homes. We were sure a lot of older people could be rehabilitated and brought back into the community. We would use our volunteer bureau to provide supportive services. Problem was, the nursing homes didn't want to hear of it. So I decided to put the screws on. I approached the Catholic and Jewish family agencies in the area and the two hospitals from which most of the referrals to these nursing homes came.

"They agreed to hold up referrals unless the homes agreed to allow voc rehab in, if I could find another place to refer their clients and patients. I don't do anything unless the timing is right. This time it was right. A new nursing home was being built in the area. I approached the backers of the project with the notion of accepting all their referrals from the two hospitals and the family agencies. These were young guys interested in a sound professional image. They wanted to shed the tainted image that many nursing homes in this town have. They liked the idea.

I then called a doctor I know who has had a good number of dealings with two of the older nursing homes. I wanted him to know directly from me that the two places he was connected with were going to lose business because of some informal arrangements I'd made. I told him that I thought there was plenty of business available for everybody, but that I was awfully anxious for those nursing homes to establish rehab programs.

"The next morning one of the nursing home operators from the northwest side called and asked for a meeting. By the end of the week, I had all three nursing home operators convinced that the rehab program would be to their benefit, because the financing arrangements would cost them very little.

"I got one of the family agencies to expand its homemaker and home handyman service and to start up a car pool transportation service for shopping. That took the wind out of the sails of one of the nursing home operators who said that rehabilitation wouldn't work because there weren't enough supportive services in the community."

This planner was convinced that informal behind-the-scenes management is much more productive than attempts to coordinate through formal organizations and structures. "I've found," he explains, "that by the time you get people to a meeting to decide on how they're going to coordinate their efforts, they've already made their decision to coordinate. We just try to help them work out the details without all that formal structure."

MANAGEMENT OF INTERDEPENDENCE

Others argue that this kind of management of interdependence is extraordinarily time-consuming and piecemeal at best. They insist that formal coordinating mechanisms are necessary to establish a process and to provide a structure within which informal negotiations can take place. "The fact is that our policy board assures that agencies will deal with each other in a focused manner," explains one planner. "Without our task forces and committees, they might arrange an exchange only occasionally. Now they do it with a sense of community good, along with occasional insights into their own self-interest."

Review

The development of coordinating linkages and inter-agency exchanges may be affected by a number of variables. These include (1) the skill and capability of the area planner; (2) the money and other resources at the planner's disposal; (3) the extent to which public opinion and environmental conditions support coordination; (4) complementarity of agency objectives; (5) complementarity of the policies and procedures which govern the functions of service providers; (6) the existence of a necessary logistical support system; and (7) other variables.

Increasing the linkages between providers can benefit both agencies and their consumers through increasing the availability of services, their accessibility to particular populations, their effectiveness and efficiency, and their responsiveness. Increasing the numbers of exchanges also increases the number of organizations to which an agency perceives itself accountable.

SUPPLEMENTARY QUESTIONS AND ACTIVITIES

1. Select an agency with which you are familiar. Then analyze this agency and its task environment in terms of the seven sets of variables discussed in this chapter that affect the likelihood if its expanding or maintaining linkages to other agencies. To what extent are they present? To what extent can they be brought to bear on a situation that concerns you?

2. Consider each of the five problems that planners focus on when trying to improve agency service delivery: availability, accessibility, effectiveness, efficiency, responsiveness and accountability. Go back over the inventory of linking mechanisms presented in Chapter 10. Which of these can be used to increase each of the five aspects of agency service delivery?

Suggested Readings

Review the recommended readings suggested for Chapters 5, 6, and 10.

12

Comprehensive Coordinating Mechanisms

From the Piecemeal to the Comprehensive

THE LIMITS OF OPERATIONAL LEVEL COORDINATION

Few planners would challenge the importance of promoting and managing inter-agency exchanges. Some planners argue, however, that linking agencies at the operational level can never achieve results commensurate with those possible by developing a comprehensive system of social services. Proponents of more comprehensive coordinating mechanisms insist that operational level coordination requires too much energy for the promotion and maintenance of structures that are themselves piecemeal, ad hoc, fragile, and subject to constant disruption. They point out that operational linkages are generally limited to only a few agencies, and that these agencies may cluster narrowly around the problems of clients in a small geographic area, or clients with a narrow range of problems and disabilities.

"I call the occasional management of inter-agency linkages, just another example of fragmented coordination and planning. We should have learned by now," argues a Rhode Island planner, "that fragmented planning is not only grossly inadequate, but that it may exacerbate problems by focusing attention on one part of the system and ignoring other parts. Even those efforts at comprehensiveness and coordination made possible through federal legislation," she argues, "are insufficient if each piece of legislation is narrow in its perspectives. What we've got to do is bring coordinating agencies in line with all the other coordinating structures that may exist in our local areas. If we are really going to serve people, we have got to *coordinate the other coordinators.*" This may be an overoptomistic view of the possible. Nevertheless, it is a position that bears close examination.

By "other coordinators" she was referring to the proliferating number of coordinating bodies, each set up in response to the needs of specific populations or service sectors. At the local level, examples may include

1. *Community Mental Health boards* responsible for planning, allocating funds, and coordinating mental health and retardation services to the population in a catchment area (established by a state authority in response to enabling federal legislation)
2. *Model Cities agencies,* responsible both for the delivery of specialized services to populations in a low-income target neighborhood, and for coordinating other agencies' services to residents of the neighborhood (funded in part through grants from the Department of Housing and Urban Development, with matching and additional local and state funds)
3. *Comprehensive Area-wide Health Planning Councils,* provided for under Section 314 of the Partnership for Health Act as amended in 1967, which are responsible for the development of area-wide plans to guide the efforts of local, state, and federal agencies involved in the funding or provision of services to a designated local population
4. *Area Agencies on Aging,* whose responsibilities include the coordination of services and the orchestration of previously untapped resources for the aging at the local level as mandated under provisions of Title III of the Older Americans Act as amended in 1973
5. *Health and welfare councils,* established by member bodies and funded through the local United Fund or Red Feather torch drive for the purposes of planning and coordinating the services of voluntary agencies, and in some cases integrating them with services provided under public auspices
6. *Sectarian federations/agencies* such as the Jewish Welfare Federation or Catholic Social Services, which undertake to coordinate and allocate funds to sectarian services at the community level.

In effect, a comprehensive social service system at the local level requires the coordination of agencies that receive their mandates, authority, and funds from a multiplicity of local, state, and national sources, both public and voluntary. Some of these agencies are in the business of providing direct services to client populations, others deliver supportive or coordinating services to direct service providers. Each of these organizations lives in its own task environment, responsive to its particular publics—those who provide its essential resources; those who provide auspices and legitimacy; those who are the recipients of its services, and those who compete for legitimacy, resources, or consumers. Within this turbulent environment efforts to consolidate and to coordinate services at the local level are often more whimsy than substance.

CONTROVERSY OVER COORDINATION

Some planners argue, in fact, that efforts to bring some order within such turbulence are doomed to failure. "Just as you can't make a bull go in the direction you want it to with a pea-shooter," a planner points out, "you can't expect to coordinate without authority. It takes big guns to make big shots!" Some planners go so far as to reject any attempt to impose central coordinating mechanisms on what they view as a natural market of services and service providers, arguing that the patchwork can be made whole only through the competitive mutual adjustment of its parts. This adjustment can be aided occasionally by a planning organization that represents the interests of those who are inadequately served. They feel that because the service system is made up of active elements rather than inactive component parts, it cannot be made to fit a preconceived pattern or central plan. Such a central plan would only perpetuate the status quo rather than unlock the system's potential for dynamic growth and change.

Some welfare economists argue forcefully against any form of coordination that would reduce "overlap and duplication." For example, at a recent conference of policy analysts a social policy analyst from MIT, suggested that without duplication the consumer may have few choices; a conglomerate service provider is in effect a monopoly. He added that fully coordinated service systems would tend to be conservative rather than innovative, and procedurally oriented rather than client- or consumer-oriented. He argued for a more natural market situation where the consumer's choice is maximized. "We're not dealing with machines that can easily be adjusted to each other," a social planner from Ohio at the conference observed. "We are dealing with dynamic entities. You can't manage an ecology. You let it work its own will."

"That's a luxury we can ill afford," disagreed a political scientist from Michigan. "We're not dealing with the simple system of an earlier time. The density and complexity of events makes a rational balance through competition and mutual adaptation more and more hopeless. A little tinkering here and there does little good." Agreeing that few service providers operate in a placid environment, he argued that centralized planning may make it possible to control some of this turbulence, or at least to "help service providers steer a course through it. Without centralized decision-making structures, the goals of coordination, integration, and comprehensiveness will slip away."

"The market analogy just doesn't work," added another planner. "Just look at what the market has produced: needless duplication or no service at all; waste of scarce resources like manpower and expertise.

The aggregate of the service programs, agencies, and facilities in our communities looks more like a patchwork quilt—often with gaping holes—than a network. Rather than providing the consumer of services with a wide array of choices, the individual needing help has neither adequate access to services, nor continuity of care within the patchwork."

THREE TRENDS

Although questions pertaining to the desirability and feasibility of coordination at the local level are likely to remain unresolved for some time to come, three trends are observable. They pervade the relationships between federal and local authorities, and they increase the likelihood that within broad limits, an increasing number of decisions about coordination will be delegated to the local level.

These trends are evidenced in (1) a progressive transfer of policy planning responsibilities from the federal to the sub-state and local levels; (2) a movement toward the functional consolidation of both special district and general-purpose local governments; and (3) the creation of programmatic and administrative mechanisms for the planning and coordination of area-wide and local services.

All three trends are observable in such mechanisms as new multi-sectoral coordinating structures; grant-in-aid consolidation and simplification; revenue sharing; and in the reallocation of legal and administrative responsibilities for programs and program development. Each may have taken hold to a greater or lesser extent in different sectors of the country, in different states or sub-state areas, and even in different communities or neighborhoods within those communities.

The beginnings of these trends were observable as far back as the early 1950s. The "701B" programs authorized under the Housing Act of 1954, for example, authorized the development and improvement of methods and techniques for comprehensive planning. They also earmarked funds to conduct research into needed revisions of state statutes which create, govern, or control local governments or their operations.

Trend No. 1: Transfer of Authority for Policy and Planning from the Federal Level

In an attempt to reverse a thirty-year process which began during the Depression and reached its zenith in the mid-60s, the "new federalism" represents a commitment to the goal of "responsible decentralization"—in other words, the transfer of programs and money for the solution of major local problems to the authority of local public officials. No single program has symbolized the aim of the new federalism more than *revenue sharing*.

GENERAL REVENUE SHARING

The major notion behind revenue sharing is to shift the position of local general-purpose government from that of being one of many local "grantsmen" applying for and operating federal assistance programs, to being in the position of deciding on how funds are to be allocated. General revenue sharing was intended to increase the flexibility by which such funds are allocated. Local general-purpose governments were made responsible for determination of how direct grants from federal departments were to be used.

Initially there was a good deal of confusion around the meaning of revenue sharing and the extent to which it could in fact transfer responsibility from the federal to the local level. Initial expectations were rarely met. Like many federal programs, revenue sharing was oversold in order to make it politically palatable. In practice so many poor decisions were made under revenue sharing, and so few dollars were in fact passed on to localities, that the program never achieved its promise. Yet the objectives of revenue sharing were and continue to be palatable to local politicians and other influential citizens, especially to those concerned with the orchestration and coordination of local services.

Briefly stated, the objectives are to:

1. relieve immediate pressures on state and local government treasuries
2. assure that total national economic growth is more directly expressed in local revenue
3. build up the vitality, efficiency, and fiscal independence of state and local governments
4. increase the progressivity of the federal-state-local tax system
5. reduce economic inequalities and fiscal disparities among states and regions within those states
6. insure that the plight of local, especially urban, governments will be given full weight
7. finance improvements in quality and level of state and local service
8. stimulate the exercise of state and local initiative and responsibility.

Taken together, these goals are intended to remediate a situation in which the federal government has the most authority and the localities the most problems. For these reasons, revenue sharing in some form is likely to be a permanent fixture in the American body politic.

That the goals of revenue sharing are far from having been realized is not in question. Local officials have charged that far from bringing more money into municipal coffers, revenue sharing has resulted in cuts in categorical programs and less money to share. Others argue that local government is apt to be controlled by cliques and factions insensitive to the needs of the poor. Those who make the first argument stand on solid ground. Too few are the dollars that were redirected from federal programs to locally generated programs. In part this is so because of the fear of many federal legislators that funds would be inappropriately spent at the local level. Many social planners have agreed with this rather proprietary point of view, which presumes that either the *planner* or *someone else* is in the best position to represent the interests of people at the local level—not those actually in need of services.

Planners and others concerned with the delivery of services at the local level are themselves partly to blame for their lack of involvement in the lack of involvement of consumer groups; especially if they have withheld themselves from involvement in local politics. Planning *is* very much a political process. The questions of who gets what, where, and how are political questions. To the extent that the answers are given on the basis of relative influence, the answers are political ones. Political decisions reflect the recognition of various interests. The question is not *whether* revenue sharing decisions will be influenced by politics, but by *whose* politics.

Planners all function in a political arena. As advocates for the needs of particular populations, planners press for the allocation of revenue sharing dollars for services to those target populations. This often requires direct involvement in the political arena through the use of pressure tactics, or it may involve working through others—politicians, civic organizations, organized consumer groups, and others.

SPECIAL REVENUE SHARING

This is as true of *special revenue sharing* as of general revenue sharing. Special revenue sharing is a mechanism whereby federal funds earmarked for certain populations or certain service sectors (known as "categorical" programs) are distributed at sub-state levels with the involvement of persons at that level. An interesting example is to be found in Title XX of the Social Security Act as amended in 1975.

Title XX brought together a number of service components mandated through public welfare (ADC, Child Welfare, and others). It authorized each state to establish a plan for the allocation of a specified number of federal dollars for the provision of social services within that state. Unlike previous amendments, Title XX specified that each state spell out what it meant by services and that broad public involvement be a necessary aspect of the plan. In many states, public involvement took place at both the state and local levels. For example, arrangements for public hearings and the establishment of both permanent and ad hoc task forces often resulted in considerable involvement of consumers, service providers, and other local influentials. It also focuses attention on the relationship of public welfare (Title XX) services to those provided under other mandates.

Trend No. 2: Functional Consolidation

Next to the categorical nature of many federally supported local or area-wide services, government fragmentation has been the largest impediment to the development of coordinated and comprehensive area-wide services.

There are more than 80,000 units of government in the United States, including states, counties, cities, townships, school districts, sanitation districts, planning districts, transportation districts, natural resource districts, and so on. They represent an almost endless variation of structures involved in an equally endless variation of relationships, some explicitly mandated by law, others based on tradition or history. In many cases, government officials must relate to two or more cities, several counties, numerous special districts, and perhaps two or three states.

These officials face both structural and procedural hurdles in any effort to coordinate policy planning and service delivery. Lacking clear-cut authority over each other, they are frequently involved in acrimonious and self-serving exchanges. In most states, the lack of decentralized state administrative bodies or strengthened county governments has made some forms of intergovernmental cooperation virtually impossible.

This piecemeal system of local and area-wide functional assignments results in inequities, inefficiencies, citizen neglect, and ineffective operations. The inequities are tied to variable local tax bases, and are expressed in unfair distributions of costs and unequal benefits or services. Inefficiencies are the result of economy-of-scale considerations with many small governmental units duplicating services. Most citizens have little if any access to the policy-making processes that relate to the service delivery; nor are there enough roles through which they can participate in service delivery. The patterns of service are themselves often illogical, rendering many of them ineffective. Policies and programs at one level of government are frequently nullified by a lack of complementary policies and programs at another level.

TYPES OF SUB-STATE CONSOLIDATED STRUCTURES

These inadequacies have led many states to develop sub-state districts or area-wide coordinating bodies such as regional councils; metropolitan planning commissions, metropolitan human service agencies and other super agencies, regional program administrations, councils-on-government, and so forth.

These bodies perform a number of functions: (1) planning and coordination for special districts; (2) fiscal mobilization and program review, including sign-off responsibilities for grant-in-aid programs; (3) technical assistance in management, planning, and service delivery.

Sub-state intergovernmental bodies have varying degrees of power and authority. In some instances, they may be designated by state government as the single consolidated regional unit with formal authority to plan and to coordinate a particular service—for example, transportation, water usage, or natural resource planning. Occasionally, such authority extends to human services, particularly in the health field.

Generally, however, councils and regional administrations depend on the voluntary delegation of authority by local government units for purposes of economy of scale. This makes them directly accountable to their local government constituents. As the executive of one metropolitan Council on Governments puts it, "We basically operate in a market situation. We have to constantly strive to sell our services and prove their importance to local government units. They in turn are free to reject our products, refuse to buy them, or force us to modify our efforts. At the same time, to do an effective job of planning, we often have to ignore the vested interests of one of our constituencies in order to press for the public good. The situation can become particularly sticky when one unit of government perceives our recommendations as favoring another government's position. It's a tough job. You are constantly fighting the battle of authority. The cities and the special districts want you to do their work the way they'd like to see it done without really giving up any of their low local autonomy. And they get mad as the dickens when your recommendations go against their perceptions of self-interest. Still, the work has its compensations. It's exciting to participate in what I'm sure is to become an essentially modern government structure of increasing importance."

There are a number of advantages to working within or closely with a large metropolitan or sub-state structure like those described. First, it makes it easier to "plug in" to the organization's central information and research capacity. Second, the planner becomes privy to its procedures for locating and cultivating new sources of financial support. Administratively linked to other planners who are concerned with population, manpower, transportation, health, education, and other areas of planning, the social planner's efforts may be supported by those of colleagues with complementary concerns.

Block grants from the federal government directly to states and localities will implement the transfer of responsibility to states and localities and also aid in functional consolidation. Although at this writing, the legislation enabling expansion of the block grant concept is still in the formative stage, it is likely to be of great importance to the social planner at the local level.

Block grants are just what their title implies: blocks of money freed of categorical restraints, transferred from the federal to a state or local unit of general-purpose government (county, city, or regional unit). These funds permit localities to develop and implement integrated plans dealing with environmental, transportation, housing, health, education, and social service issues.

Trend No. 3: The Creation of Coordinating and Planning Mechanisms

Regardless of a planner's administrative location, a knowledge of how functionally consolidated governmental units operate will be beneficial. In fact, thorough familiarity with a variety of federally created planning and coordinating mechanisms as well as voluntary coordinating structures is essential to social planning at the community level.

TYPES OF MECHANISMS

Conceptually, these mechanisms can be grouped into four basic types: *review and comment mechanisms; planning agencies; federations;* and *ad hoc coalitions.* Two review and comment mechanisms will be discussed: (1) OMB circular #A-95 which establishes a system of notification and review; (2) Model Cities sign-offs on HEW and other similar programs. Despite the fact that each of these programs has been administered by a different federal or state agency, they are similar in both process and intent. For example, while these mechanisms do not provide local or regional government structures with automatic veto power on proposals, they do authorize designated agencies to review and comment—or to "sign-off"—on them. Although the final decision on the funding of local projects and programs remains with the relevant federal agency, this agency will take into consideration the recommendations made by the designated local or area review authority.

At the very minimum, such arrangements give state or local government officials access to information about grant applications from service providers before grants are awarded. This provides them with an opportunity to negotiate with applicant organizations around the issues of potential conflict and concern. Even where formal sanctions are not exerted, informal suasion tactics on funders as well as on the potential recipients (local service providers) can be felt.

While social planners at the local level are rarely accorded sign-off authority, they are in the position of being able to influence those parties that do have sign-off authority. For this reason, familiarity with the following two mechanisms can be of strategic importance.

Initiated in 1969, the Office of Management and Budget Circular #A-95 set up an intergovernmental effort that covers more than one hundred federal assistance programs. Its objective is to bring the projects supported under these programs into conformance with comprehensive planning objectives of state, area-wide, and local government units. Area-wide clearinghouses for A-95 projects are generally located in a designated state agency, a council-of-governments, or a regional planning commission. In those parts of the country that do not have functionally consolidated sub-state planning bodies, clearinghouses are located in the state capitol.

Local agencies applying for grants under A-95 procedures are required to submit brief descriptions of their proposals to the appropriate clearinghouse prior to formal application for funds. The clearinghouse in turn is required to forward "notices of intent to apply" to other agencies and to local governments which may have interest in the projects. Within a period of 30 days, local government units and other relevant agencies may then conduct their own review of the proposed project and, via the clearinghouse, negotiate independently with the applicant and make recommendations. The applicant (service provider) is then required to forward written comments by the clearinghouse to the federal funding agency, along with the formal application. A statement of how these comments influenced the application must be included. Approximately 14 billion dollars per year in federal grants-in-aid are affected by A-95 grant review procedures.

MODEL CITIES* AND OTHER SIGN-OFFS

In support of the planning and coordinating role of the Model Cities agencies in designated neighborhoods, the Department of Health, Education and Welfare requires a sign-off by the Model Cities director on applications by service providers for grants from HEW. The Model Cities agency was further expected to consult with the local elected council or chief executive as part of its review process. Similar agreements to grant sign-off responsibilities to other agencies also exist. In many states, area agencies on aging have sign-off authority over all state funds going to local agencies to provide services to older people. The same may be true for community mental health agencies. While sign-off responsibility is no guarantee that better coordination will occur at the local level, it does provide the planners with considerable leverage.

"We had no authority to fund anyone," explains the Director of a Community Mental Health Center, "but our Board does have sign-off respon-

*Note: At the time of writing the entire model cities program was undergoing serious review. The sign-off procedures described in this section, however, are prototypes and will undoubtedly become incorporated into any successor program.

sibilities on the funding applications of every local agency to the State Department of Mental Health, and by agreement, we're supposed to be consulted on all funding to prospective mental health problems. That means that the Department of Public Welfare will check with us on its Title XX planning, and that both the lab training and the voc rehab folks will also check with us.

"So when the state hospital decided to discharge 200 patients into the community, we could hold up their plans until we could design a procedure whereby a program of continuity of care could be established. We put together a task force and designed an integrated program of group homes, independent living arrangements, vocational rehabilitation, medical care, counseling for ex-patients and their families, and job placement."

PLANNING AND COORDINATING AGENCIES

Even when sign-off authority is not present, agencies with responsibility for planning and coordinating can do a great deal. Some may have a great deal of clout by being designated the sub-state funding agency for a particular field of practice. Examples include some of the organizations mentioned earlier: area agencies on aging, Community Mental Health boards, and comprehensive area-wide health planning councils.

These organizations are generally legitimated by boards or advisory committees representing the interests of other service providers, the consumers of services, and community influentials. In general, their staffs work with members of the board or advisory committee (and its subcommittees or task forces) on one or more of the following tasks:

the conduct of needs assessments

the development of both annual and long-range plans for service delivery and integration

evaluation of services provided and monitoring of the plans developed

consultation and staff training

the establishment of funding priorities and provision of technical assistance to other agencies on resource and program development

They have patterned much of their work on procedures developed in the voluntary welfare field by councils and federations of agencies.

FEDERATIONS

Some of these planning and coordinating agencies are established along federation lines. Health and Welfare Councils and Service Federations are good examples. Federations are made up of member agencies from the voluntary sector, but they need not be so limited. In one medium-sized metropolitan area, for example, the United Community Services (a health and welfare council supported primarily by the Torch Fund–Red Feather campaign) was made up of representatives of all the relevant service providers in the area.

Members of its board included (1) administrators of social agencies and private nonprofit professional service providers; in some cases, proprietors of profit-making institutions may be included as well; (2) representatives of participating community service associations and of self-help groups; (3) related government "general public" agencies such as transportation, recreation, and education; (4) local educational and training institutions with adult education; and, in some cases, (5) representatives of business and industry or labor unions with special retirement or pre-retirement programs.

Some federation member units are themselves federated organizations. These may include hospital federations and sectarian federations such as a Jewish Welfare Council, Association of Black Social Agencies, or Catholic Charities. Some member units may be local chapters of national associations such as the Family Services Association of America, the Child Welfare League, or the National Council of Churches.

Since each of the organizational units within the federation has its own separate goals, formal mechanisms must be established to put the emphasis on common goals. "Problem-oriented" or "sectorially oriented" program committees are established to carry on much of the federation's business. A problem-oriented program committee may concern itself with the problems of minority groups in certain neighborhoods or with the lack of coordinated community-based care for the permanently disabled. Sectorially oriented program committees will include federation members concerned with specific service sectors such as transportation, housing, employment, or education.

These program committees can be responsible for (a) problem identification and fact-finding; (b) programmatic or policy recommendations; and sometimes (c) preliminary review of project proposals that have been submitted for outside funding. Review may be limited to judgments about whether or not the proposal is consistent with overall federation policies, or may actually include the program and policy committee's recommendation to fund or reject the proposal. Committees may strive primarily to effect better interorganizational coordination, or planners may use them as a device to open up the more controversial aspects of interorganizational exchange.

Federations are generally governed by a policy board which may include representatives of each program committee. Frequently, the board will include a balance of agency representatives and others who represent consumers and broader community interests. While policy tends to be made at the board level, decisions are often subject to ratification by member units. This highlights an underlying contradiction between planning and policy-level coordination. Because federations are partnerships of independent organizations on whose good will the federation depends, planners may find it difficult to press for basic programmatic changes in member agencies. They may find it equally difficult to focus on specific problems that are not of direct interest and concern to all member units.

Federations are also organizations with their own identity, unique purposes, and survival needs. Thus, planners often find themselves in a quandary. What proportion of their efforts should be spent on trying to effect changes within the member organizations, and how much effort should be spent on maintenance or development of the federation as a system?

Because the interests of member agencies do at times conflict with each other and also with those of the federation, federated structures are generally unable to deal with anything but noncontroversial issues. They are best at handling matters which foster maximum agreement and commitment to the federation, and which cause the least friction between member units.

AD HOC AND SEMI-PERMANENT COALITIONS

The fourth type of coordination structure is found in the ad hoc or semi-permanent committees and task forces organized around specific issue concerns. Typically, coalitions will be formed when (1) a threat to an agency causes an emergency or crisis situation requiring collaborative effort to reduce the possibility of threat to "sister" agencies; (2) several agencies find that without collaborative efforts, they cannot succeed in pressing for some needed reform or reallocation of dollars for local uses; (3) new funds become available requiring some evidence of comprehensiveness in program design or of consortium arrangements in program implementation.

Planners often find the use of ad hoc coalitions much more effective than permanent structures in creating specific changes in the delivery of services. Permanent structures may in fact impede innovation. "We found we had to spend half our time outwitting the coordinating structure we'd built," explains the former director of a community action agency in a larger midwestern community. "If we wanted to talk an issue to death or to find all the reasons why we shouldn't move ahead, we went to our policy board and program committees. When we wanted to get something done, we got together a few powerful people who cared, and off we went."

Regardless of the structure or mechanism used, organizations will tend to be more willing to cooperate with each other when (1) they depend on each other for commodities, materials, or resources, or for the output of their efforts; (2) they find that competing with others for scarce resources is dysfunctional; and when (3) some shared or coordinated activity is critical to the organization's goal accomplishment or its survival needs.

The social planner who attempts to manage coordination between service providers without recognizing the agencies' multiple levels of interdependence may find his efforts counterproductive, ineffectual, or ritualistic at best. This may be the reason why such formal structures as federations and councils of agencies are frequently unsuccessful. The real need for coordination may exist at a much less inclusive or comprehensive level. Ad hoc coalitions may be much more effective in the short run, although they do not persevere over time.

In our discussion so far, we have assumed that agencies are horizontally interdependent at the local level. However, the situation is not so simple; the fact is that many local organizations are heavily dependent on or interdependent with extra-community groups. Some receive substantial funding from sources outside the community. Many are branches of national agencies or are regulated by state and federal agencies. Some are accredited by extra-community professional associations. Almost all are dependent on outside organizations for trained personnel.

Attempts to develop formal structures with a hierarchy of relationships, as in federations and councils, always create tensions between those who push for local horizontal coordination and those who strain toward better vertical integration with elements in the extra-community system. Because many local agencies have commitments elsewhere, it becomes extraordinarily difficult to plan for a concerted policy. Organizations brought together for cooperative purposes are frequently so diverse in functions, ideological commitments, personnel, and perceptions of local problems, that attempts to force inclusive cooperation may fail. Cooperation and coordination in pursuit of comprehensiveness must be based on the interests of the parties involved.

Review

Three long-term trends support movement toward greater integration and coordination of services at the local level. These are (1) the progressive transfer of planning responsibilities from the federal to the local, sub-state, and state levels; (2) a movement toward functional consolidation of governmental units; and (3) the creation of programmatic and administrative mechanisms for the planning of local and area-wide services. The transfer of planning authority from the federal government is best expressed through general revenue sharing and such special revenue sharing programs as Title XX of the Social Security Act as amended in 1975. Functional consolidation is found either in multi-government organizations like councils-of-governments or in multiple function agencies like metropolitan human resources councils and other types of superagencies.

Programmatic and administrative mechanisms refer to review procedures such as those embodied in A-95 grant reviews and Model Cities sign-offs, and in a larger variety of ad hoc and permanent planning structures. The latter include voluntary federations like health and welfare councils and such public agencies as area Agencies on Aging, Community Mental Health boards, and comprehensive area-wide health planning councils.

1. Explore the ways in which the trends discussed in this chapter have affected service delivery in your area.

2. What is the principle behind revenue sharing? Who is involved? Design a strategy to procure a larger share of the available revenue sharing dollars for a specific target population.

3. Which of the planning and coordinating mechanisms discussed have been utilized in your area? What kind of impact could you as a planner have on these mechanisms to increase the quality and quantity of services to populations of concern to you?

4. Describe the procedures used in your state's Title XX planning. What impact does it have on the coordination of services at the local level?

Recommended Readings

MAYER, ROBERT, ROBERT MORONEY, and ROBERT MORRIS. *Centrally Planned Change.* Urbana, Ill.: University of Illinois Press, 1974.
In 1972, Brandeis University and the University of North Carolina sponsored a conference to reexamine the subject of centrally planned change. Participants were asked to reflect on past problems and future prospects of central planning by government. This book is largely a synthesis of the views and perspectives presented at that conference. The authors provide an analysis of basic concepts, issues, and requirements of centrally planned change in contrast to several decentralization strategies. The contribution of various alternative technologies (PPB, Evaluation) to planning is also discussed. The authors conclude that, despite setbacks and problems encountered in the past, central planning is a relevant tool for societal guidance.

FRIEDMAN, JOHN. "The Future of Comprehensive Urban Planning: A Critique." *Public Administration Review,* 1971, *31,* 315.
Friedman offers a general overview and critique of comprehensive planning as it has developed in the urban setting. The author discusses those characteristics of the metropolis which have been highly influential upon the planning process. He pinpoints major problems and failures committed by comprehensive planners in the past and offers several proposals to facilitate future planning efforts in urban America.

GARDNER, SIDNEY. *Roles for General Purpose Governments in Services Integration.* Project Share Human Services Monograph Series. Washington, D.C.: Department of Health, Education and Welfare, August 1976.
Following historical overviews of the origins of general-purpose governments and of the emphasis on service integration, Gardner analyzes the trends that have catapulted both the government structure and its chief executive into the role of integrator for human services. Both the constraints imposed on the integrator and the dimensions of integration deemed most feasible are documented.

Suggestions for Further Reading

ALTSCHULER, ALAN. "The Goals of Comprehensive Planning." *Journal of the American Institute of Planners,* August, 1965.

BLOEDORN, JACK C., ELIZABETH B. MACLATCHIE, WILLIAM FRIEDLANDER, and J. M. WEDEMEYER. *Designing Social Service Systems.* Chicago: American Public Welfare Association, 1970.

CALLAHAN, JOHN, et al. *Government Functions and Processes: Local and Area-Wide.* Washington, D.C.: Advisory Commission on Intergovernmental Relations, 1972.

Coordinating Federal Assistance in the Community: Use of Selected Mechanisms for Planning and Coordinating Federal Programs, Community Development Evaluation Services No. 8. Washington, D.C.: U.S. Department of Housing and Urban Development, August, 1972.

Decision-Makers' Guide to Program Coordination and Title XX. San Francisco: Department of Health, Education and Welfare, Region X office, 1976.

"Evaluation of Human Services Planning Approaches at the State and Local Levels." Washington, D.C.: Department of Health, Education and Welfare, Office of the Undersecretary for Planning, 1976.

GANS, SHELDON, and GERALD T. HORTON. *Integration of Human Services.* New York: Praeger, 1975.

Governmental Functions and Processes: Local and Areawide, Volume IV of *Substate Regionalism and the Federal System.* Washington, D.C.: Advisory Commission on Intergovernmental Relations, 1974.

Human Resource Agencies: Creating a Regional Structure. Lexington, Ky.: Council of State Governments, 1974.

Human Services Integration. Lexington, Ky.: American Society for Public Administration, 1974.

MEYERSON, MARTIN. "Building the Middle-Range Bridge for Comprehensive Planning." *Journal of the American Institute of Planners,* 1956, *22* (2).

MOTT, D., and E. MOTT. *Meeting Human Needs: The Social and Political History of Title XX.* Columbus, Ohio: National Conference on Social Welfare, 1976.

NATHAN, RICHARD P. "Federalism and the Shifting Nature of Fiscal Relations; General Revenue Sharing and Federalism." *The Annals,* May, 1975.

REIN, MARTIN. "Social Planning and the Search for Legitimacy." *Journal of the American Institute of Planners,* 1969, *35.*

Roles of Cities in Human Services, Project Share Human Services Bibliography Series. Washington, D.C.: Department of Health, Education and Welfare, September, 1976.

SUNDQUIST, JAMES L. *Making Federalism Work.* Washington, D.C.: The Brookings Institute, 1970.

ZALD, MAYER. "The Structure of Society and Social Service Integration." *Social Science Quarterly,* December, 1969.

IV

People and Planning

Social planning is *for* people. At the community level, it is often also *with* people. Social planners work with local people in designing plans and in developing and implementing service programs. Often these programs are designed to accommodate to and reinforce the natural helping system that exists in every community and thus require the collaboration of representatives of civil and other public interest groups.

Many of the planner's efforts are advocacy efforts, aimed at serving the interests of particular populations. In Chapter 16, two forms of advocacy are described: integrative and distributive. Integrative advocacy includes a range of strategies oriented toward bringing the individual into the network of available services, assuring proper or appropriate service. Partisan advocacy is oriented more toward the redistribution of power or authority over resources and the policies which govern the delivery of those services. The relationships between advocacy and citizen participation are explored in Chapter 15 which focuses on citizen and consumer involvement in plan and policy making. The planner's work with policy boards, advisory committees, task forces, and ad hoc coalitions are described. In many instances, planners work with citizens groups and with representatives of various organizations in order to legitimate their own planning efforts, or to petition on behalf of a particular project, cause, or population. They often use citizen participation as a buffer against criticism or opposition. Some planners view participation as an end in itself, a concomitant of participatory democracy. Others view it as a strategic means toward accomplishing specific substantive ends. It can be both.

Participation can also lead to expansion of services through the volunteer efforts of individuals and of members of civic associations. Chapter 14 describes three ways in which planners involve volunteers in the provision of services and in their development. Volunteers can undertake clerical and administrative tasks, engage in policy-making decisions, perform a public relations function on behalf of service agencies or the needs of particular populations, or provide services directly to those populations.

In the latter role, their efforts are similar to the people who participate in the natural helping system that exists in every community and which is discussed in Chapter 13. This system is composed of lay care-givers and "extra-professional" providers of services. The lay system is made up of friends, relatives, neighbors, and others who interact on an ad hoc basis on behalf of particular clients or client populations. The lay system may become semi-formalized through the development of lay referral networks.

"Extra-professional" care is often provided by self-help groups and mutual aid societies. These include local chapters of national organizations like Alcoholics Anonymous and Synanon. They also include local consumers' cooperatives, cooperative living arrangements, and the like. The planner's role in promoting these organizations and in linking them to the professional and institutionalized system of services is too often left to chance.

13

Natural and "Extra-Professional" Helping Systems

In earlier chapters, the social planner's efforts were described as oriented toward improving the delivery and coordination of social services. The services discussed tended to be those provided by professionally trained personnel under institutionalized auspices. But there is another, far larger and more ubiquitous service delivery system at the community level. It is composed of ordinary citizens who partake in a natural or "extra-professional" system.

Until recently, this system remained virtually invisible. While everyone participates in it, there were few concepts to describe it. Few social scientists paid much attention to it. Professional care givers, if they made use of it, tended to do so in an ad hoc way, guided by their common sense and practical wisdom rather than by any set of professional principles learned in school or gleaned from the literature.

The reasons for this avoidance are not difficult to fathom. First, professional and institutionalized services were developed in response to the inadequacies of a natural helping system to provide all the care needed in an urbanized, technological society. Moreover, professional services often had to be justified in contrast to the inadequacies of a natural system. Second, the continued growth of a natural helping system is in part a response to the inadequacies of the professionalized and institutionalized system. For these reasons, it became a political impropriety to deal with it other than to deprecate it—or occasionally to give it some begrudging recognition.

In a time of scarce resources and growing demand, however, social planners can ill afford to ignore any efforts at helping those in need. Without an understanding of the natural helping system, planned efforts to modify or expand services are bound to be limited in both scope and effectiveness. In order to understand why this is so, it may be helpful to find out where people go when they need help and how they get there.

Where Do People Go For Help?

"We're here when people need us," explains the director of adult services in a county welfare department. "We know we provide a residual service, but that's what we're here for. When families and friends can't help, when people can't cope on their own any more, they come to us, just like others go to a hospital or a psychiatric clinic."

Certainly not all social services are residual. Many complement the natural coping capacity of the individual or bolster the coping capacity of families and friends. Some are preventive in nature, aimed at heading off the breakdowns that cause client dependence on professionally provided services.

Yet, whatever the availability of professional or institutionalized services, most people make relatively little use of them. Even in times of crisis, many people apply for service to a department of public welfare, to a public housing authority, to the mental health agency, or for that matter, to a private physician as a last resort, when all else has failed.

WHERE PEOPLE DON'T GO

"In this country," a Kansas physician reports, "60 percent of the aging have never seen a doctor and will never be seen by one." He explains that many older people prefer to use home remedies or the help of family, friends, and neighbors rather than seek professional medical care. Often, especially in many rural areas, professional or institutionalized medical care may just be unavailable. In other cases it may be available but unacceptable, or it may require supportive services. For example, an 87-year-old Chicago man in immediate need of a serious operation will not enter a hospital because during the previous year his wife and three of his closest friends died there. He sees it as a place of no return. A 40-year-old Newark, New Jersey woman cannot go to the hospital for minor surgery, because as she puts it, "If I left the apartment for a week, the hoodlums around here would steal everything. I wouldn't even have a bed left when I came home. Besides who would take care of my kids?" For want of supportive services she can get no medical care.

The Chicago man might have been willing to risk the hospital had he known what was in store for him, if he had been able to talk to other people like himself who had undergone similar surgery, or if he had been assured of some home care during his convalescence. The Newark woman would have been willing to undergo surgery if she'd had a house sitter or a neighbor to help care for her children.

People may make even less use of other services. A United Auto Workers study indicates that very few union members in certain areas make use of a mental health insurance benefit. This finding is consistent with other research which shows that as many as half of all adults with serious psychological impairments may never receive or seek any kind of professionalized help from the mental health system. Yet many of these people are able to remain in the community because of some natural adaptive capacity, or some supportive help from others.

If the larger proportion of all Americans do not receive services from institutionalized care-givers or professional providers, where then do they go for service?

HELP FROM THE LAY AND EXTRA-PROFESSIONAL SYSTEMS

Many Americans simply do not receive any help when they are in trouble. Others make do with whatever their own resources or capacities allow. "Most people have a remarkable capacity for coping," reports a psychiatrist. "They treat themselves." For many, however, self-help is not sufficient; particularly those situations where older people are left completely to their own devices are unacceptable.

Fortunately, help is frequently available through a system of ad hoc and "extra-professional" lay care-givers. The ad hoc lay service system is composed of friends, relatives, neighbors, and key individuals knowledgeable about community resources. Extra-professional services are offered through self-help groups and mutual aid societies which may be outgrowths of the ad hoc system. A discussion of these groups is included in this chapter. Services are also provided by volunteers who may act as junior partners to professionalized care-givers, and by members of civic associations who undertake various service activities at the community level. These service providers will receive separate treatment in the chapter that follows.

The Ad Hoc Lay Service System

HOW IT WORKS

In times of trouble most people look to themselves first. They attempt to diagnose their own problems and to treat them. Frequently, they seek help or advice from friends, relatives, or neighbors. Even with health problems, most people tend to diagnose and treat their own symptoms or to seek aid from friends and relatives before seeking professional help. "It's just my lumbago, a little linament will fix me up in no time." "What you need is to get off your feet for a couple of days; let me fix your meals." Or, "Try lying out in the sun during the day and using an electric heater at night. That'll fix you up."

Friends and relatives may also suggest the need for professional help. "If the heat treatments don't work, I know a good chiropractor." Often, people pass through an informal network of lay helpers on their way to professionalized services. "The Salvation Army people will help you out; they understand." "You don't have to be a member of my church to join the Golden Age Club. It'll do you a world of good." "When I had my foot problem, nobody could help me as much as the chiropodist on the corner of Main and South. Why don't you try him?"

This lay referral system also helps the client or patient evaluate the professionalized services. Most first visits to a professional service provider may be tentative probes to see whether the service is acceptable. An older person referred to a professional or service agency by friends may check with those friends later to discuss the care received or promised. They may help him make some decisions about whether to continue receiving professional care.

Everyone is familiar with this kind of help. Some observers term it the "natural helping system"; others call it an informal, community-based "lay service network." It includes the kinship and friendship network in which the person is involved and which can be mobilized for help in defining a problem, treating it, referring the individual to professional care-givers and institutionalized providers, and assessing and evaluating their services.

Effective professional care often requires an effective lay service network. A physician prescribing a home treatment program may know his recommendations are impractical without the help of friends or relatives. He may attempt to reach out and activate the lay service system through his patient. "It's impossible," a doctor explains, "for me to be available to consult with every patient of mine about what he eats, about every ache and pain, about every decision he has to make about going out or staying in. If I tried to make that kind of decision for even three or four persons, it would take up all of my time. And my decisions wouldn't even be as good as their own." The same may be true in other situations where needs for housing, transportation, and other services are so unpredictable or change so rapidly that even the most expert professional service provider cannot respond quickly. In such cases, the lay service network may be the first line of help.

Lay services are sometimes available from professionals or business people in other areas of practice. Often, for example, the pharmacist may suggest approaches to hygiene and self-care. The grocer may refer older people to a self-help group or recreation program. The post office may be a center for literature and information on still other services. The barber may dispense all kinds of advice. The beauty parlor may serve as a social gathering point and as a center for an information exchange on the health and social needs of its clientele.

ADVANTAGES OF AN AD HOC LAY SERVICE SYSTEM

Because the system is ad hoc, it can be quickly mobilized to respond to individual needs. There are no long waiting lines or red tape, no waiting until the doctor is in or until the agency opens its doors. A natural system, it provides a set of lay services for which technical and professional knowledge is not necessary. Professionals are often unwilling or unavailable to help older people shop, select clothing, prepare meals, and do the many other things which are required to maintain full or partial independence. In many cases, nevertheless, professionals find themselves forced to assume responsibilities for care or for advice just as adequately and much less expensively provided by neighbors, friends, relatives, or others in the lay system.

This part of the natural system has other advantages as well. It does not require that a person surrender his or her independence by relying on professional experts for direction. It can be scheduled at one's own convenience, and because care is given by others who are like oneself, or in similar situations, it generally poses no value conflicts. It also avoids what Elliot Freidson has called a potential culture conflict between patients and medical or other professional personnel, each of whom are governed by different sets of norms and expectations about appropriate behavior. A physician, for example, may attempt to shape a patient's behavior according to his professional perspectives or in relation to bureaucratic and organizational needs. The patient, on the other hand, may prefer a more personalized, warm, and responsive relationship—a relationship that is rarely possible within institutionalized service systems.

Generally speaking, the lay services system provides a more personalized type of help, given with more affect, more feeling, more individualization. It is more readily understood by its consumers and so may be less threatening. Institutional care and use of professionalized services is, for many, an admission of defeat or incompetence. It is where they go when no one else seems to care or to be able to help.

DISADVANTAGES OF LAY SERVICES

There are some obvious disadvantages to total reliance on the lay service system. Many persons are outside a network of caring relatives, friends, or neighbors. Professional and institutionalized care-giving has developed primarily to answer the need of such persons. Manpower services, literacy training, recreational programs, home health care, homemakers services and meals on wheels would not have to be organized under institutional auspices, if such help were readily available to all those in need through a "natural" system.

Further, because the lay services and referral systems are not based on professional knowledge or technical expertise, they are unable to provide in-depth diagnosis and remediation of a problem. Home remedies for abdominal pains and friendly visits to an isolated older person may be helpful. But they are not sufficient when the pains are caused by a cancerous growth, or the isolation is symptomatic of psychiatric illness. Lack of expertise may result in poor advice and bad treatment. There is no system of accountability to govern the lay system.

In many cases, the person's need drains the kinship or friendship systems to the point of exhaustion, resentment, guilt, and retaliation. "When I couldn't manage any more, I just had to move in with my daughter," explains a widow of 15 years. "We wanted mother with us, even if we didn't have much room," her daughter adds. "It was when she became too ill to care for herself and medical expenses mounted that we went to the Welfare Department. Next week she's going to a nursing home. It breaks my heart, but the tensions and pressures on everyone in the family are too great. We just can't cope with her needs anymore. And she can't cope with them herself."

In earlier interviews, this same daughter alternately expressed deep affection for her mother; resentment bordering on hatred because of the tensions her presence imposed on the rest of the family; an occasional wish that her mother would die (a wish which caused deep feelings of guilt); and anger at the social "system" which permitted the woman no alternatives between institutionalization and complete dependence on her daughter's hard-pressed family.

Extra-Professional Care-Givers: An Overview

If many professional care-givers and planners are dimly aware of the existence of a natural or ad hoc lay system, they may be only slightly more aware of other elements in the natural helping system. These include *providers of other services* incorporated into the lay service network, such as banks, grocery stores, pharmacies, and the post office; *self-help and mutual aid* groups that focus on members' problems; *junior partner* associations and *volunteers; community service, religious,* and *civil associations* which include in their purposes the provision and support of services to others; and *social action organizations* or coalitions that are issue-focused and whose concerns are to effect some changes in the professional service system on behalf of some of their own membership or some other constituent population.

Like the lay service network, the first three types of helping groups are bona fide service providers—potential allies of service agencies. The other two may supply personnel to the professional and extra-professional systems, but may be even more concerned about supporting or changing elements in that system. They are potential allies of the planning agency.

Self-help groups may include unions, fraternal groups, neighborhood associations and block clubs, community corporations, and consumer co-ops. Some, like Weight Watchers, Alcoholics Anonymous, and Synanon, are national in scope and have developed quasi-professional technologies. Others are less known, usually local in scope. Examples of these are consumer and living cooperatives, social clubs, and other types of mutual aid groups whose prime beneficiaries are their own memberships.

Unfortunately, most social agency personnel are barely aware of either the lay service network or of self-help groups. Many do, however, recognize the need for lay services. Accordingly, they may organize or coordinate the work of volunteers to expand or complement the work of their own staff. Volunteers recruited from the general public or from the membership of civic associations serve a vital function in the social network discussed in the next chapter.

In practice, the many distinctions along the continuum from lay to professional care-giver often become blurred. An association may assume any one of a number of roles at different stages in its development. While there is no straight line of development, the process of change from one type of association to the other can be viewed as evolutionary: some systems adapt to new needs and services; some disappear when their particular characteristics are no longer functional.

Former mental patients or former drug addicts, for example, may form a temporary lay service network until the individual participants are no longer of service to each other. Or, they may find these services so important that they form a mutual aid group that meets regularly, insists on membership conformity to rules, and creates a quasi-professional technology. Some groups reach beyond the needs of their members and offer services to others in need. Sometimes they even employ one or more professionals, thereby becoming transformed into professionalized or institutionalized service agencies. At other times, they may establish regular liaison with professionally staffed agencies such as counseling centers and medical clinics. In turn, these professional service providers may seek the cooperation of self-help and civic groups, sometimes using their members as volunteers.

Self-Help Groups

Many self-help groups are organized for expressive purposes—that is, to satisfy membership interests for socialization, education, and mutual support. Others are organized for instrumental purposes. They may be outward directed, attempting either to influence some aspect of society or to change specific conditions that affect their membership, or perhaps they aim at concerting resources for the benefit of their members (as through a buyer's co-op, a welfare rights group or other agency pressure group, or a cooperative living arrangement).

Self-help and mutual aid groups are formalized expressions of the lay service network. In many respects, they are a substitute for the extended family and the integrated community. They are necessary in a society where geographic and vertical mobility is frequent, and where rapid and almost wrenching changes in personal status would otherwise be disruptive to both the individual and society.

Self-help or mutual aid groups develop when a group of individuals formally agrees to meet and act together in order to attempt the satisfaction of some common need, or to help each other around a shared problem or set of problems.

There is some evidence that participation of people in self-help groups and mutual aid societies has increased considerably in a number of American communities. The reasons are expressed vividly by the president of the Golden Age club in a mid-sized California community.

"Want to know why older people are getting more active and more and more involved in activities that help themselves? I'll tell you. First of all, we're healthier and we keep our health longer. Secondly, when you lose your job, and when your family moves away, you have to find some other places and some other way to get a little recognition. A third reason is that there are lots more older folks than there ever were before, especially in the big towns and suburbs out here on the West Coast. Fourth, you don't find too many older people living with their children nowadays. If they haven't got their kids and grandkids to take care of and worry about, they're going to have to take care of and worry about themselves. The last reason is that young people don't understand us too well. We're sort of an embarrassment to them. They don't feel comfortable with us, and sometimes we don't feel comfortable with them."

The disadvantages of relying on self-help groups are similar to the disadvantages of ad hoc lay services. Self-help groups may not be able to provide technical competence when required, and may substitute a quasi-ideological mystical belief in a method or a relationship for professional knowledge and skill. Unlike the ad hoc system, members of self-help groups may discover that they are required to give up even more autonomy and independence in certain areas than they would in seeking professional services. Critics of therapeutic communities, for example, have charged that residents become so dependent on the supportive system within those communities that they cannot survive outside. Most self-help groups have only limited tolerance for deviant behavior. Members who do not ascribe to the group's norms or fulfill their membership obligations may be expelled. Because many self-help groups are exclusive, they frequently have none of the relationships to other care-givers that a deviant member might need.

Differential Uses of the Natural and Professional Systems

Despite many similarities, the professional and the lay and extra-professional systems have distinct and separate characteristics. Care-givers in each system are guided by different kinds of knowledge and experience. Lay knowledge arises out of individual or shared experiences; professional knowledge tends to be more technical in nature, representing the collective wisdom of experience combined with the ordered knowledge of science and research. Practitioners in each system are governed by different norms and values. Lay care-givers are governed by those norms inherent in their subcultures or communities; professionals are ruled by values inherent in their occupations or reflective of the organizational and bureaucratic norms of the agencies in which they work.

A client's decision to participate in one or the other system will depend on his actual or perceived vulnerability; his acceptance of the norms, values, and knowledge inherent in each system; the referrals made within each system; his knowledge about, or the availability of, services in one system or the other; and the benefits he anticipates or actually receives in each.

In a sense, the consumer may be viewed as having a "career choice" within each system. Like any career, the person performing it must develop the skills necessary to prune it and the relationships required to support those skills. Later other career choices, the choice of what systems to enter depends on (1) knowledge about the services available via one method or the other; (2) the accessibility of each system and the ease with which the person in need gets help; (3) the compatibility between the consumer's reward-value hierarchy and the benefits he or she can accrue in each; (4) the extent to which the consumer feels comfortable with the norms, values, and culture of the agency or natural helping system.

No matter how extensive or well developed the professionalized network of services, extra-professional helpers will always be needed to individualize and humanize the overall system and to perform many less complicated tasks. Eugene Litwak points out that specialized knowledge and formal organizational structure are not terribly important when (1) little specialized knowledge is required to provide a service; (2) the tasks to be performed are so simple that the ordinary citizen has enough knowledge or expertise to perform as well as the expert; (3) the situation requiring intervention is so complex, unpredictable, or urgent as to make it difficult for the professional service providers to act in time.

RELATIONSHIPS BETWEEN BOTH SYSTEMS

In fact, both systems usually operate side by side and simultaneously. They may be indifferent to each other or they may be in opposition and in conflict. Sometimes they will accommodate each other, or even collaborate to the point of merging. Generally, however, participants in each system are unaware of the existence of the other system. For example, persons in need are often unaware of official programs in housing, recreation, health, or transportation designed for their use. On the other hand, professional providers often function with total disregard and complete indifference to the existence of a lay service network of quasi-institutional care-givers.

Sometimes, the professional system perceives the lay or extra-professional systems as a challenge to or a criticism of its services. In such an adversary relationship, each group may find itself trying to shape the other to its will or perception of appropriate behavior. At other times, the two systems may attempt to achieve some form of mutual adjustment in which elements of one system may attempt to incorporate all or a portion of the other system.

While the relationships between the two systems frequently produce strain, they just as frequently produce meaningful symbiotic relationships. In the field of services to the aging, for instance, both networks operate to increase the scope and responsiveness of programs for the elderly.

INCREASING LINKAGES BETWEEN THE SYSTEMS

The planner's task is to examine the points at which the systems may converge and to promote the relationships between them that will increase the availability, accessibility, appropriateness, and responsiveness of human service.

Planners addressing the problem of increasing linkages between the two systems should consider (1) how aware each system is of the other; (2) whether they view each other as collaborators or as protagonists; (3) the extent to which their structures are or can be made sufficiently compatible to permit coordination and integration. The following suggestions are drawn from the experience of a number of social planners interviewed by the author.

1. *The social planner can foster use of the natural system through training aimed at members of the professional system.* "Most professionals are only dimly aware that an extra-professional service system exists," explains a planner. "Our job is to help them understand how it works, what decisions are best left to it, and how to use it." For example, a physician can hardly expect his diagnosis and treatment of a severely disabled patient to be effective unless the treatment plan is supported by members of the lay service network. Someone has to help the patient with the prescribed diet, remind him to take medication, help him with shopping, help him reduce personal tensions, keep him active, and so forth. It seems clear that training can help professional service providers —physicians, recreation directors, housing specialists, transportation planners, and others—by making them aware of how the extra professional service network can enhance or nullify their efforts.

2. *Information about the professional care system should be made easily available and accessible to consumers and potential consumers and to those in the lay and extra-professional systems.* All too often, people in need or their friends and relatives don't know where to go for specialized help. They are unfamiliar with the range of available services, uncomfortable or unsophisticated with regard to negotiating through the maze of bureaucratic regulations and intake procedures, or unaware of the range of alternatives.

"We've been wanting to do something for older folks in our town for some time now," explains the president of the Kiwanis, "but it's harder than the dickens to know where to start. We don't want to just plunge in and duplicate some service that already exists. Our members want to do something, but we don't know what's needed." Just trying to put the information together on the range of professional services available may be difficult enough. Deciding how a civic organization can collaborate may be even more difficult. An effective information and referral service may be able to put the Kiwanis in touch with one or more social agencies, and suggest a significant task to perform.

3. *Even when information about certain federal or local programs is highly publicized or well known, people may find it difficult to maneuver through what they may perceive as a maze of obstacles to service.* "So many forms," a widow complained after a visit to the Social Security office. "I'm not too good at reading, so I just left."

Although she was an isolated individual, the widow was also a potential member of the lay service network and may, in fact, have been referred to the Social Security office by someone else. Her withdrawal effectively cut her off from service, and her relation of this experience may cause others to be leery of the system as well. Similar experiences of being cut off are often expressed by other potential lay care-givers. Sometimes, planning or service agencies employ an ombudsman to help members of the lay system work their way through the maze of bureaucracy that surrounds much of the formal professionalized system. By the same token, volunteers and outreach workers from the community are sometimes employed to help the formal system expand its contacts and its bridges to the informal system. The ombudsman, the paraprofessional, the volunteer, the junior partner association, are "common carriers." They bear messages between the two systems.

4. *Some social planning efforts may be aimed at increasing the professionalized system's control over and access to elements in the lay and extra-professional systems.* Planners may help service agencies establish advisory groups or neighborhood associations composed of clients, or seek to augment an agency's authority over that population. Thus, the agency can expand its own services by reaching out into the lay service network.

Agencies may also attempt to incorporate or absorb self-help and mutual aid groups by making them junior partners, giving them roles as volunteers, fund raisers, or client recruiters. Aided by social planners, agencies may co-opt members of social action coalitions by giving them leadership positions on boards and policy committees; by agreeing to a coalition demand in return for getting a lay association to assume a junior partner stance; or by "employing" the coalition's leadership as adjunct staff or in a paraprofessional capacity.

5. *Conversely, social planners may* help consumers to exercise more control over the professional system *in order to increase its responsiveness to the needs or wishes of the lay service network.* The range and extent of professional accountability to consumers varies considerably. On the one extreme, client groups or their representatives might monitor a service agency. They might exercise veto power over the hiring or firing of staff or serve on a board to appoint a new director. Consumers may also make up the bulk of advisory panels on specific issues.

Consumers or their representatives can also influence service agencies by developing their own advocacy structures, such as a welfare rights group, a consumer co-op with its own officers, or a consumer union. Local chapters of welfare rights organizations often help an agency's clients to gain access to the formal system. They also express the members' grievances toward that system. Partisan advocacy and social action are discussed more fully in the next chapter.

Consumers may also make use of the services of an ombudsman, consumer relations commissions to aid them in fighting discrimination, and indigenous experts who have sufficient credentials to deal with service agency experts. A retired teacher, for example, can deal with the board of education or a retired doctor can deal with the hospital. An information and referral service is also helpful. An area planner can help develop any of these resources. At other times, consumers will attempt to serve on policy boards and committees which have varying degrees of autonomy, or perhaps influence the service system from the inside by becoming staff members or volunteers within it.

POTENTIAL RISKS

Such linkages entail risks for each side. One system may be sufficiently bent to the will of the other so that its autonomy is reduced or it is diverted from what it had perceived as its primary mission.

Incorporating elements of the lay system into an agency service program may have negative or unanticipated consequences. In one New York settlement house, a local block club leader was placed on the staff as a paid worker. Other residents rebelled. "Now that you have Mrs. Williams on your staff, you won't find me at your meetings anymore," complained a long-term member. "I have lots of old people to talk to in my apartment complex. I don't want one of us on the staff. Why should Mrs. Williams know about my personal life? I used to feel that I could talk to a professional when I needed help." No one ever complained when Mrs. Williams was performing the same service informally.

Lay people are not the only ones who may be upset by closer relationships between systems. Professional staff frequently resist making effective use of volunteers and paraprofessionals, whose presence may threaten the claimed "expertness" of professionals, alter accustomed modes of communication, and challenge existing structures of authority. Often a delicate balance, an "ecology" exists between the extra-professional and professionalized service systems which planners must be careful not to upset. *It is when this ecology is unbalanced, or when it inadvertently excludes certain persons from service, that the planner must intervene.*

Management of the linkages between systems is, at best, a tricky business. Planners have had little experience in it. While they are certain to make mistakes in attempting to manage this interaction and be criticized for them, they cannot be absolved of the responsibility to engage in the effort. As professionalized service providers learn how to work with community groups to solve problems which do not require their expertise, they will be freer to utilize their technical skills and expertise efficiently.

The planner, as the central figure in this drama, is ideally suited to unlock the doors between both systems and to facilitate movement between them. Self-help groups, volunteers, and junior partner organizations, civic and community service associations, and groups organized for social action and advocacy all play a role in the development and delivery of services. Their particular characteristics and specific functions are explored in greater detail in the next chapter.

Implications for the Social Planner

The implications of knowing about, understanding, and working with the extra-professional system may be of considerable significance for the area planner. Although there is currently only a minimal amount of research literature available, it seems safe to suggest that planning with and for elements of the extra-professional system may have a number of advantages.

Planners who are knowledgeable about both systems are quick to become aware of successful helping mechanisms developed in one which may be transposed to the other. The technique that works well in a self-help group should be shared with professional providers, just as professional knowledge and skill in certain areas may be shared with members of the lay service system.

Professional care-givers are probably only a small minority of all care-givers. Assessments of need and of available resources for the provision of services to the aging are more accurate if they take into account the lay and extra-professional systems. So, too, can professional services and service agencies be rendered more effective, efficient, responsive, accessible and accountable through articulation with extra-professional care-givers.

The drain on the lay service network and the pressures on the quasi-institutional elements of the extra-professional system can be reduced through linkages with professionalized providers. Comprehensiveness is increased by linking both systems—fewer potential clients may "fall through the cracks" between care-givers. Another advantage of articulation is that services can be more rationally organized. First, preventive interventions are possible through increasing the adaptive capacities of lay networks, self-help groups, and civic associations. Second, functional alternatives to current care-giving patterns may be increased. For example, institutionalization may be deemphasized in favor of personal care systems which maintain emotionally and physically disabled people in the community with an optimal degree of independence. Third, making information about both systems available to potential clients could increase consumer choice by increasing the range of alternatives. Planners should be responsible for providing consumers with a mechanism through which they can judge the advantages and disadvantages of the systems.

By developing linkages between both systems, planners can broaden community participation and consumer involvement. In so doing, they increase the dialogue and reduce the cultural distances between planners, professional providers, lay providers, and consumers. Finally, in working with elements of the extra-professional system, planners reduce their isolation. They increase their access to a variety of community-based resources such as legitimacy and manpower. They also increase their access to other resources and to elements in the system requiring change or providing needed support.

Many planners are convinced that their impact on professionalized service providers depends on their effectiveness in increasing citizen and consumer inputs into the planning and service-providing processes. They may devote much effort to working with a large number of disparate voluntary associations (formally or informally organized) concerned with the provision or promotion of social services outside the system of professionalized service providers, funders, and planning bodies.

This extra-professional system is composed of (1) a network of lay services; (2) mutual aid and self-help associations; (3) associations of volunteers and junior partners of the professionalized service system; (4) community service and civic organizations; and (5) other permanent and ad hoc groupings of citizens.

The lay service network is made up of friends, neighbors, and relatives of those needing help. For most people, it is generally the first place they seek help. Professionalized service providers may be sought only when the lay services are inadequate, or when potential clients are referred to professional agencies by friends and relations.

The lay service network is often particularly effective in providing (a) immediate, emergency, and short-term care; (b) referrals to other elements in the lay service network or to components of the professionalized service system; (c) supportive services to complement those prescribed by professionals; (d) help in evaluating the utility of professional service; and (e) feedback to the professional system on how its programs and services are perceived and received by elements in the consumer population. The other components of the extra-professional system serve similar functions.

Both the lay and extra-professional and the professional service systems have distinct and separate characteristics. At times this causes them to be indifferent to each other, each pursuing its separate, distinctive existence. At other times, the systems may compete for clientele or resources. Each may perceive the other as a threat and enter an adversary relationship. More often, they achieve some form of mutual adjustment through which one system tries to incorporate the other as an extension of itself, or somehow to shape its activities in accordance with its perceptions of consumer need.

Sometimes professional care-givers encourage formalization of elements in the lay service network into self-help groups that can handle some of the lesser problems brought by clients to agency staff. These self-help groups thus offer services that are supportive of the agency's program.

The planner can play a key role in establishing the linking mechanisms between both systems and in utilizing those linkages in such a manner as to increase the range and effectiveness of services to a particular population.

To increase the linkages between both systems, planners have used the following techniques: (1) setting up instructional programs that introduce professionals to the lay service network, and consumers to the way in which professionalized services operate; (2) initiating an ombudsman or "common-carrier" service between both systems; (3) helping agencies increase their access to or control over elements in the lay service network so as to increase the efficacy and effectiveness of their services; and (4) enabling elements of the extra-professional system to exercise increased control over the professionalized service system in order to increase the latter's responsiveness to needs of its consumers.

The implications of planning for and with elements of the extra-professional system include (a) reducing the planner's isolation; (b) increasing the accuracy of assessments of need and available resources; (c) sharpening the efficiency of the professional service system and simultaneously reducing the drain on the lay service network; (d) increasing comprehensiveness through early intervention; and the choice of a wider range of functional alternatives; and (e) broadening consumer and citizen participation.

SUPPLEMENTARY QUESTIONS AND ACTIVITIES

1. Inventory and describe at least five self-help groups in your community. Are any listed in the yellow pages?

2. Draw a map of an actual or potentially available lay service network with which you are familiar. You might begin by using a schema such as the following. Make it more specific by filling in the names of various groups or agencies. How can a planner make effective use of this system or increase the flow of resources from one branch to another?

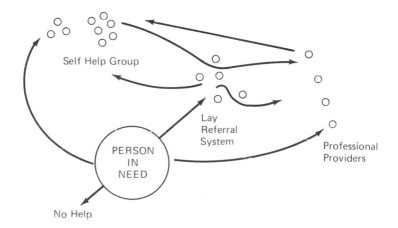

3. What connections exist between self-help groups and professional provid-ers? Are any of these formalized? Should they be?

4. Read over the vignette that follows. Give three arguments that contradict the position taken. Can you present three additional arguments *in favor of* the position taken? Three arguments *against* it?

PINBALL REFERRALS

"Running this Information and Referral service is almost like playing a pinball machine. If agencies have services or programs for children, they register with us. Sometimes we dig them out ourselves. Then we sort of set them all out on a board, like stations on a pinball machine. A mother with some sort of child-related problem walks in the door, or calls us up, and we shoot her out to those stations. That's really what we do. We tell her about four or five stations that might be of interest to her, point her in the right direction, and shoot her out. If she makes it, well and good. If she doesn't, one of those stations might bounce her somewhere else.

"For all we know, she might rebound from one agency to another—or back to the first. She might fall into an empty hole where we have no station. She might make it all the way through the board quickly, or it might take forever; she may or may not get service. Other than through statistical checks, we've just got no way of knowing. It's a lousy system, but it's the best we can afford at the moment.

"It would be better if we had some overall policy to govern all our member agencies and help us determine who should be treated where and when. That would require effective central communication and planning that just doesn't exist. This type of system would allow us to take the client directly to that agency we think could handle the problem best. Each agency would have a clear domain, and a specific number of clients it could take. They'd be interdependent. If one couldn't provide the entire service, we'd make arrange-ments with another to provide another aspect of the service. That's how it should work, but of course it doesn't.

"Know how it does work? It works best when the clients themselves know what the system's all about. They're the best referral agents we have. When we've got some clients who have been helped, we ask if they'd be willing to help others. When people help themselves, they begin being self-propelled balls through that pinball machine. They start off with our push, but then they can direct their own way across the board."

Suggested Readings

LITWAK, EUGENE, and HENRY MEYER. "A Balance Theory of Coordination Between Bureaucratic Organizations and Community Primary Groups." *Administration Science Quarterly,* June, 1966, p. 468.

The "balance theory" is based on the notion that both bureaucratic and community primary groups are essential for achieving adequate social control. At the same time, they are viewed as having antithetical, mutually destructive atmospheres. Bureaucracies stress specificity, rules, and impersonality, while primary groups operate on personal, affective bases. Thus, if linked too closely, conflict will arise between these groups. If they remain too far apart, they will not be able to coordinate efforts to solve mutual problems. Optimum social control is most likely to occur when their relationship is "balanced" at a midpoint of social distance. In this article, Litwak and Meyer suggest eight possible mechanisms for coordination (voluntary associations, the mass media, settlement houses, etc.) that can link bureaucratic organizations to primary groups.

FREIDSON, ELLIOT. "Client Control and Medical Practice." *The American Journal of Sociology,* January, 1960.
Friedson's article is one of the first pieces found in the literature that shows the connections between professional and natural care-givers. It explicitly discusses the lay referral process.

WARREN, ROCHELLE B., and DONALD I. WARREN. *The Neighborhood Organizer's Handbook.* Notre Dame, Ind.: University of Notre Dame Press, 1977.
Chapter 1 describes the functions of a neighborhood, providing a solid analytic framework of use to the planner interested in understanding the natural helping system. It also provides important information on the neighborhood as a base for recruitment of citizens for participation in social action and in the planning process.

Suggestions for Further Reading

LEFTON, MARK, and WILLIAM ROSENGREN. "Organization and Clients: Lateral and Longitudinal Dimensions." *American Sociological Review,* December, 1966.
LITWAK, EUGENE. "Technological Innovations and Theoretical Functions of Primary Groups and Bureaucratic Structures." *American Journal of Sociology,* 1968, 73.
ROSENGREN, WILLIAM. "The Careers of Clients in Organizations," In *Organization and Clients,* W. Rosengren and M. Lefton (Eds.). Columbus, Ohio: Charles E. Merrill, 1970.
SILVERMAN, PHYLIS R. "The Widow as a Caregiver in a Program of Preventive Intervention with Other Widows." *Mental Hygiene,* 1970, *54,* (5).
WELLMAN, BARRY et al. *Community Ties and Support Systems.* Toronto: Centre for Urban and Community Studies, University of Toronto, Research Paper No. 11, July, 1972.

14

Volunteers and Civic Associations

No amount of planning is ever likely to assure the availability of social services to all those in need, when that need is most urgently felt. Nor is the natural helping system a proper substitute or alternative source of care for those not currently or adequately served by professional providers. One of the ways that social planners at the community level attempt to overcome the deficiencies of both systems is by linking them in partnership relationships. Invariably, the professional service providers are the senior partners, and members of the natural helping system, the junior partners. This is so because the junior partners are often dependent on the professional or the professional's agency for their mandates, for their access to client populations, and for directives on what to do and how. Volunteers need not be lay persons. Often, they are professionally trained, giving of their time to programs for which they are not paid. These points are illustrated in the following vignette.

Making One Program Do the Job of Another

"This is a rural state. We are never going to get enough resources to provide all the services that are needed. So we've got to make one program provide the services that another one should offer.

"I'll give you an example. We couldn't possibly recruit enough home handymen, let alone pay them to visit all the places where the handicapped live. So we sat down with the head man from the city housing authority. We persuaded him to let our staff train his code enforcers as "housing consultants." Now, they notify us when the level of repair in a handicapped person's home is particularly low, and we send one of our home handymen out.

"That's another way of killing two birds with one stone. The handyman is usually a retired senior citizen with a special trade background. He may have been an appliance repairman, a carpenter, a cabinetmaker, or an electrician. We know he's got the handyman skills, and we're not concerned about training him for that. Instead, we train him as an emergency counselor and intake worker.

"If he spots a serious emotional or health problem when he visits a home, he tries to let the person know about the services provided by our intake and referral unit. If necessary, he'll place a phone call and hand the phone to the person whose home he is visiting. It's a way of getting something started. If he is not successful in referring the handicapped person over the telephone to the necessary service, or in getting the person to come in, we'll try a couple of other things.

"We send one of our friendly visitors out. In this town, the visiting service is part of the Information and Referral Center, staffed by volunteers from several civic groups. The friendly visitor often acts as a link between the Referral Center, homebound individuals, and other agencies that might serve homebound persons in a particular neighborhood. As a matter of fact, the director of homebound services spends much of her time interpreting the program to other agencies.

CONSULTANTS AND VOLUNTEERS

"Recently she coordinated a training program for hospital social workers and geriatric physicians. She found they were referring patients directly to nursing homes because they were not aware of the possibilities for personal care in the community. Her relationship with the hospital people turned out so well that she was able to enlist a hospital nutritionist as consultant for one of our other programs.

"About sixty elderly people had been attending a school lunch program once a week, with the schools subsidizing the program. The school nutritionist insisted she knew all she needed to know about putting out a balanced diet. The problem was that the food kids need isn't necessarily the kind older people need. But the nutritionist at the hospital knew the school nutritionist personally. At the request of our homebound services director, the two were brought into contact, and it was found that the school nutritionist had been resistant only because she didn't have the time or the manpower to prepare more than one kind of meal. I knew just what to do. I approached the Homemaker's Club at the Methodist Church and arranged to have two members volunteer on a rotating basis to work with the school nutritionist.

ON BEING A FACILITATOR

"What I'm trying to say is that I'm a behind-the-scenes worker. I keep a low profile. What I've described may not seem like big stuff, but to the people who are helped, it is. There are lots of other people who can be recruited and trained—bus drivers, for example.

"I trained one group to spot people in trouble. They are among the best referral agents we have. I've given those city inspectors a feeling of doing a public service. I've gotten what had been a self-centered cooking club to begin to help others. You see, it's not just me. People want to do good. They just don't know how. Even in a rural area like this, problems are complex and people aren't sure what to do about them. They'll ignore a problem unless someone can show them a way of helping. They need a facilitator. That's what services are all about. That's how I got into this planning business."

Volunteers as Junior Partners

When an agency recruits and assigns volunteers, the volunteers' mandate stems directly from that agency. In a sense, they belong to the agency and are its nonprofessional, nonpaid staff. When a social agency reaches a negotiated agreement with another group to provide volunteers, the volunteers generally belong to the organization that supplies or recruits them. This organization may have its own ideas about how its recruits or members should be used. Thus, a happy working relationship frequently calls for a process of mutual adjustment in which agreements may have to be renegotiated frequently. The benefiting agency may view its supplier as a junior partner in the provision of services, a designation that is often agreeable to both organizations. At other times, however, the "junior partner" may not be comfortable or satisfied with its assigned role. The resultant tensions in such situations will be examined in more detail in the next section.

Much of the time, agency administrators welcome the notion of using volunteers, although they are not always clear about the volunteer's role. "Volunteers bring volunteerism back into the voluntary agency," says the director of a family agency. "By donating money to the United Fund, most people feel they can get away from their responsibility for voluntary participation in the community. People buy their way out of volunteering. In practice, a lot of agencies have discouraged people from volunteering their efforts. They find it hard to coordinate volunteer and professional staffs, and they fear that too much volunteer participation may ultimately reduce the amount of financial contributions. For example, the Health and Welfare Council in this city has long paid lip service to volunteer effort, but has done very little to organize it.

"We know better. We do everything we can to get our volunteers to participate fully in the provision of services. We don't view it as either meddling or interference. We view it as an extension of our work. We don't like to think of our volunteers as junior partners, but I guess in a sense you might say they are. They make it possible for the professional staff to do things which they otherwise couldn't do. The truth is that without volunteers, this wouldn't be much of a voluntary agency. It would be a purely professional operation."

TASKS PERFORMED BY VOLUNTEERS

While not all agency administrators would agree with the foregoing statement, it is a reflection of the opinion of a growing number of professional people in the human services. Unfortunately, many service providers have neither the experience to organize volunteers nor a clear conceptual framework with which to begin.

It may, therefore, be helpful to examine the kinds of tasks volunteers might assume. The work of volunteers can be classified in four general categories: (1) providing direct services to clients; (2) performing administrative and clerical tasks; (3) policy-making functions; and (4) public relations functions.

In the provision of direct services, volunteers do everything from performing practical tasks, such as driving people back and forth to agencies and arranging telephone contacts with isolated older people, to tasks requiring specialized skill, such as tutoring eighth grade math, retirement counseling, short-term or emergency therapy, providing information, diagnosis and referral, practical nursing, cooking, and nutritional counseling. They may work with individuals and families in residential group settings, in emergency care facilities, or in recreation and group service agencies.

Some volunteers perform technical or administrative tasks requiring clerical or filing skills, bookkeeping and budgetary management, and advertising experience.

Still others serve as members and officers of agency boards, committees, and task forces. In this capacity, they provide legitimacy to the agency's services, or facilitate linkages with other associations to which they may belong. On occasion, their efforts result in effective public relations. If they are knowledgeable about the agency's programs, they can interpret them to potential contributors, participants, and users.

The rewards of volunteering are many, both for the volunteer and for the recipients of these services. Being a volunteer is not easy, however. A volunteer must be able to work with people who are sometimes rude and disagreeable, tolerate snobbishness by some professional staff people, and risk assuming responsibilities beyond his capacities. Tensions sometimes exist between volunteers working in different agencies or in the same agency, between volunteers and clients, and between volunteers and professional staff.

"We're all for this volunteer business," proclaims the harried administrator of a housing project. "Lord knows we've little enough staff to provide the services needed. But sometimes the volunteers take on responsibilities that are just inappropriate, or they commit the professional staff to things they just shouldn't be committed to. It would be different if we could get enough of the right kind of volunteers. But the pressures are so great that I've just no time to recruit them and, certainly, no time to train them." Many agencies find it difficult to recruit, organize, and supervise volunteers. For this reason, the planner's involvement in recruitment and training is very important. Training programs for the professional staffs who will be working with volunteers may be just as important.

"Introduction of the volunteer program into our agency just threw us for a loop. We weren't ready for them," reports the director of a Catholic Family Service agency on the West Coast. "No matter how hard we tried, we couldn't work out their jobs so that it freed up our professional staff. They resisted doing the menial tasks, like bookkeeping and recording. Frankly, they couldn't perform those tasks very well without knowing what the professional caseworkers do anyway. They wanted to get out in the field or interview clients. When we got good volunteers, the only way we could make their work satisfying enough to keep them was to give them the same responsibility and autonomy we give our professional staff. And our professional staff didn't like that. Some of our best volunteers were beginning to wonder why they couldn't be paid.

"Morale suffered and we found ourselves doing all we could just to mediate the disputes that were cropping up. The only times things worked out were when volunteers took on a whole caseload by themselves. But then how could we differentiate between professional and volunteer workers? My supervisor of adult programs was furious half the time. She even threatened to quit. Finally, the volunteers just quit coming. I was glad to see them go."

Quite obviously, this agency was not prepared to use volunteers. Problems may be even more severe when the volunteer belongs to a junior partner association which has an identity of its own and may not wish to be viewed in a subsidiary role.

One way junior partners maintain their independent identity is to provide voluntary service to more than one social agency. "This way," explains the president of a civic group, "we are identified as an organization that cares for the blind but we avoid being too closely identified with any particular service agency. Of course, once our members are assigned to an agency, they develop close ties with it, but as an organization we retain our identity and have enough options to keep from being swallowed up." Other civic groups may not have leadership that is as astute or aware of the difficulties in maintaining their organization's identity.

In many ways, the advantages of providing service through volunteers are the same as those of providing service through other lay care-givers. Volunteers frequently provide a more personalized service, are able to give more time, and are not subject to the same bureaucratic norms which inhibit professional staff; nor are they always bound by the exigencies of red tape. Unlike the ad hoc elements of a lay service system, they are organized or recruited explicitly to extend the capabilities of the professional staff. In this way they can serve as a link between professionals and clients, mediating differences in their perceptions, values, and norms. Their work may also result in increasing the efficiency of the professional staff who are no longer required to perform routine or non-expert functions.

However, there are some valid reasons not to use volunteers. Clients may object. They may feel volunteers are not as capable as professionals of providing adequate services or being objective. Professional staff may themselves object to the intrusion of lay people and to what they have considered to be a professional service arena. They may also protest the real difficulties in coordinating and managing volunteers, who many feel are not as dependable as professional and paid staff.

The Planning Agency and Volunteers

Despite the difficulties of recruiting, supervising, and managing volunteers, their contributions to the provision and extension of services can be significant. For this reason, planning agencies are frequently asked to develop and coordinate volunteer efforts. In most major American cities, volunteer bureaus exist that are often affiliated with the local health and welfare council, with a human services commission, or with some sectorial planning body.

Many planning and coordinating agencies establish special task forces on volunteers. Often the planner or someone on his staff provides specialized professional services to volunteers and to user agencies that employ volunteers. Such services might include (1) assessing the needs for volunteers within the professional service system or among specific populations in need; (2) recruiting and training volunteers; (3) allocating volunteers to agencies and self-help groups; (4) establishing standards for the use and supervision of volunteers; (5) administering those standards so as to avoid misuse or exploitation; (6) assuring that effective supervision and help is available to volunteers when necessary by training agency supervisors of volunteer programs; (7) providing opportunities for volunteers to exchange experiences and to receive mutual encouragement from colleagues located in other work settings; (8) helping agencies establish volunteer job classification charts; and (9) monitoring and evaluating the volunteer system.

These are herculean tasks, with which most planning agencies are not currently equipped to deal. Often a planner will delegate many of these activities to special task forces or will subcontract certain responsibilities to public and private social agencies, community colleges, or community service and civic associations such as the Kiwanis, Junior League, and church or ethnic associations. In other instances, those planners who are exclusively concerned with a particular agency may contract with a local health and welfare council that already has a volunteer bureau. While an increasing number of communities have semi-independent volunteer bureaus linked to a national association, many others have associations of volunteers who take on the tasks of "manning" volunteer bureaus.

Civic Associations

Throughout the text, mention has been made of civic associations and service groups. Most American communities boast a large array of such organizations. In addition to their community-oriented service functions, they may also perform fraternal and mutual aid functions for their own members and take on occasional social action projects. A partial listing of organizations would include the Junior League, environmental protection groups, civil liberties groups, local business associations, and such fraternal/service clubs as the Rotary, the Lions, the Masons, the Elks, the Kiwanis, and others.

Each of these groups may have its own preferred projects in accordance with its membership in a national association. If this is the case, the local group may have neither the time, energy, nor will to engage in or contribute to a community services project. The planner may then have to help the agency make use of the services provided by the association on its own terms.

More than likely, however, it will be possible to enlist assistance from a civic association around an issue of local importance. This is especially true when working with church or ethnically related groups. Included among these are the congregational men's and women's clubs, various service committees, and chapters of national organizations like the B'nai B'rith and the National Council of Jewish Women.

Unlike self-help groups which are oriented towards their own members, community service associations aim at benefiting the public at large, or a specific segment of that public. They differ from professional service providers and care-giving organizations in that they generally do not charge fees or pay those who give service. In addition, their staff do not require professional credentials or extensive specialized training, nor are they subject to the same kinds of regulations as paid professionals. At times, their involvement may be no more than to provide funding for a project or service. But at other times, they may act as advocates in generating public interest in and support for services to particular populations in need.

Because their memberships often represent a substantial portion of the local citizenry—and a varied cross section of the population—social planners often involve representatives of civic associations on task forces, committees, and boards. These devices will be discussed in the next chapter.

Review

Planners often work closely with representatives of civic associations and with others in the community who serve as junior partners in the planning process or in the provision of services to those in need. Volunteers include both lay people and professionally trained persons whose efforts extend and complement those of professional service providers.

Volunteers perform a variety of tasks: direct services to clients; administrative and clerical services; policy making; and public relations. Some agencies are not properly prepared to make the best or most effective use of volunteers. Their involvement may be upsetting to agency staff and disruptive to routine operations. These problems can generally be overcome, however, through proper planning and orientation procedures for both volunteer and paid staff.

The advantages of engaging volunteers in the provision of services are much the same as those inherent in the natural service system. Volunteers may be able to give more personalized attention to a help seeker. Also, they are often drawn from the same social group as the help seeker, and thus can mediate between the values and norms of the professional care-giving system, and the clients being served.

The planner's work is also augmented by the efforts of members of civic associations. These include both sectarian and nonsectarian groups. Some are mandated by their national charters to provide service at the local level. Almost all take on specific service tasks on either a regular or ad hoc basis. Social planners have found that these invaluable groups not only in the expansion of a community's service capacities but also in implementing a variety of planning efforts.

1 Starting with the Yellow Pages, draw up an inventory of all the civic associations in your community. Now find out what they do and whom they serve. For each organization, draw up a card with the following information:
   a. name, address and telephone number
   b. size of membership and peculiar demographic characteristics if any (for example, ethnic affiliation, socioeconomic level, professions or occupations principally represented, age, where members reside, and so on)
   c. service projects currently managed by the association (describe the extent of involvement, whether part of a national effort or local in scope, whether a regular [annual] project or ad hoc in nature)
   d. extent to which any of these projects are conducted in collaboration with other community groups
   e. extent to which they are conducted in collaboration with one or more human service agencies; also who initiated the project and how is it managed
   f. key contact person(s) within the association

2. Examine a social agency that makes extensive use of volunteers. Find out how they are recruited and by whom; whether and how they undergo orientation and training for their assignments; the relationships between their work and that of paid staff at the agency; the extent to which their efforts extend or impede the agency's ability to accomplish its missions.

3. Contact one or more of the following national organizations to find out what services they provide that might promote the development or expansion of volunteer services in your community.
   a. Action
       806 Connecticut Avenue
       Washington, D.C. 20625
   b. American Association of Volunteer Service Coordinators
       18 South Michigan Avenue, Suite 602
       Chicago, Illinois 60603
   c. Association of Junior Leagues of America
       825 Third Avenue
       New York, N.Y. 10022
   d. Center for A Voluntary Society
       1785 Massachusetts Avenue
       Washington, D.C. 20036
   e. National Center for Voluntary Action
       1785 Massachusetts Avenue
       Washington, D.C. 20036

f. United Way of America
    345 East 46th Street
    New York, N.Y. 10017

Recommended Readings

LAUFFER, ARMAND, and SARA GORODEZKY. *Volunteers.* Beverly Hills, Calif.: Sage
   Publications, Inc., 1977.
One of a series of *Guides for the Human Services* published by Sage in cooperation with
   the University of Michigan School of Social Work's Continuing Education Program in the Human Services, this slim volume is replete with "how-to-do-it"
   information for the planner and agency administrator interested in developing
   a volunteer program. Individual chapters focus on recruitment, orientation,
   training, supervision, program management, relationships between volunteers
   and paid staff, evaluation, and financing.

STENZEL, ANNE K., and HELEN M. FEENEY. *Volunteer Training and Development: A
   Manual for Community Groups.* New York: The Seabury Press, 1968.
Still one of the best pieces around for a nuts-and-bolts guide to recruitment, training
   and assignment of volunteers. The book includes a series of exercises and activities that can actually be used in volunteer training.

Suggestions for Further Reading

ASH, PHILIP (Ed.) *Volunteers for Mental Health.* New York: MSS Information Corp.,
   1973.
CULL, JOHN G., and RICHARD E. HARDY. *Volunteerism: An Emerging Profession.*
   Springfield, Ill.: Charles C Thomas, 1974.
ROUTH, THOMAS A. *The Volunteer and Community Agencies.* Springfield, Ill.: Charles
   C Thomas, 1972.
SCHINDLER-RAINMAN, EVA, and RONALD LIPPITT. *The Volunteer Community: Cre-
   ative Uses of Human Resources.* (2nd ed.). La Jolla, Calif.: University Associates
   Press, 1975.

15

Citizen Participation
in the Planning Process

Social planners are often heavily involved with citizens and citizens' groups. Representatives of the general community, of client populations, and of other organizations may serve on a planner's board of directors or advisory committee. They may participate on a task force dealing with an issue of prime concern to the planner. Often the planner brings them together in a permanent or an ad hoc coalition.

Planners also work directly with civic associations, fraternal organizations, and service groups. These organizations may become partners in the planning process, expanding the planner's resources, petitioning for change, buffering against criticism.

The reasons for involving citizens are many. Some social planners view participation itself as a rightful goal of the planning and organizing processes. Others use participation as a means toward the achievement of other ends. In part, the differences stem from ideological disagreement; in part from differences in strategy. Planners who hold that participation is an end in itself view involvement as a major opportunity to restore the meaningful human interaction that they find missing in contemporary society. For them, the substantive outcomes of that involvement—the specific health and welfare services to be developed or the service programs to be coordinated—are means toward long-term objectives.

These planners view participation in terms of democratic values that call for the broadest possible involvement of those who will be affected by policies

269

and programs. Both positions can be held by the same planner as was apparently illustrated in the first illustration in Chapter 1.

While few planners might admit to a less democratic ideological position, most generally opt for the more short-term and pragmatic uses of participation discussed throughout this chapter. They tend to view participation as a *means* that should be employed selectively to accomplish specific program or service goals. They point out that participation may result in substantive losses rather than gains, or divert a planning process from the accomplishment of its objectives to sustenance of the participatory process.

One planner fears the backlash possibilities. She describes a situation in which her efforts to organize the consumers of an agency's services resulted in punitive action by the agency's administration against the clients involved. "In a political game, you have to be prepared to lose," she cautions, "but is it fair if the clients are the ones to lose?"

Another planner suggests that "when you open up the process to everybody, you no longer have control over it. The more people you get into the act, the less likelihood that you'll be able to travel a straight path to your objective." He claims that an increase in the number or range of participants in a planning process also increases the range of agendas. He dismisses much of the talk about participation as "process for the sake of process." On the other hand, he makes effective use of boards, task forces, and advisory committees. As he explains his position, "When the group's mandate is clear, and everyone knows what the task is all about, it may be worth a minor diversion from your goal to secure the resources that the right people and the right numbers can provide."

Participants as Members of Boards, Task Forces, Advisory Committees, and Ad Hoc Coalitions

BOARDS

Many human service agencies—those providing direct services as well as those in the business of planning and coordinating those services—are governed by a policy-making group that provides the organization with its mandate or sees to it that a legislative mandate is carried out. Whether it is called a board of directors, a commission, or a policy board, this body is responsible for establishing policy guidelines; reviewing and adopting budgets (or recommending them to policy bodies at a higher level), evaluating major programs or actions; hiring and firing the agency's chief executive (and sometimes other staff as well); and establishing job classifications.

Boards may be appointed or elected. If appointed, participants may be selected by a public official such as the mayor or governor, or by the chief executive of a larger organization under whose auspices the local group operates. For example, the director of the state drug abuse agency may be responsible for appointing board members of local drug abuse committees.

Some boards are composed of persons elected by community groups. In these instances board members are expected to represent their constituencies. Other boards may be self-perpetuating, with new members selected by current members. Alternatively, board members may be selected through a general election process in which all members of an organization or residents in a neighborhood have a right to vote.

Much of a board's activities may be conducted by its standing committees and special committees and task forces. Standing committees may be responsible for nominating new members, for personnel, for budget review, for program development and evaluation. Ad hoc committees and task forces are established for specific purposes from time to time.

TASK FORCES

Task forces are generally appointed. Unlike boards, they do not endure over the lifetime of an organization or program. Task forces, as their name implies, are limited to the accomplishment of a specific task. Typically, task force assignments include the conduct of studies or surveys of needs; development of plans for action or program designs; recommendations for solutions to specific problems; design of mechanisms for better coordination of services, and similar issues.

Task forces may be composed of experts in performing the assigned task, representatives of the population directly affected by a proposed change, or a combination of both groups. Thus, if a health planning council establishes a task force on drugs, members of the task force may include professional providers of drug abuse services plus client or consumer representatives and other concerned citizens.

Task forces are rarely responsible for action or implementation. The findings or recommendations of a task force are fed back to the policy board or to the executive or the organization that has established it. The executive may be the mayor or governor, the superintendent of the board of education, the head of the transportation authority, the chairperson of the city council, or the county administrator. Task forces always receive their mandates from some external and well constituted authority. They almost never are self-constituted; nor do they draw their mandates directly from those groups to which their individual members belong.

ADVISORY COMMITTEES

Advisory committees, on the other hand, may have authority only to the extent that they are representatives of populations or groups whose advice and support a planning agency values. Advisory groups differ from task forces in that they rarely possess a well defined set of responsibilities; they differ from policy boards in that they command nowhere near the same degree of authority. Advisory committees may influence decisions, but they rarely make them. Decisions on policy, employment, budgets, and the like are made elsewhere. Thus, the policy guidelines for a local area agency on aging are found in the "state plan," which is established by a state committee on aging. This plan, in turn, is approved by the Administration on Aging in HEW and must be in conformance with the provisions of Title III of the 1973 amendments to the Older Americans Act. The area agency's local advisory group does just what its title implies; it advises on staff, programs, and allocations, but does not determine who or what they will be. The state unit on aging hires the local chief executive, while the state plan provides policy guidelines and general program directions.

Members of advisory groups also provide a sounding board for the planner, reflecting on his or her ideas and providing insights on how those ideas may be received by the community at large, by a potential funder, by other service providers, or by the recipients of services. They may provide specific information on the attitudes, opinions, or needs of particular populations, for example, residents of the barrio or older persons living in rural sections of a county. In almost all cases, they confer some added legitimacy to the planning process, to the plan itself, or to the planner's agency.

Unfortunately, the distinctions between advising and deciding are not always clear. Members of advisory groups may not know what is really expected of them. Frustration when one's recommendations are not followed may lead to lack of commitment and even resentment. For these reasons, the responsibilities of advisory committees should be as clearly defined as possible.

AD HOC COALITIONS

In addition to boards, committees, and task forces, planners often work with ad hoc coalitions of persons or organizations representing specific interests. Planners are frequently responsible for convening such coalitions. Thus, a mental health planner concerned with the increasing numbers of runaways in the community or with teen pregnancies may convene a coalition of agency representatives who also are concerned with the needs of adolescents. The group may decide to lobby for a change in legislation permitting more extensive sex education in the schools. It may press the local health and welfare council for the establishment of a new counseling program for teens or the County Board of Commissioners for money to establish a temporary home for runaways.

Once the limited objectives of the coalition have been met, it generally dissolves. It is not necessary for all members of the coalition to have similar objectives. It is only necessary that they agree on the limited objectives that hold them together.

TIPPING THE SCALES

Equally important as convening a task force or a committee is the assurance that the *right* participants are involved. Depending on the project or activity, the planner may try to involve representatives of social agencies, the providers of professional services, political interests, the community as a whole, and the population to be served. Yet when representatives of all four groups are brought together in an advisory committee, one or more groups may be at a functional disadvantage.

Those people who represent consumer interests may not have had much experience working in professional or bureaucratic settings. They may be unable to cope with the issues at hand, particularly if these are technical and require an understanding of management, budgets, and research terminology. When it comes to service delivery issues, agency representatives often defend their own interests through their access to specialized knowledge, their control over information, their reliance on staff resources to back up their positions, and the skills acquired through experience. Representatives of political interests and other community influentials may have similar skills and will generally back up their positions through the social standing and political influence they can bring to bear or the money and credit potentially at their disposal.

In such situations, social planners sometimes attempt to "tip the scales" by involving a larger number of consumer representatives or advocates. Planners sometimes set up special training sessions to prepare these people for their participation on boards and committees. They may compile fact sheets so as to strengthen their participation and to balance the information presented by others. Some planners devote considerable effort to organizing consumer groups and to recruiting people who represent existing consumer organizations. The actual number of consumers on a committee or task force may be less important than the numbers and the strength of the groups they represent.

Planners also work directly with existing groups organized for their own purposes—civic associations, fraternal organizations, and service groups.

Working With Civic Associations and Service Groups

WHAT THEY ARE

Service groups and civic associations include such organizations as the National Council of Jewish Women, the League of Women Voters, the Chamber of Commerce, neighborhood associations, and others who seek to help the public good through some provision of public services. Fraternal organizations such as the Elks, although organized primarily for social reasons, frequently take on service or civic activities. Professional associations and special interest groups such as local chapters of the National Council of Senior Citizens also perform similar functions.

Despite their occasional role as junior partners to service agencies, civic associations generally maintain a distinct identity. Fraternal groups, self-help groups, business enterprises, and other organizations may perform civic functions and community services from time to time, although they are organized for other purposes.

HOW THEY ARE USED BY PLANNERS

In addition to taking on special service projects or providing volunteers for social service agencies, civic associations also perform other functions in the planning process. They are frequently used by planners to (1) legitimate a planning effort or service project; (2) act as petitioners on behalf of some project, cause, or population; and (3) serve as a buffer against criticism or opposition.

The endorsement of a well established civic association adds both prestige and credibility to a project. By seeking support of civic associations for specific projects, or by incorporating the leadership of community service organizations into task forces, boards, and advisory committees, planners increase the likelihood that their programs will be legitimized and that consumers will use them. Support from one organization sometimes brings the support of still another. "If we get the Junior League involved, it won't be long before the Downtown Business Association will be knocking on our door," reports the executive of a planning agency. But this may not be true in all cases or all communities. "Half the time, the involvement of one group drives away another," reports a planner from Iowa. "There is so much competition for prestige around here and so much animosity between groups, that getting one group involved almost automatically means that another group will be against the project."

While planners may quite appropriately seek the support of civic associations, such support is rarely without cost. Organizations may have their own reasons for lending their support and their own ideas of the direction a project ought to take. The planner must be prepared to (a) modify a project in return for desired support; (b) spend considerable time in managing the relationships between the planning agency and the civic organizations involved and among the various organizations themselves; and (c) return some prestige to the giver.

"A civic association does not often lend time or a name to a project without something in return," explains a United Fund planner. "We make sure that the press and the right people know who's involved. There is some status, after all, to be gained by being associated with us, too." Community leaders and members of civic associations often perform active petitioner functions on behalf of the planner of a particular project. They may promote the interests of the planning agency, its member agencies, a particular project, or a population that concerns them. Petitioner functions may be performed by general membership organizations such as unions, fraternal groups or the Junior Leagues, or by ethnic and religious groups organized primarily to work on behalf of their "brothers" and "sisters" or coreligionists.

As petitioners, these associations can intervene with funders, with legislative or administrative officials, and with the public at large. "We get attention a lot faster when the chairperson of the state Developmental Disabilities Committee or some of the key people in the Association of Parents of Retarded Children speak on our behalf. The leaders in these groups tend to know key people at the state capital and in Washington. It works best when they put in a good word for us long before we submit a formalized proposal. It works even better if their hints prompt the funder to ask us to do something we've been wanting to do all along."

Much of today's legislation is the result of successful action by petitioner organizations. Members of state legislatures or congressional committees and the bureaucracy need inputs from interested community groups or knowledgeable individuals. They are frequently apt to trust the judgment of people who represent various interests at the local level.

These organizations are in turn used by planners to buffer unpleasant or unpopular aspects of their local programs. The fact that prestigious organizations are involved may stave off excessive criticism. Inclusion of recognized leaders from these associations on a task force may prevent criticism from the associations' membership. Support from several associations gives the appearance of community-wide support, buffering potential opposition.

"But things are not always as simple as they seem," cautions a New England health planner. "If you're seeking some association's influence in support of your project, people who are not members of that organization or who may not like it may wind up rejecting the project. To be honest, we have sometimes found it to our benefit to leak the news of some organization's opposition when we really are trying to get somebody else's support. And conversely, if we want a project killed, leaking information about a particular organization's support to the press is sometimes a pretty effective way of blocking something." Buffering, as the commercial puts it, is a "two-way action."

Other Issues in Participation and Involvement

"Merely working with civic associations," suggests the administrator of a regional Council on Governments (COG), "even putting community people on advisory committees or boards, doesn't really get at the issue of true involvement and participation. The idea behind participation should be to get people to act on their own behalf. What I'm talking about is social action."

This is an appealing posture for many planners. Yet it is not without some danger. Organizing people for social action may result in the planner's identification with a particular population or cause and thus result in loss of support or access to others in the community. Some planners feel that the risks are worthwhile. "We have no choice but to support social activity, even if it takes the form of protest action," argues the COG planner. "But we don't have to do it foolishly. We can provide technical assistance to groups interested in social action, even seek them out, just as we seek out agencies to involve and to advise. We can arrange for funding of agencies or professional advocates to provide the technical assistance in our stead and get us off the hook—without absolving ourselves of the responsibility. Furthermore, it is not necessary for us or anyone else to staff all the potential action groups that develop. Most action groups don't last forever. They mobilize around some particular issue and don't necessarily last even long enough to see it through."

Experienced planners are well aware of the ephemeral nature of most protest actions and of most protest-oriented groups and action coalitions. Some planners have adopted the strategy of bringing together those who might serve as a core or nucleus for social action activities. "We train them. We make them aware of the possibilities. We bring them together and introduce them to each other. And we provide them with information about issues and about successful activities in other areas," explains the information officer of the mayor's office in a southwestern community. "The issues they choose to work on together are up to them. Of course, we're not entirely neutral. We select the information, after all. And when we think an issue is hot or support for a particular change exists in the broader community, we push it. That's what we're here for."

PLANNERS AS ORGANIZERS AND MEDIATORS

Other planners argue for the formation of constituent groups that can put pressure on their own coordinating or planning agency. "We're under a lot of pressure from the service agencies we're supposed to be coordinating," explains a planner. "Why should they be the only ones putting pressure on us? We would all be more effective if consumers were also organized and applying some pressure. Then we wouldn't have to respond to the agencies alone. We could point out to agencies that their claims compete with those of our other constituencies. What could be better than playing the mediator role between competing interests?"

It is not always that simple. When planners are relegated to mediating between competing interests, they may have very little time or resources left to accomplish other planning objectives. In most communities, citizen participation of a militant nature tends to be thin and sporadic. But when it does get organized, the planning organization may find itself unable to cope with the pressures. "We should have learned our lesson in OEO and the Model Cities program," complains a planner for a metropolitan board of education. "Organizing neighborhood associations so that we could have our own consumer-based constituency to promote support for education seemed a neat idea. But neighborhood representatives had their own ideas about what they wanted. We became the goat, not the agent of deliverance." Like many of the community action agencies of the late '60s and Model Cities agencies of the early '70s, the board of education found that it had incorporated community-based conflicts into its very structure, leading to a perpetual state of indecision and endless dispute.

ARE PARTICIPATION AND THE SHARPENING OF ISSUES ENOUGH?

Some planners argue that a forceful exchange of ideas among planning board members may be a sufficient goal in itself. "Why shouldn't conflicts get sharpened and fought out within our own agencies?" asks a former poverty worker. "What better place is there?" In encouraging citizen participation, he argues, it is more important to liberate ideas and to get people involved than to win on specific planning objectives.

"I'm not worried about the possibility that involvement might impede innovation," explains a social planner. "That's a short-term consideration. I'm concerned about the long-range effects of participation. Too many people have been squeezed out of the system. I want them to do some squeezing now—to squeeze their way back in and put the squeeze on others. I want to get the disenfranchised back into the body politic. Until we do, no amount of mucking around by well intentioned, even skilled, planners is going to make any difference." The goal is a political one in the best American tradition.

Sometimes the political process backfires, however, as the following vignette illustrates. In part this may have been because the planners were not fully comfortable with the end-means dichotomy discussed earlier. In part it failed because participation was not perceived in the same way by those organizing and those being organized.

Task forces were used to conduct surveys by the Governor's Office on Aging in a New England state prior to the development of a bill to establish new service centers. "The process was phenomenal," reported a staff member of the Governor's Office. "We had every area of the state blanketed by task forces. Half the members of each task force were people over 65 or others who we knew had the interest of older people at heart. Other task force members included local government representatives and service agency administrators. We know our people, and we knew we could make our task forces representative.

"Each task force was organized around a special area of concern—transportation, health care, nutrition, education, home supportive services, and so on. We didn't just want citizen input in deciding what the problems were and identifying the program—we also wanted task force members to become involved through real jobs. These people went out and administered our state-wide questionnaire to thousands of concerned individuals, many of them senior citizens. By the end of the process, not only had we gathered all the information we needed, but we assured ourselves of good PR—we had gotten out to the communities and the communities knew they were involved. What's more, they knew we cared.

"When we finally published our report and submitted it to the legislature, it documented what we had been saying all along, but this time in the words of older people themselves. As one of our volunteers put it when he saw the report, 'Hey, that's what I said, that's tellin' 'em. It's about time the politicians got the word directly from us.' " But not everyone agreed.

"Talk about manipulation," wrote a retired social worker about our procedure in a letter to the editor of a widely read morning paper. "The state planners had us gathering their data for free. Think of all that manpower going out there filling in the blanks in a prestructured questionnaire. All people had to say was *yes* or *no* to a list of pre-established priorities. They had no voice in what went on those priority lists. This was the biggest piece of 'public relations' imaginable."

The state planner was thunderstruck on reading the letter. "We did everything we could to give people a sense of involvement," he protested. What he did not understand was that there are many levels of involvement, and that involving older people or community residents at one level when they want to be involved at another is not satisfactory. Nor is it necessarily sufficient.

THE DILEMMAS OF PARTICIPATION AND PARTISANSHIP

Although almost all social planners subscribe to the notion of "participatory democracy," for many this notion poses a dilemma. It is not easy to exploit the potential vitality of participation while at the same time subordinating it to instrumental objectives.

Reform in America has always been achieved through the tugs and pulls of vested interests. Reform is based on partisanship. Unfortunately, partisan efforts at reform often collapse for lack of secure and true representation of the interests of particular populations. Building a base on perceived client or consumer interests may result in expanding only the most parochial and unimaginative of concerns.

Social planners may face other dilemmas as well. They may be committed to institutional cooperation on the one hand and to particular populations on the other. Partisanship strategies are not always easily reconciled with cooperative and integrative strategies. Even if *pooling* a number of interests and *distributing* the benefits to those populations in need are part of the same process, planners who make a commitment to one mode sometimes find themselves branded as partisan advocates or as do-nothings. Faced with difficult choices, planners may at times choose to assuage dissident populations and organizations. At other times they will seek compromise and accommodation, perhaps through helping dissidents redefine their interests.

In other circumstances, a planner may attempt to put the confrontation of differences in sharper perspective. Treating local areas as communities of homogeneous interests may keep the waters superficially calm but may also submerge the interests of those citizens with the least political clout. Yet, stirring up the waters often results in loss of control and may reduce the likelihood of specific goal accomplishment.

These dilemmas are not easily resolved. They are the outgrowths of a competitive, pluralistic society. They are, perhaps, inherent in the very structure of American society.

Review

Citizen participation in the form of volunteer groups, ad hoc lay service networks, self-help groups, and the like can be used effectively to increase the capability of agencies and professional providers to give service. Participation and advocacy are related when planners use participation for political purposes. The participation of community groups often serves to buffer the planner's activity, to legitimate his efforts, or to petition for a planning objective.

Participants are often involved as members of boards, task forces, advocacy committees, and coalitions. Boards set policy, review programs and budgetary decisions, hire or fire key personnel, and establish job classifications. Members are either elected or appointed. Task forces may be appointed by a board, by an executive officer, or by the planner. They are generally limited to a particular assignment to be completed within a designated time. While a task force may gather data or make recommendations, it is rarely responsible for the final decision or its implementation. The same is true of advisory groups. Members of advisory groups, however, may draw this authority from other groups or populations they are deemed to represent rather than from the presumed expertise of individual members. Yet their function and authority are generally circumscribed.

Coalitions are generally convened by the planner or some other interested party. They do not depend on any outside authority for their mandate or existence. Generally ad hoc in nature, they remain together until they have accomplished their common goal.

Although participants are often recruited individually to work on task forces, boards, coalitions, and committees, planners frequently encourage citizen participation by involving civic associations. Many of these groups are concerned with the general welfare of the community. Others, including professional associations, fraternal groups, and mutual aid societies, may be motivated by self-interest or by a desire to be of service to particular populations in the community.

Some planners work directly with citizen groups to solve specific problems they perceive in the configuration of services or the distribution of resources. These planners may view participation as a goal in itself or as a way of ensuring the perpetuation of democracy at the grass roots level. However, this may lead to the dilemma of having to choose between the goals of participation per se and that of implementing explicit changes in the human services system.

Such dilemmas are not easy to resolve. They are the outgrowths of the pluralistic society that is both the cause and the consequence of such participation.

SUPPLEMENTARY QUESTIONS AND ACTIVITIES

1. Using a planning agency familiar to you, examine the extensiveness with which it has employed consumer or citizen involvement in its planning efforts. Does the agency state in its policy directives why these persons are to be involved in the planning efforts? What reasons are given? Do these "stated" reasons differ from the "real" reason for their involvement? How?

2. Examine the extent to which you (or a planner whose work is familiar to you) become involved with groups representing the general community. Do you think that work with civic associations might detract from the time you (or the planner) could spend working directly with representatives of minority populations or the poor (especially when neither the poor nor the minorities are heavily involved in those associations)? Is the cost in time worth the investment?

3. Identify the potential conflict between involvement of citizens to support planning in general and their involvement to support development of services for particular populations.

4. Are there contradictions between the strategic uses of citizen participation to buffer, legitimize, or petition on behalf of a program or project, and the objectives of involvement of low-income and minority persons? What are they? How may they be overcome, or better still, made more complementary?

5. Define the responsibilities of an agency's board, advisory panels, or task forces. Are these responsibilities clear to everyone concerned? How are members selected? Who does the selecting and how? To whom are they responsible?

6. Analyze the reasons why an agency known to you personally has participated in one or more coalitions. How did the agency benefit? Who else benefited? How? Why did the coalition not last indefinitely? Did it evolve into another more permanent structure or pattern of relationships?

7. Three vignettes on citizen participation follow. Read them over. Then answer the following questions. You might find it useful to discuss your thoughts with others in a class or social agency.
   a. Does this planner's perspective, style, or ideological position differ from your own? How?
   b. In the situation described, does the planner make the correct strategic decision? Would you have acted in a similar manner? If there is more than one correct decision, what are others?
   c. Under what circumstances might you act in the way or ways described by the planner? Do you act that way now? Why or why not? Are the circumstances in your situation different? How?
   d. Do you have the knowledge and skill needed to perform at the level described in the vignette? At a higher level? In which areas do you need more training, experience, or just plain information?

MR. CARMADY TELLS IT LIKE IT IS (VIGNETTE NO. 1)[1]

"When I first got to this city I decided the best way to get to know it was to walk through it. I wanted to get a feel for its neighborhoods. I wanted to get to know the downtown area, to speak with the shopkeepers, find out where all the people lived.

[1]Note: This is an expanded version of a vignette appearing in Joan Levin Ecklein and Armand Lauffer, *Community Organizers and Social Planners*. New York: John Wiley & Sons, 1972.

"It was late August when we moved here. The first thing that struck my eye was how many older people seemed to hang around the downtown area aimlessly with almost nothing to do. A park at the civic center was always full of older people. I decided to call on some of the clergymen and the downtown businessmen to talk about what we could do. Someone suggested I contact the recreation department. I did. They were sympathetic, but explained they were already expending a larger share of their budget on older people than the numbers of the elderly warranted. I got their brochure on adult education classes and occasional senior citizen square dances. It was obvious that a lot of people were interested but nobody was concerned enough to take the bull by the horns.

"As the new staff planner with the Welfare Council, I thought it would make sense for me to take the bull by the horns. I called together a 'downtown advisory committee'—somebody from the Mayor's office, somebody from the recreation department, a priest from the archdiocese, three people from the Junior Chamber of Commerce, two merchants from the Downtown Business Association, and a couple of retired school teachers who lived in the area and were well respected. It was 'textbook perfect' in its composition: all the right people.

ADVISORY COMMITTEE AND EXPERTS

"Our first advisory committee meeting was in early September, right after Labor Day. I put a small notice in the paper indicating that anybody who wanted to come was welcome. I invited a couple of sociologists from the university who had made studies of the downtown area. They were ready to testify on the needs of senior adults in the city. One of them had already told me that their studies showed the top priority was development of a downtown multi-service center for older people. I had done my homework, too. One of the merchants had a large store building that had remained unrented for several years. If the area Agency on Aging or somebody else would fix it up, he would donate it rent-free as a downtown walk-in.

"The meeting was going well; people seemed to agree that they wanted to work together. My sociologists said all the right things. My merchant made his offer. I was already congratulating myself on the big success I was going to be after only two months on the job. Others began to suggest how they might contribute their services to the development of a program at the center. It was incredible. I was just about to ask for a subcommittee to work on writing out a project proposal, when one of a handful of older people who had dropped in to observe the meeting raised his hand.

" 'We don't need a downtown center for older folks,' he protested. 'Most of the older folks don't live in this area. We just come here during the summer months, because it's warm and there's nothing to do in our neighborhoods. Come October, it'll be too cold to come downtown. And then we won't have anything to do and no place to go. All those old people in the park are there two months of the year, that's all. Besides, there are hundreds of older folks who can't afford the bus fare. They never come downtown. Some of my friends can't even step up on the steps of the bus. Look mister, I don't want to hurt your feelings. But I'm telling you like it is.'

"For a couple of minutes I didn't know what to say. The old man had really taught me something. How was it that I had never thought of asking any of the old people I'd seen what they thought was needed? How come I asked people to a meeting who were in the prime of their lives? I had to do a doublethink about older people. After all, they hadn't always been older people. They were in the prime of their lives once, too."

Picking Leadership for Advisory Panels and Task Forces (Vignette No. 2)

"I'm not one of your professional planners. I started out being active on more committees and association boards than you could shake a stick at. I guess it's because I'm pretty well known and can count almost all the community influentials in my circle that I was offered the job of directing the coordinating council. So I'm pretty savvy about leadership.

BALANCING MEMBERSHIP

"I try to balance my committees and task forces with different kinds of people. All depends on what my objectives are. If I need to confer a lot of legitimacy on a project, give it high visibility, if it's a project of large scope or magnitude, I'm going to look for the people who are leaders because of their positions—top corporation executives, powerful clergymen, those with a big social reputation. These are the people who are known to be "doers." Now, I know they're not doers. I know they play only ceremonial roles. They're doers in their jobs, where they play their primary community role. When I put them on a committee or a panel, that's a secondary role, and they expect the staff to do all the work. But their presence sure makes it easier for the staff to do the job. Up to a point, that is.

"Most of these top leaders, the ones with the reputation for action, don't work well together. It's hard to get them to operate as a team. They're more interested in giving sanction to a project than in getting it accomplished. You can't get much other than newspaper publicity, maybe an occasional evening soiree and some good pictures from them. But maybe that's enough.

COMMITMENT

"If you want a committee of people who will work together on things, you've got to select them on the basis of their interdependence and their commitment to a particular goal. The project you've got them working on has to have payoff for them in terms of their primary jobs. Unlike that first group of top leaders, who are proponents of good "things in general," these are going to be your proponents of "things in particular." You pick them because they know what they want and they know what they're here for. And you pick them because you can trust them. You put them on a task force, because you know that each needs the other in order to get the task done.

"You've got to be careful, though, about task force composition. If you put a guy with a big leadership reputation on there, will it intimidate the others? If you have the head of the public transportation agency and the director of the public welfare agency, can you put the woman who heads up the volunteer services bureau on that task force too? Or—even if she's the most knowledgeable and most logical person in terms of commitment—will her lack of status and position count against her? It's a little like teaming up agency administrators with caseworkers and paraprofessionals and expecting them to interact around common concerns. It hardly ever works that way.

"Still, you do have to load the task force with the people who have the most at stake in getting something done, or in stopping something from happening. I always fill every committee or task force two-thirds with people who have a big stake in the task, and up to one-third with people who are neutral or opposed.

"That means you've got to know your people, and you've got to check them out in advance. There's no taking chances in this business. Things don't happen just because you get a lot of nice or well-meaning people together. It's who the people are, how you group them, and what the task is that makes the difference."

Mental Health Services for Teens (Vignette No. 3)

"Most mental health programs in my city are geared to middle-aged adults and children. Almost no services are provided for teenagers. I've wanted to do something about that for a long time. I got my chance when my boss, the director of the Community Mental Health Center, allowed me to set up a task force on problems of teens. The impetus was clearly some news articles about teenage alcoholism. But I didn't care what the reason was. I welcomed the opportunity.

"At first there was a reluctance on the part of my task force members to look deeply into the needs of teenagers. It meant examining the services that their agencies were currently providing or not providing. The task force people were mostly mental health agency administrators who had not been directing much service to teens and young adults. Some in fact refused to regard them as a distinct population. But I'm a 'doer' and a 'prober' and people expect me to play my role that way.

PROBING, PUSHING, AND SELLING

"People know when they sit on one of my task forces that I'm not going to let them sit back until we identify the real issues. So when I begin playing my usual role, they say 'Oh, here he goes again.' But they let me do it. You see, I press hard, but I also build up people's egos. I congratulate them for their past efforts. I try to build up their contributions. I say everything positive I can about their agencies. And I don't force anybody to make a commitment in front of his colleagues.

"Once I get something on the table, I'll wind up with, 'Well, I'm glad we started discussing this; we'll work it out. Charlie, how about you and I talking on the phone?' or 'Marie, I've wanted to take a charming gal like you to lunch for a long time. How about Thursday?' That's how I work. Half of me is doing a major selling job, and half of me is charming the pants off my colleagues. I talk up the opportunity of doing something significant for people who are really in need. I talk up the possibility of a pioneering effort, something that might have state-wide or national significance. I bring in examples of things done elsewhere that were almost as good as what we could do here, but not quite as good. What I'm trying to do is show them that something *can* be done, that it already *has* been done, but that with some imagination and a little gumption we can do it better. I don't use the same selling techniques with everyone. For those who are sharp, I use a very direct and open approach. They'd read through me any other way. For others, the job may require selling myself, making sure they will have confidence in my suggestions. It may even mean promising some resources or offering help in getting resources they need for something else. I'm the first one to suggest or respond affirmatively to a tradeoff. If you want to get anything done in this business, you've got to know what the other fellow needs.

OPERATIONALIZING AN IDEA

"Once the decision was made to develop a mental health program for teens, it was my job to do the really hard work of spelling out the possibilities. I had to find a location for the new program. I had to find somebody who was willing to take it on. I had to consider organizing the new program separately under its own board of directors, or incorporating it into one of the existing agencies. It meant checking with the agencies to find one that might want to take it on, and then feeling out the reactions of the others. It also meant finding new sources of funding and promising to help the sponsor of the program get the needed staff, as well as retrain some of his current staff. If you get someone to meet you halfway, you've got to meet him too.

"I get involved very intensively in these initial stages of the project. I don't do all the work myself, but I spend a lot of time with task force members helping them to understand and clarify the issues. I do a lot of spade work, a lot of telephoning, and a lot of opening doors. By the time we get to the stage where we can start to write a proposal, I begin to withdraw. I feel I've done my job. But I'll come back in and offer my assistance when the new service system gets off the ground. They'll need my help again in finding the right personnel, defining the task properly, developing their advisory groups and boards. I've developed a reputation for not letting people down. I don't talk anybody into anything he can't handle or that I'm not willing to help him handle. Being a doer means being around when they need you."

Recommended Readings

BURKE, EDMUND M. "Citizen Participation Strategies." *Journal of the American Institute of Planners,* September 1968.
Although contributions to the literature on citizen participation have been extensive during the past ten years, the reader will still find most of the critical issues discussed in this article. Burke lays out a number of citizen participation strategies, pointing out that they emerge from the planner's ideology, the ends to which participation is employed, and the means most readily available.

Journal of the American Institute of Planners, July, 1969.
This is a special issue devoted exclusively to the use of citizen participation in the planning process. Although *JAIP* generally focuses more extensively on urban and regional (physical and economic) planning, social planning seems to be the major focus here. In particular, see the following:
Sherry A. Arnstein, "A Ladder of Citizen Participation"; Melvin Mogaloff, "Coalition to Adversary: Citizen Participation in Three Federal Programs"; Martin Rein, "Social Planning: The Search for Legitimacy"; Roland L. Warren, "Model Cities, First Round: Politics, Planning and Participation."

Suggestions for Further Reading

AUSTIN, DAVID M. "Dilemmas of Participation." Paper presented at the Annual Forum of the National Conference on Social Welfare, Chicago, May, 1969.

BARBER, JAMES D. (Ed.). *Power to the Citizen: Introductory Readings.* Chicago, Ill.: Rand McNally, 1972.

BRAEGER, GEORGE, and HARRY SPECHT. *Community Organizing,* The Social Work and Social Issues Series. New York: Columbia University Press, April, 1973.

CLAVEL, PIERRE. "Planners and Citizens' Boards: Some Applications of Social Theory to Plan Implementation." *Journal of the American Institute of Planners,* May, 1960.

COX, FRED M., et al. (Eds.). *Strategies of Community Organizations: A Book of Readings.* Itasca, Ill.: F. E. Peacock Publishers, 1973. See especially the articles by Rothman, Erlich, and Alinsky.

ECKLEIN, JOAN LEVIN, and ARMAND LAUFFER. *Community Organizers and Social Planners: A Volume of Case and Illustrative Materials.* New York: John Wiley and Sons, 1972. See chaps. 2 and 3.

FISCHER, CONSTANCE T., and STANLEY L. BRODSKY. *Human Services Knowledge, Power, and Responsibility.* New Brunswick, N. J.: Transaction Books, 1977.

FREDERICKSON, GEORGE. *Neighborhood Control in the 1970's: Politics, Administration, and Citizen Participation.* Scranton, Pa.: Intext Educational Publishers, 1970.

GLENN, NORVAL, and MICHAEL GRIMES. "Aging, Voting, and Political Interest." *American Sociological Review,* August, 1968.

GURIN, ARNOLD, and JOAN ECKLEIN. "Community Organization for What?—Political Power or Service Delivery." *Social Work Practice.* New York: Columbia University Press, 1968.

HARTOGS, NELLY, and JOSEPH WEKER. *Boards of Directors.* New York: Oceana Publications, Inc., 1974.

MARRIS, PETER, and MARTIN REIN. *Dilemmas of Social Reform.* New York: Aferton Press, 1967.

McSURLEY, ALAN. *Getting and Keeping People Together.* Louisville, Ky.: Southern Conference Education Fund, 1967.

MELVIN, ERNEST E. "The Planner and Citizen Participation." *Journal of the Community Development Society,* 1974, *5*(1), 40–48.

MOGULOF, MELVIN B. *Citizen Participation: The Local Perspective.* The Urban Institute. Washington, D.C., 1970.

NOLL, RACHAEL P. "Can Elderly Volunteers Help the Elderly?" *Journal of Human Relations,* January, 1967.

Participation Today: Proceedings of a Staff Conference. U. S. Department of Housing and Urban Development, Regions IV and V, Chicago, June 1968.

PERLMAN, ROBERT, and ARNOLD GURIN. *Community Organization and Social Planning.* New York: John Wiley and Sons, 1972. See especially chap. 5.

Public Welfare. The Journal of American Public Welfare Association. Spring, 1972. Special issue on the question of advocacy.

REIN, MARTIN, and S. M. MILLER. "Social Action on the Installment Plan." *Transaction,* January–February, 1970.

ROSENGREN, WILLIAM R., and MARK LIFTON. *Organizations and Clients: Essays in the Sociology of Service.* Columbus, Ohio: Charles E. Merrill, 1970.

ROTHMAN, JACK. *Planning and Organizing for Social Change: Action Principles from Social Science Research.* New York: Columbia University Press, 1974. See especially chaps. 7 and 8.

SHOSTAK, ARTHUR B. "Promoting Participation of the Poor: Philadelphia's Anti-Poverty Program." *Social Work,* January 1966.

STEELE, MARILYN. "Citizen Participation in the Planning/Evaluation Process: Brief Case Studies of Wilmington, Grand Rapids, Genesee County Drug Commission and Mott Children's Health Center." *Community Education Journal,* 1975, *5,* 28–31.

TRECKER, HARLEIGH B. *Citizen Boards at Work: New Challenges to Effective Action.* New York: Association Press, 1970.

VON HOFFMAN, NICHOLAS. "Reorganization in the Casbah." *Social Progress,* April, 1962.

WARREN, RACHELLE B., and DONALD I. WARREN. *The Neighborhood Organization Handbook.* Notre Dame: University of Notre Dame Press, 1977.

16

The Planner as an Advocate*

Social Advocacy and Legal Advocacy

The term "advocacy" figures prominently in social legislation on behalf of youth, the mentally retarded, the aging, oppressed minorities, and others. It refers to efforts to represent the interests of specific populations, to reallocate resources in their favor, or to provide services to them. Although rooted in the history and tradition of legal advocacy, social advocacy has characteristics of its own. The distinctions between social and legal advocacy are instructive.

In general, the legal advocate derives the authority to represent a client's interests directly from that client as prescribed by law. The planner, as social advocate, usually does not; his or her authority may stem directly from a legislative mandate, or from the stated purposes of the organization in which he or she is employed. Thus legal advocates are almost always directly accountable to those they represent, but social advocates are accountable to the organizations that employ them—not directly to the population on whose behalf they advocate. This status may create a problem for some planners.

It is not unusual for there to be conflicts of interest between clients or client populations, on the one hand, and social agencies and service providers,

---

*Many of the concepts in this chapter were developed by John Tropman and William Lawrence of the University of Michigan when they, together with the author, worked on a project to train area planners in the field of aging.

on the other. Whether the agency is the planner's employer or one with which the planner must regularly interact, a dilemma is inevitable. Sometimes planners find themselves playing down client interests when these conflict with the aims of social agencies whose trust they perceive as essential to maintain. This, of course, may jeopardize needed trust and support of consumers. At better times the planner must try to hang loose, disassociating him or herself from the interests of service providers whom the planner's target population may view with mistrust, with those of the population for which the planner advocates. It is never easy to decide with whom to align oneself at any planning stage.

There are other conspicuous differences from the legal model. For one thing, it presumes no need for a personal commitment on the part of the advocate to his or her client or the client population represented. The converse is usually true of the social advocate. Without a strong personal and professional commitment to a population in need, to their rights, or to a cause, the social planner may not be sufficiently fortified to perform his advocacy functions appropriately or consistently.

The procedures used by the legal advocate are generally prescribed in traditional law. Legal mechanisms exist through which an attorney represents his clients—courts, review boards, and so on. This is rarely the case for the social advocate. Few structures or mechanisms are yet standardized for the resolution of conflict when it occurs. This means that the social planner–advocate may find him or herself challenged on the means if not on the goals of his or her advocacy.

It also means that social advocacy often becomes highly political. The merits of a case are argued not in legal, but in political terms. The questions are: "Who gets what, when, and where?" and "Do we have enough power or good will on our side to get it?" In the American legal system, the adversary posture is the basis upon which clients are represented and conflicts resolved; it is also the standard by which lawyers are often evaluated. But the adversary role is often problematic for the social planner. On the one hand, the political nature of social advocacy requires that the planner represent the interests of a particular client population. On the other, the political process itself requires that the planner be willing to compromise, to delay action, or to drop an issue altogether when its pursuit may adversely affect attainment of another goal.

Planners and the Plurality of Interests

"When we first started out," explains a planner concerned with expansion of child welfare services, "the word 'advocacy' was the highest on our list of priorities. But we hadn't fully thought through the implications of an advocate position. You can't just assume that everybody really wants to help kids, or that it's simply a matter of coming up with some ideas, some good public relations, and some new money. Far from it, as we discovered. Service agencies, especially, were often more concerned with their own survival or growth needs and the interests of their staff than with the interests of their clients.

"When I tried some gentle pressure, they pushed back. Before I knew it, my own boss was telling me to tone it down. I did, and I didn't. I decided to take a back seat and leave the driving to those groups who felt themselves most directly affected—the Association of Parents of Retarded Children and a number of civic associations that had done a lot in the field. My work, I reasoned, was going to be more effective, if I could help them become more effective."

Every planner knows that there may be a plurality of interests around any issue. Because it may be difficult to advocate "out front" in promoting the interests of one group over another, some planners direct their efforts toward helping client populations form to advocate on their own behalf. Thus, client populations are helped to: (1) formulate their own opinions about what needs to be done and how to do it; (2) gain access to the technical skill or ability they may need for formulating strategies to rectify problematic situations; and (3) represent their own interests where it counts—where decisions are made, resources allocated, and services provided.

For some planners, the logical consequence of assuming an advocacy position is to subject themselves to control by those groups for whom they advocate. Although rare, this is closest to the legal model, in which the advocate is employed by a particular interest group. In other situations, where the planner is not employed directly by the client group, he or she may try to ensure that the interests of certain populations are represented through their participation on boards, panels, and advisory committees.

ADVOCATE PLANNERS AS PROTAGONISTS OF PARTICULAR INTERESTS

"As far as I can see, all plans are the embodiments of particular interests," explains an area planner for the aging. "We're not here to represent the public interest or the general good. We're here to represent the interests of older people, especially the most disadvantaged older people. Objectively, there is no 'best' plan," he continues. "What's best is what the people we represent feel is best. It's not something you figure out on paper and come to some rational agreement on; it's something you fight out in the interorganizational arena. As an area planner, I can't afford to look out for everybody's interests. Let others do it for their own constituencies. We'll fight for ours."

As the area planner quoted above so forcefully summed it up, advocate planners generally attempt to make the most effective case for their positions, not necessarily the most reasoned one. They must be willing to accept the possibility—often the necessity—of confronting groups whose interests clash with those of the populations or clients they represent. But victory does not have to be absolute. Nor does it have to result in absolute losses for the other side. When planning is viewed in its sociopolitical context, planners often scale their demands for change to strategic considerations. "It's not how much you *should* get or settle for; it's what you *can* get without endangering your position or the position of the people on whose behalf you're advocating," explains another planner.

Many planners assume that the conflicts of interests that lead to an advocacy posture are best resolved when they are made explicit. Some argue that promoting change on behalf of any group requires explicit confrontation.

REDISTRIBUTIVE AND INTEGRATIVE ADVOCACY

A number of planners quoted throughout the text express a position termed *partisan advocacy* (see Chapter 1). Redistributive in its orientation, this position is based on the assumption that some members of society have been unfairly deprived of access to needed services, and that the planner or planning agency has a duty to strengthen the position of the deprived population vis-à-vis those social institutions that provide or distribute human services. The underlying assumption is that a conflict of interests must necessarily lead to a redistribution of resources among competing parties.

INTEGRATIVE ADVOCACY

Many of the other planners quoted tend to reflect another form of advocacy in their practice, one that assumes a difference in interests but does not necessarily lead to conflict. These planners' advocacy activities are generally directed at securing for their clients those rights and services that are mandated under existing law or policy, but are denied them in actual practice. Denial, they assume, may not be intentional. It may stem from ignorance or lack of skill on the part of service providers, or ill will and inappropriate attitudes on the part of some staff members of a human service agency. Or perhaps it results from the use of administrative methods or of service approaches that are inappropriate to specific client populations.

Although the interests of clients and of agencies may not be identical, the goals of each may be met through better integration of the two; that is, through the establishment of better linking mechanisms between them. Such mechanisms, we recall, include the establishment of information and referral systems, volunteer bureaus, and staff training and community education, as well as the use of ombudsmen, grievance machinery, and social brokerage techniques.

The creation of an information and referral system may reflect the planner's interest in making services more accessible or in assuring referral to appropriate services and follow-ups. In many instances, an I and R system may provide complementary benefits to service agencies by reducing agency intake costs and enhancing the organization's own efforts at referral or coordination of services. Similarly, as volunteers find new cases, foster more personalized services, and even engage in social brokerage, they extend the agency's ability to provide services and become integrative forces in their own right.

Frequently the distinctions between integrative and redistributive or partisan advocacy are not all that clear in practice. For example, grievance machinery may be used to correct systemic flaws and right individual grievances, or it may be used to redistribute decision-making power within an agency. Demands by residents of a housing project for proportionate representation on the tenants' council may result in greater integration of residents into many other community activities. Whether a particular strategy is labeled integrative or redistributive depends on how it unfolds. Many strategies are both, simultaneously or sequentially.

Selecting the Right Approach

To be an effective advocate in a variety of situations, the planner must be able to shift from a redistributive to an integrative strategy, from conflict to cooperation, from a vigorous and highly visual style, to a more low-keyed or behind-the-scenes approach. The factors to be considered in the conscious selection of a strategy and approach include the issue itself; the planner's position on the issue and the stances of relevant others; the salience of the issue to the population affected; the degree of political solidarity of the target population; the extensiveness of public support for the issue or for the population in question.

THE ISSUE ITSELF

How "hot" is the issue? Whether or not the state correctional agency should locate a halfway house in a particular suburban community may be a hot issue. Reduction in property taxes for retired persons may not be. When an issue is hot, it often makes sense for the planner to take a low-keyed, mild approach. Playing the game behind the scenes may make more sense than becoming a highly visible torch bearer. Most planners, after all, can't afford to be single issue proponents. They must deal with many issues and maintain ongoing working relationships with many groups.

When an issue is buried somewhere and threatens to remain so, it may make sense to take a more robust stance. For example, the planner may choose to become personally identified with a movement to remove the architectural barriers for handicapped persons in order to make the issue itself more visible.

No single issue ever stands in isolation. The problems of architectural barriers for the handicapped may be related to zoning regulations, to the scheduling and routing of public transportation, and other issues. When more than one or two issues intersect, choices may have to be made. Will a strong partisan stance on removing architectural barriers (high steps) from city buses result in such conflict that an integrative strategy that might call for slight alterations in bus routing or scheduling be rendered ineffective?

THE PLANNER'S POSITION

Planners can get typed. If they always take a partisan or redistributive position on issues, these actions tend to become predictable and may lose effectiveness. "Jerry's brilliant, and usually right on most issues," the director of a welfare council explains. "But he always comes on so strong for kids in trouble that his contributions are rejected before he ever makes them. It's not that he is dismissed for being a single issue man. He's dismissed because he always comes on the same way."

Although planners must generally be consistent to be effective, they do not have to be fully predictable in their actions and responses. No matter how justified a cause may seem, it may be necessary to drop one issue in favor of another one. It is rarely possible to fight all battles on all fronts at the same time. The selection of an issue may be militated by the choice of preferred strategy. If a planner is convinced that the partisan strategy needed to win on one issue would do irreparable harm to other agency relationships, he or she might opt for another issue that requires a more integrative approach. Sometimes letting an issue ride today makes it possible to win on a larger and more important issue tomorrow.

Changing one's specific objective, or one's strategy and approach, need not reflect inconsistency. On the contrary, accommodating one's course of action to changes in an issue environment may be the way to be consistent. Consistency can be best measured over time; not in relationship to a temporary strategic shift or tactical side step.

The planner's stance is often affected by the attitudes of the other participants. How do employers, funders, or policy makers stand on the issue? Are they strongly in favor of a given objective or recommended action—strongly opposed—neutral? Are they preoccupied with the issue? Will they let the planner win this round in order to get support for their positions on another issue? Last but not least, the effect of the various personalities involved must be taken into account. Is conflict natural or comfortable for the planner? Or is a cooperative strategy more congenial? Is the planner more effective working out front or behind the scenes and through others? The advocate must know not only his or her own strengths and weaknesses, but those of his subordinates and collaborators as well. In that way, maximal use can be made of everyone's talents.

SALIENCE OF THE ISSUE

As we saw in the vignette entitled, "Mr. Carmady Tells It Like It Is," strategic decisions should not rest entirely on the predispositions of the planner and those with whom he or she interacts. The choice of a strategy and approach must also reflect the salience or importance of an issue to those affected most directly. The interests of older persons, for example, may be promoted through tax relief and/or housing subsidies; meals on wheels and/or more liberal use of food stamps; escort services and/or reduced fare for public transportation. One or more of these programs may have a great deal of public support but be of little interest to the aging. Another program may be of interest to a vocal group of senior citizens, but may not generate even a note of recognition from others.

How are choices to be made? Who determines which choice is of greatest importance or salience? If it is impossible to poll members of the population in question, the planner may be forced to use indirect means such as consumer analysis in seeking information on preferred programs. At other times, the population(s) whose interests are being considered may be sufficiently cohesive to permit direct polling.

Some planners, in fact, organize constituencies for the explicit purpose of involving them in choices about programs and services. In the first vignette of Chapter 1, the planner consciously developed cohesive groups of older persons in order to build up his constituency and to make their interests more visible. But in the third illustration, the planners who were no less advocates in their positions chose to identify the most salient issues through staff conducted studies. Both approaches are equally correct. They depend on the planner and his style, what is considered appropriate by his or her employing organization, and the extent to which the population in question is or can become politically cohesive.

POLITICAL SOLIDARITY

Where it already exists or can be generated, the political power of the population for whom the social planner advocates can be a significant factor in the choice of a strategy. Situations in which there is actual or perceived solidarity in the ranks of a population are rare, however. More often, the planner may find him or herself in the role of organizer, attempting to generate both solidarity and clout so that members of a socially disenfranchised group can more adequately advocate on their own behalf. The planner may concentrate on locating those issues around which an organizational effort might be based. At times this requires selecting an issue around which broader public support may be generated.

PUBLIC SUPPORT

The political power of a target population often depends on the public's willingness to support that group on a particular issue. As a result of any number of factors, the interests or needs of a particular population may be highlighted and a great deal of public sympathy may be expressed toward them. Other groups or causes may be temporarily unpopular. More often, perhaps, the general public will be indifferent to the needs of particular populations such as the aging, developmentally disabled children in need of adoptive placements, and similar groups.

By making people aware of an issue's potential relevance to them, public apathy can often be converted into public support. For example, everyone is growing older, and most adults have aging parents or relatives. Perhaps harder to see, the early care of children with special problems may reduce the costs of more extensive services at a later date; and services to the mentally ill and to offender populations may reduce the likelihood of extended illness and repeat offenses. Yet these societal concerns may be far removed from everyday interests. Even if perceived, public support does not follow automatically. Thus the planner may find that an effective advocacy strategy requires an effective public information and community education program as well as other supportive activities.

Supportive Activities

Activities that are supportive of integrative and redistributive advocacy have been discussed throughout the text. They include the use of (1) studies; (2) consumer analysis; (3) technical assistance and consultation; (4) legislative action; (5) community education; and (6) citizen and consumer participation. Each activity is recapitulated briefly.

STUDIES

Studies may be focused on selected problems or on the needs of deprived populations in the community such as the rural poor, residents of an inner-city neighborhood, or a minority group. They may be used to highlight problems, to suggest solutions, or to develop priorities. They may also be used to involve or to recruit citizens and consumer groups to take on the mantle of partisan advocacy.

CLIENT ANALYSIS

Client analysis focuses on the discrepancies between actual and potential client populations. It examines the reasons potential clients do not seek or receive service. It frequently emphasizes the obstacles to service in agency procedures, regulations, resource distribution, or systems of accountability. It plots the anticipated growth or decline of consumer needs over time and examines the implications of manipulating the identified blockages. Client or consumer analysis is discussed in more detail in Chapter 11.

TECHNICAL ASSISTANCE

Technical assistance and consultation may be offered either to the provider or the consumer of services. An advocate planner might choose to concentrate his or her efforts on increasing the knowledge and skill of agency personnel, believing that this will lead to the provision of more adequate services. Or the planner may provide consultation to individual consumers through development of an ombudsman service or an information and referral system. Another advocate will feel that only organized consumers and an alert public can effect needed changes in service programs. This may lead to the provision of technical assistance to interested civic associations and self-help organizations. The planner may organize or recruit such groups to work on a specific project or limit his or her efforts to helping them identify the issues they think are important.

LEGISLATIVE ACTION

Many advocate planners feel that influencing the legislative process may have the greatest payoff in the long run. They argue that government is too often the province of a few. These planners often attempt to influence the drafting of new laws at the local, county, and state levels that will affect the delivery of services. Changes may also be needed in other laws not directly concerned with services—zoning regulations, park development appropriations, or bonding bills, for example—that affect the quality of life and the choices available to specific groups of people.

COMMUNITY EDUCATION

Community education is often a critical step in effective planning and advocacy that usually precedes legislative action. Community education programs involve work with the press and allied news media; presentations to civic groups, churches, and fraternal organizations; information exchange with staff of social agencies and allied service providers; and publicity campaigns through any of the above. In many instances, the involvement of the population to be helped may optimize the effectiveness of an educational campaign.

Many planners view citizen participation and consumer involvement as tools of advocacy. The two terms, however, should not be confused. Advocates are concerned with *who benefits* from a process or action, while the citizen participation approach concentrates on *who is involved* in the process or activity.

Although conceptually distinct, participation and advocacy are often linked strategically. This is particularly true when planners involve consumers on their own behalf, or when they enlist other citizens in the aid of particular target populations.

The Costs and Benefits of an Advocacy Position

Although effective advocacy strategies may be rather complex, the advocate's posture per se is relatively uncomplicated. The planner's choices are all made within the context of a single question: "Will this particular course of action advance the interests of my clients or constituents relatively more than any other action?"

An advocacy position also assures the planner of a greater opportunity to deliver for a particular population. When one's efforts are concentrated, the chances of success are often improved. Social planners frequently achieve only limited success because they address diffuse issues and tend to be advocates in general rather than advocates for a particular group.

However, the costs of maintaining an advocate posture are considerable and should be well understood. The advocate must represent constituent interests whenever such representation is necessary, not just during the working day. Timing can be highly important. Once an action process is under way, the planner may be the only person able adequately to represent the interests of his or her constituents at meetings, conferences, and in private sessions.

A second cost lies in the stress of advocacy. Successful advocacy involves more than pushing constituents' interests at the expense of others' interests. It also involves maintaining a calculating posture toward others. The advocate planner may find it difficult to relax.

It is perhaps a truth that "everyone likes to be liked." It is sometimes easier to compromise on a client's interests than to take on one's colleagues at a staff meeting. Yet to be an advocate requires being a "difficult person" at least some of the time, and perhaps much of the time. Being a "nice guy" to some may seem like selling out to others. Advocates are not always liked, but good ones are respected.

"You have to be on constant alert against turning into just a nice guy," explains a planner. "The change too often occurs unconsciously. You find yourself spending more time with other planners and agency administrators than with the people you are supposed to be working for. Maybe it's necessary because agency administrators control the allocation of resources. But you find that there's an insidious and invidious pressure to develop greater appreciation for administrators' problems than for the problems of those you are trying to help."

At the worst, the advocate planner, removed from the pressing interests of his or her clients, may come to see him or herself as part of a community-wide human services elite whose mission extends beyond the narrow partisan-ship of specific parochial interests. If this happens, the planner's usefulness as an advocate is severely curtailed.

The danger of letting a client's interests slide is inherent in the position of advocate, but is perhaps a greater temptation among social than among legal advocates. The legal profession provides its practitioners with three years of intensive training in advocacy methods. Partisan advocacy is central to the courtroom drama. It has not yet been defined as central to social service work, and it receives very little attention in the curriculum of services preparing practitioners for work in the human service professions. The lawyer is able to avoid taking attacks personally, realizing his opponent is just another lawyer pressing for advantage on behalf of his client. Social services workers have no such rigorous training in advocacy, and so are less well equipped for the role. In fact, the norms in many human service professions generally operate in the direction of cooperation rather than redistribution, reducing the range of strategic approaches available to many social planners at the community level.

Review

There are two forms of social advocacy. One is integrative. It assumes com-plementarity between the goals of consumers and those of providers, and that these goals may be met through better integrative mechanisms. The second, redistributive or partisan in its orientation, assumes actual or potential conflict of interest.

Integrative advocates use a variety of linking mechanisms to bring pro-viders and consumers together, among them Information and Referral systems, volunteer bureaus, community education, and social brokerage techniques. They may also engage in the use of studies, the provision of technical assistance and consultation, legislative action, the promotion of public relations, and the encouragement of citizen and consumer participation.

Redistributive advocates generally use more political and conflict ori-ented means. Both integrative and redistributive advocacy, however, should not be viewed as opposite approaches to representing the interests of particular population. Rather, these strategies represent points at different ends of a continuum. An advocate planner may move from a distributive to an integrative strategy as the situation requires. This situation is often affected by the issue itself, the planner's position on the issue, its salience to the population affected, the degree of solidarity of that population, and the extensiveness of public support for the issue or the population in question.

SUPPLEMENTARY QUESTIONS AND ACTIVITIES

1. Identify an issue around which you or your agency performed an advocacy role. Was it redistributive or integrative? At which stage or phase of the process? Which approach did significant others expect you to take? Who were these other persons?

2. List five issues around which a redistributive advocacy strategy is warranted.

3. List five issues around which a nonintegrative strategy is warranted.

4. If an issue appears on both lists, why? Is one strategy more appropriate than another? Or should both be used at different times or under different circumstances?

5. Look over the following vignette. How would you characterize the planner's advocacy posture? Is it integrative or partisan, or does it combine both approaches? How does it contrast with that of the social advocate whom you met in the first chapter of this book (illustration I)? If you had to make a guess, do you think both planners quoted are one and the same person? Why or why not?

WHO GETS WHAT, WHEN, AND HOW

"Practically everybody's a potential advocate of something. Those who aren't advocates are potential conservers of something. The trouble is, those who've got it want to keep it and those who don't have it aren't organized to get it. I don't mean to sound like a wild-eyed radical, but I am convinced the reasons Chicanos are overlooked by most service agencies is that they're simply unable to present their problem forcefully. The providers of service either don't see them or can't hear them because of a language problem. Minority groups have to make it clear that they have needs, and they want those needs to be met. Joe Hill once said, "Don't mourn for me, guys; organize!" I say, "Don't mourn your minority status, organize!"

"Look, it's like this. We're supposed to have freedom in this country, right? Well, most of the decisions that affect minority people aren't made by minorities. They're made by others who don't know anything about the needs of the Chicanos or orientals, or native Americans. When somebody at City Hall decides how public housing is to be designed he doesn't take into account the living patterns of the barrio. When the architect designs a low-income housing unit, he doesn't arrange the living patterns to reflect the social interaction among Chicano families.

"Spanish-speaking people are a minority. As individuals they are minorities of one. No one's going to listen to them. Together, they make up at best from one-eighth to one-fifth of the population. So they have got to get organized—that's the issue. Talk to some Chicanos like I did when I first got here. Here's the kind of attitude I heard expressed:

> The people in City Hall don't give a damn about us. It's a government for Anglos, not for us.
> Participate in your committees? Why? We have no influence. Nobody cares about us. You're just trying to con us. I've been conned enough in my time.
> Listen man, it's nice to know somebody's caring at last, but it won't make any difference. The decks are stacked against us. They just passed a new tax and put it on food and clothes. That's how much the power structure cares. They got a need and we pay for it. It isn't fair.

"He's right, it isn't fair. These people are alienated. We've got to bring them together, give them some sense of solidarity, of purpose, the ability to participate and be heard. Failure to be heard just results in frustration, and frustration is debilitating and demoralizing. This causes them to retreat further. Planners worry that agencies aren't responsive. How can they be responsive? They don't even know what minority people want or need. Chicanos can't tell them. They're afraid. They're afraid of authorities.

GIVING MINORITIES SELF-DETERMINATION

"I'll tell you what my strategy is. On every task force and on every study committee, every review panel, put at least 75 percent minorities. If I can get away with it, I'll put more on. I know the state guidelines require only a one-half representation of client groups. And I know some people will say that it's important to get the people with status and prestige on committees, those who have authority to make decisions—agency administrators and the like. I disagree.

"Some of the minority people on our committees now may not be as skilled or as competent or have as much access to decision-making power as other people we leave off, but they will. You'll see some changes around here as they get more sophisticated, get to know who is making the decisions and who's affecting them by not making any decisions, and as they develop relationships with each other."

Recommended Readings

PEATTIE, LISA. "Reflections on Advocacy Planning." *Journal of the American Institute of Planners,* March, 1968.
In a complex, rapidly changing world of pluralistic goals, reliance upon technical tools and expertise has made it possible to keep our cities running. As a consequence, however, a set of "bureaucratic management institutions" have evolved which seem impersonal and alien to the average citizen as well as to the disadvantaged. Peattie views advocacy planning as a means through which localized urban interests can be expressed. In this article, the author offers comments on some of the major problems which appear to be inherent in the nature of advocacy planning, and discusses the potential contributions it can make toward managing social conflict in urban areas and humanizing public planning. Incidentally, this issue of *JIAP* is "loaded" with important articles on advocacy.

BLECHER, EARL M. *Advocacy Planning for Urban Development.* New York: Praeger, 1972.
The practice of advocacy planning is examined via a comparative analysis of six OEO demonstration programs in urban planning. The analysis addresses two basic questions: (1) What are the nature and characteristics of advocacy planning when translated from theory to practice? (2) Under which demonstration models can advocacy planning be most effective as a process of urban planning? The author concludes with a description of the nature and characteristics of advocacy planning "as a new social concept affecting urban planning and decision-making processes."

Suggestions for Further Reading

CORSO, ANTHONY. *"The Urban Planner as an Inside Advocate,"* 31-page bibliography. School of Public Administration and Urban Studies, San Diego State University, 1977. Available from Council of Planning Librarians, Exchange Bibliographies, P.O. Box 229, Monticello, Ill.
DAVIDOFF, PAUL. "Advocacy and Pluralism in Planning." *Journal of the American Institute of Planners,* November 1965. Reprinted in Neil Gilbert and Harry Specht, *Planning for Social Welfare: Issues, Models and Tasks.* Englewood Cliffs, N.J.: Prentice-Hall, Inc., 1977.
KAPLAN, MARSHALL. "Advocacy and the Poor." *Journal of the American Institute of Planners,* 1969, *35,* 2.
KAPLAN, MARSHALL. "Advocacy and Urban Planning." *Report of the National Council on Social Welfare.* New York: Columbia University Press, 1968.

KRAVITZ, ALAN S. "Mandarinism: Planning as Handmaiden to Conservative Politics," in *The Politics of Planning,* Thad Beyle and Terry Lathrop (Eds.). New York: Odyssey Press, 1970.

MARRIS, PETER, and MARTIN REIN. *Dilemmas of Social Reform.* New York: Afterton Press, 1967.

PEATTIE, LISLE R. "Reflections on Advocacy Planning." *Journal of the American Institute of Planners,* March, 1968.

RICHAN, WILLARD C. "Dilemmas of the Social Work Advocate." *Child Welfare,* 1973, *3* (4).

V

Gaming and Social Planning

In the southeastern section of a "corn belt" state, sixty representatives of senior citizens' groups, social agencies, and civic associations were brought together by the staff of an area Agency on Aging to establish area-wide priorities for the coming year. The results of their efforts were to be integrated into an area plan to be submitted to the Governor's Office. Before they had finished drinking their coffee and being introduced, they found themselves playing TURN-ON*, a gamed simulation of the planning process. As the morning wore on, they analyzed data on needs and available resources, studied federal and state funding guidelines, and began the process of establishing local priorities. Some participants found themselves embroiled in a political process of give-and-take. A number formed coalitions aimed at the development of specific service programs.

By the end of the morning, they had designed the outlines of an area plan and had written seven program proposals. Their experience was very similar to that of a group of mental health agency administrators in a large northeastern metropolitan community. Attracted to a workshop on grantsmanship, they found themselves playing the Mental Health Planning Game. As they concerted their available money, political influence, and organizational energy, they too found themselves entering into coalitions leading to the design or expansion of service programs and to the coordination of these services.

Both games are offshoots of COMPACTS, a *Com*munity *P*lanning and *Act*ion *S*imulation game. COMPACTS has been redesigned dozens of times and used in hundreds of settings for purposes of teaching and learning and for collective problem solving. One version of COMPACTS is found on the following pages. Called the Inter-Agency Cooperation Game, it was designed for a conference of state and local planners in the field of vocational rehabilitation. It can be used as presented in the following chapter, or modified by the game leader to articulate more closely with the players' interests. Alternatively, it may be used as a "priming" mechanism; played as is for one round and then redesigned by the participants to deal with issues of greater relevance to them.

Simulation and gaming techniques are finding increasing utility as training, model building, and decision-making instruments. Social planning games draw in part from experiences in military gaming and in the use of business strategy games. Participants create a simulated social system. Representing individuals or organizations within that system, players engage in decision-making exercises, negotiations, and other instrumentally oriented behaviors. Their concerns are with the accomplishment of certain goals.

As in other kinds of games, the participants' behavior is rule-governed. Rules regulate the choices they can make and the chance events which affect these choices. Rules also specify the objectives of play.

*TURN-ON is an acronym for *T*apping *U*ntapped *R*esources, *N*ow *O*r *N*ever, a game designed by the author for the Administration on Aging, Department of Health Education and Welfare.

Unlike other games, these "gamed social simulations" need not have final scores for individual winners. Paralleling the real world, participants in the system may be playing for very different objectives. Sometimes they will compete for scarce resources. At other times they may be able to increase their resources by pooling their efforts.

Game playing has been used by some planners to elicit information about the real world they are trying to modify, to train administrators and consumers in more appropriate behavior, to identify problems and issues, and to experiment with various strategies in a system in which participants play "for real" but not "for keeps."

17

The Inter-Agency Cooperation Game

Unlike other chapters in this volume, Chapter 17 is comprised of a game that can be played in the classroom, in a social agency, or in an inter-agency or community setting. The Inter-Agency Cooperation Game includes roles for representatives of consumer groups and civic associations, for a variety of community influentials, for human service agency administrators and planners, for funders, and for process observers.

As in the real world, resources are unevenly distributed between individuals and organizations. These resources include money, facilities, personnel, energy, political influence, and legitimacy. In the community simulated, twelve issues provide the context against which planning and cooperation may occur. These deal with the hard to employ; area vocational schools; racism; sheltered workshops; special problems of the disabled living in rural areas; the lack of coordination between public school and vocational rehabilitation programs; community facilities; indicators of effectiveness; the availability of professional personnel; and citizen participation.

In the pages that follow, the reader will find:

1. Instructions for playing the Inter-Agency Cooperation Game
2. Game components that may be duplicated as is or modified by the game leader for distribution to participants
3. Suggestions for post-play activities, and
4. Information on the availability of other games of interest to social planners

Instructions for Playing the Inter-Agency Cooperation Game

Before proceeding, skim over the entire chapter. Pay particular attention to those sections of the chapter that may be duplicated for distribution to participants. Decide whether or not you will use the game as found in this chapter. If so, follow the instructions given. If you prefer to modify the game by changing the roles, the procedures, the issues, or the forms, feel free to do so. Guidance for game modification or redesign is given under "Suggestions for Post-Play Activities."

PREPARING THE GAME FOR PLAY

1. Draw up a role badge (stick-on tape will do) for each player. Use the *"Inventory of Player Roles"* as a guide. Notice that a color for each role badge is suggested. You may find that play proceeds more smoothly if all the social agency administrators wear role badges drawn up in red, if the consumer groups wear black badges, and so on. Alternative colors will work just as well. Whatever ones you choose, we think you will find that color coding the badges will help players locate each other during play.

   Feel free to add or subtract roles to accommodate the number of players you anticipate. By making up more badges than you need, you will be able to accommodate extra players. If you run short, you can always add more process observers.

   The Inter-Agency Cooperation Game can be played with as few as 16 or 17 players, and as many as 60. You will have to decide which roles to keep and which to drop or add.

2. Place role badge in a plastic baggie of its own, and add a limited number of resource chips. You can use any small colored objects to designate the different resources used in the game. These can be poker chips, bits of colored paper, lego blocks, etc. For each type of *strategic resource,* you will need a different color. Any set of colors might work. To remind players what each chip represents, you might want to draw up a wall chart or poster that looks like the following.

Money	=	Green
Facilities	=	White
Personnel	=	Blue
Energy	=	Red
Political Influence	=	Black
Legitimacy	=	Grey

You will have to determine how many of each resource goes into each plastic baggie. Remember that different sectors have access to different amounts of each resource. Try varying amounts from 0 to 10 per resource chip. But try not to let any player have more than 30 chips altogether, or less than 10. Life is not always fair; some players will not have the same access to strategic resources as others may.

Funders will tend to have most of the green (money) chips, although some agency administrators and community influentials may also have some. Members of civic associations and consumer groups may not have much more than personal energy (red chips). Agency administrators will tend to have most of the personnel and facilities needed for new or expanded services.

3. You are now ready to prepare the room for play. Set up tables so that each category of people sit at one or two tables with others in the same category. Lay out the plastic baggies with the name badges and resource chips at the appropriate tables, one by each chair. A typical set-up might look as follows:

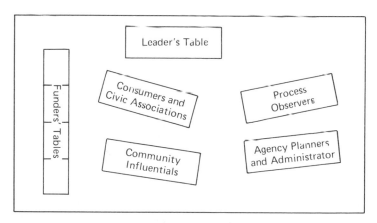

Put up the wall chart telling people which color is used to designate each strategic resource. Have sufficient chairs at tables. Have extra newsprint or board and chalk available for players to work on.

It is not essential that you group players according to the types of roles they are to perform, but you may find that doing so will reduce the likelihood that they will form coalitions only with others at their table. Players will quickly discover that coalitions made up of only agency administrators or of consumers are not likely to be as effective as those more broadly constituted.

4. If you wish, duplicate enough copies of the appropriate pages which give an orientation to the game and list the protocol for playing. If you do not duplicate these pages for distribution, you will have to communicate their

content verbally when giving participants instructions prior to play. One way of helping players remember what you tell them is to summarize some of the information on wall charts or posters. Consider making a poster with the titles of each of the issues on it and summarizing the order of play on another wall chart.

5. Now look over the descriptions of the 12 community issues that follow this preparation section. This version of the Interagency Cooperation Game was designed to deal primarily with vocational rehabilitation and job training issues. You may prefer to use another set of issues. If so, eliminate these or substitute others you consider to have greater salience. (If you do, don't forget to make changes on the titles on the reverse of the protocol sheet or on your wall poster.)

You may find, however, that the game works quite well the way it is, even if participants may have greater interest in some other field of service such as aging, drug abuse, or corrections. After playing one round, you might ask the players to identify the issues that concern them, to write up new issue descriptions, and then redesign some of the roles accordingly. Whether to redesign in advance or following play is a choice you will have to make yourself.

Whatever set of issues you decide to use, you should duplicate enough copies so that every player can find out what the issues are. Consider the following possibilities: giving only those players who would tend to be interested in certain issues, copies of the issue information; giving all players all the information on all the issues; duplicating only enough issue information to leave one or two copies at each table. (Make sure, however, that the funders have some way of finding out what the local issues are.) Which alternative seems most closely to simulate reality? Any other thoughts?

6. Look over the sheet entitled "Players by Role and Status," decide which player roles you are going to include, or add to, in a particular run (play) of the game. Consider duplicating this sheet or a new one if you are changing the rules for distribution to all players or affixing it on a bulletin board. Are there advantages to making this information public? Which of these roles would you identify with the title of social planner? Consider also duplicating or posting the information found on the sheet entitled "Helpful Hints of Players."

7. Duplicate sufficient copies of the Inter-Agency Cooperation Game "Proposal Form" to assure that they are easily accessible to all players. Leave a stack of 10 or so at the funders' table(s) and some at each of the other tables. Between 5 and 10 at each table should do. Duplicate several copies of the "Funder's Priorities Form." Make them available to the funders.

8. *That's it, you're ready to introduce players to the game!* The following activities are suggested.

   a. Welcome participants. Ask them to find a place to sit that includes a baggie with a badge that represents the role they might like to play. Ask players to pin their badges on. If you have duplicated materials and located them at each of the tables, ask them to look over the materials as they are waiting for the rest of the participants to come into the room.

b. When everyone is settled, explain that you will be playing the Inter-Agency Cooperation Game and what the purpose of play will be (to simulate the community planning process, to learn something about the proposal development and grantsmanship processes, or whatever other purpose you may have in mind).

   Ask players to stand up one at a time, table by table, and tell the group who (for the purpose of the game) they will be.

c. Tell participants how the game is to be played. Go over the information on the orientation and protocol sheets.

   Say something about the issues around which play will take place, but don't bother reading or having each issue paragraph read out loud. It takes too long. Participants can read and discover the issues on their own.

d. Show them how the "Proposal Forms" are to be filled out. Do the same for the "Funder's Priorities Forms."

e. Tell them the fiscal year has begun. While play takes place, it is not necessary for you (the game leader) to play an active role. Be available to coach players and to help them over the hurdles.

   Get the process observers together and help them decide what to look at. Some may be wise to study the coalition-forming process, the way in which funding decisions are arrived at, the extent to which leadership emerges at the local level, differences in behavior of agency representatives and consumer group representatives, and so forth. Process observers should be prepared to report on what they observed at the end of the fiscal year.

Suggestions for Post-Play Activities

1. The first thing to do after the play of the Inter-Agency Cooperation Game is to *debrief* or to discuss and evaluate the experience. Participants will be anxious to talk over what happened. You might want to focus on some or all of the following:

   a. Which proposals were successful and which ones were not? Why? Ask players who worked on a successful proposal to explain why things worked out the way they did. Ask the same of those who were not successful. Probe for real-life parallels and for principles that might be applied in practice.

THE INTERAGENCY COOPERATION GAME

Community Issues*

ISSUE #1   HARD TO EMPLOY

The State Rehabilitation Agency puts a high priority on its on-the-job
training program. The major portion of a trainee's salary is assumed
by the state during the initial months of training. As the individual
becomes more productive, the employer takes over an increasingly larger
share of the salary until the person becomes a productive worker and an
employee.

Employers have been extremely resistive to efforts to implement this
program with the hard-to-employ, especially those with physical or
social disabilities. Employers feel that these students will create
more problems; may damage materials, supplies, and equipment; and
are unreliable and unmotivated. In a few instances where OJT programs
are initiated, the employer refused to hire the trainee at the end of
the training period. Some employers seem to be using the support funds
from the State Rehabilitation Agency as an "industrial subsidy."

ISSUE #2   AREA VOCATIONAL SCHOOLS

The community is in desperate need of an area vocational school. Local
schools do not have the capacity to expand their present vocational programs.
The number of students wanting vocational training is increasing rapidly.

Taxpayers have been lukewarm to the idea, as evidenced by their failure to
pass proposals in the past two special elections. School administrators feel
an area vocational school will remove a tremendous burden from their shoulders.
Course listings and program descriptions seem to preclude the retarded
and physically disabled from enrolling, however.

ISSUE #3   RACISM AND DISABILITY

A state survey indicates that between 25 and 30 percent of the population
in the ghetto have some kind of vocational handicap. Included are physical
disabilities, mental retardation, emotional problems, poor job skills, and
lack of personal attributes necessary for employment.

Many educators feel extremely uncomfortable and ill-equipped to serve
this population and see special problems in the students' lack of job
skills, their relatively poor attitude toward the agency, and their limited
prior work experiences. Some black activists tend to view local services
as foreign enclaves established to filter cheap labor into white business
enterprises. There is little communication between staffs and local
residents. Poor whites in the area complain of differential treatment,
with blacks and middle-class whites getting all the situations.

*These cards may be duplicated for use in playing.

ISSUE #4   SHELTERED WORKSHOPS

Goodwill Industries and the Jewish Vocational Service each operates a large sheltered workshop as part of its total complex of agency services. None of the other workshops in town provide professional counselling and other supportive services. The other organizations include a small workshop serving male indigents and alcoholics and several private centers in which disabled persons may engage in work-like activities for little or no pay. Some have built-in federally financed training programs and may have connections to industry. One has a sliding pay scale, in relationship to number of weeks on the job and level of worker productivity.

Although a considerable amount of money is spent on these programs, many disabled people are unable to find their way into them. Fragmentation and spottiness is aggravated by a poor information and referral system. Hardly any agencies in the health, mental health, education, welfare, or poverty fields know where and how to refer disabled people for work training experiences. Narrow eligibility criteria and long waiting lists in others discourage potential clients. Earlier efforts at consolidation of these programs met with resistance. To add to the difficulties, administrators fear that a shortage of contract work may result in less adequate services to each agency's current clientele.

ISSUE #5   LOCATING SERVICES

The city can be divided into four socioeconomic sections. The section just east of downtown contains the poorest white and the poorest black neighborhoods. The areas north, west, and south of the downtown district contain the lower middle-class, middle-, and upper-class housing respectively. The state and county office buildings are located on the western edge of the downtown district; most education, rehabilitation, health, and welfare agencies are located north and west of downtown.

There are no neighborhood service offices to which people in the east section can walk. State agencies have a practice of centralizing offices for purposes of efficiency and because they have experienced difficulty in recruiting staff willing to work in low-income neighborhoods. High crime rates have forced the few training centers that were once located in the ghetto to seek new homes.

ISSUE #6   JOINT REFERRAL AND ASSESSMENT CENTER

There is no organized system for screening and assigning clients to the various agencies within a service area. Clients are not assessed with regard to which agency is best prepared to serve them. Many clients are inappropriately referred. Many times clients will be seen by an agency several times before they are referred to the proper helping agency. A standardized assessment system is vital.

Participating agencies have been reluctant to make a commitment for funding a referral and assessment center even though almost everyone agrees on the need. Clients would obviously benefit through more timely and appropriate service.

ISSUE #7   RURAL AREAS

The rural sections of the state have few programs, facilities, or staff
to serve the developmentally disabled. Families are unable to secure
services without long trips to urban centers. Diagnosis and evaluations
frequently have little impact on the individual, since the management plans
cannot be implemented.

The parents associations for the retarded, cerebral palsied, and
epileptic have been unable to coordinate their demands for services,
each feeling that they require a special focus to new programs.
State departments of education, mental health, health, and social
services agree that there is a real need in the rural areas, but are
unable to provide additional services.

ISSUE #8   COORDINATED SCHOOL/VOCATIONAL REHABILITATION PROGRAMS

The pre-vocational experiences in the public schools are unrelated to the
needs of disabled students. There is little relationship between the
school activities and the actual work requirements in the employment sector.
Many disabled students are excluded from vocational training programs.
Whenever possible, at graduation time, the school tries to place these
students in jobs. Some of the teachers working in the community on job
development activities are not very effective and may, in fact, have a
negative impact. If placement is not accomplished, a referral may be
made to the State Rehabilitation Agency.

The rehabilitation counselors are unwilling to spend much time with school-
aged children or with the teachers in developing and upgrading programs.
There is enough to do with adults. They are very much concerned, however,
that "good" clients are being placed by the schools and that the only
referrals they get are of problem clients.

ISSUE #9   COMMUNITY RESIDENCE FACILITIES

Despite the emphasis on the return of residents of state schools for the
retarded to the community, there have been many indications that local
communities are unable to meet the need. Insufficient numbers of
facilities, shortages of trained staff, limiting zoning regulations,
and community distrust and fear have all added to the problems being
faced by nursing homes, hostels, and other community residences.

Tentative efforts to correct these problems have been minimally effective.
Nevertheless, there is a continuing and growing pressure to establish a
network of necessary community living situations.

ISSUE #10   EFFECTIVENESS INDICATORS

All agencies within the community issue reports to their sponsors
(voluntary agencies to their boards and to the welfare council,
public agencies to their government sponsors such as state rehabilitation agencies), and they all gather or use available information
on clients and on social conditions.

Most of this information, and most of the issued reports have little
comparability in language, categorization, or measurement units, however.
Information used in one setting cannot be applied to another.

No standard measures of effectiveness exist. Job placement rates,
physical rehabilitation counts, and job training measures, for example, are subject to multiple interpretations. It is virtually impossible to measure or to predict the impact of new services.

ISSUE #11   PROFESSIONAL MANPOWER

The growing awareness of the problems and needs of the developmentally
disabled has not been matched by an increase in trained manpower to
provide services. A study group has identified the need for (1)
additional manpower in the field; (2) in-service training to permit
upgrading; and (3) development of broader roles for paraprofessionals.

Few university-based programs exist either for basic training or in
continuing education that relate to agency needs. Agency administrators
are unable to find staff who can meet their present and changing program
needs or who are comfortable in interdisciplinary or multi-professional
settings.

ISSUE #12   CITIZEN PARTICIPATION

A number of groups advocating on behalf of people with certain kinds of
handicaps exist. There are no groups of organized agency clients or
potential clients, however. As a result, agencies find it difficult
to find representatives of certain interests or concerns that might
support expansion of their services. Many agencies might not welcome
organized client groups, however, perceiving them as a threat to professional service and organizational autonomy.

There is no history of client involvement. Existing citizen participation in service models is subject to challenge by newer models
developed in Model Cities, OEO, and Community Mental Health settings.

THE INTER-AGENCY COOPERATION GAME

Orientation to the Inter-Agency Cooperation Game*

PLAYER   The Interagency Cooperation Game includes roles for (1) rep-
ROLES   resentatives of <u>voluntary associations</u> or <u>consumer groups</u>
          (black badges); (2) <u>community influentials</u> (blue badges);
(3) <u>service agency administrators</u> (red badges); (4) <u>planning and allocating</u>
<u>agencies</u> (funders) (green badges); and (5) <u>process observers</u> (orange badges).

RESOURCES As in the real world, resources are unevenly distributed between
           individuals and organizations. Color coded Lego blocks are used
to represent

1.	money and credit	(green)	4. energy	(red)
2.	facilities	(white)	5. political influence	(black)
3.	personnel	(blue)	6. legitimacy and legality	(grey)

ISSUES   Twelve issues exist in this community that might serve as the
         impetus for social planning efforts. These issues deal with

1.	Hard to Employ	7.	Rural Areas
2.	Area Vocational Schools	8.	Coordinated School/Voc Rehab Programs
3.	Racism and Disabilities	9.	Community Residence Facilities
4.	Sheltered Workshops	10.	Effectiveness Indicators
5.	Locating Services	11.	Professional Manpower
6.	Referral and Assessment Center	12.	Citizen Participation

OBJECTIVES All players are concerned with correcting for deficiencies or
           inequities in the service delivery system. Funding agencies
seek to finance projects that meet their priorities for service and for
populations to be served. Voluntary associations and consumer groups seek
to develop new services for their members or their constituents. Service
agencies attempt to expand their services and to create new services for
their client populations. Community influentials sometimes seek the public
good, at other times to increase their own power.

HOW THE   Participants decide on their objectives and seek support from
GAME IS   other players. Coalitions may be formed; projects designed;
PLAYED   proposals submitted. Action coalitions made up of any combin-
           ation of players may decide to pool their resources in efforts to
develop new service programs. Other players may try to block projects not in
their interests. Play takes place during a one-hour playing round representing a <u>fiscal year</u>.

* The orientation section may be duplicated for player usage.

PROTOCOL -- ORDER OF PLAY*

GETTING   Check your resources. How many of each do you have? Study the
STARTED   12 issues. Which are you interested in? Who else seems to be
            interested? Do they have the kind of resources that complement
your own? What resources are needed to develop a program you are interested
in? Do you expect anyone to block your efforts to design a proposal around
this issue? If you are a funder, you must complete your Priorities Form and
post it on your table within the first 15 minutes of play. Other players
would do well to know what the funders' priorities are.

FORMING   You may choose to form or join an action coalition working for
COALITIONS or against the resolution of any particular issue. Coalition
            members (a) determine their own program objectives; (b) recruit
additional coalition members with necessary resources; (c) manage the resources
(stacking them up on the resources board and graph); (d) write the proposal.
Funders do not join coalitions but may attempt to influence their composition
or the projects they are working on.

PREPARING   Be certain all parts of the proposal form are completed. Did
A PROPOSAL you specify the issue or issues to be addressed? Are your pro-
FOR   gram objectives clearly spelled out? Do they match the criteria
SUBMISSION established by the funder(s) to whom you will be submitting your
            proposal? Has agreement been reached on auspices and sponsorship?
Is your statement on resources complete? Be careful. Poorly designed or
incomplete proposals may not be accepted by funders. Completed proposals
require supportive documentation. Funders want to see how much support
(in the form of resource chips) you've got backing your proposal. There is
space on the proposal form to keep your records.

SUBMITTING To determine whether your proposals fit the guidelines or priorities
PURPOSALS   of the funding agencies, discuss your proposals with them prior to
            final submission. Try to submit proposals to funders that are not
inundated with requests, or that have sufficient financial resources. Early
submissions may have a better chance than last minute submissions. No proposals
may be submitted after the close of the fiscal year.

If your proposal is rejected, you may take your resource chips back and use
them for another project or to resubmit your proposal to another funder-time
providing!

REVIEWING   Funders may review proposals on the spot (if they are submitted
PROPOSALS   early enough and the funder has time), or held until the end of
            the fiscal year. In reviewing proposals, the funder should
ascertain that (a) all sections have been clearly filled out; (b) there is
evidence of community support through resources committed; (c) the applicant
has commitment of local mating funds (if required); (d) the proposal fits the
funder's priorities. If the funder does not have sufficient funds to approve
all proposals, he will have to make a choice among those submitted.

---

* The protocol section may be duplicated for player usage.

FUNDERS   (Green Badges)

Funders centrally concerned with community issues described in this game+	Other Funders
State Rehabilitation Agency	State Department of Social Services
Department of Vocational Education	State Department of Mental Health
Department of Special Education	Regional Health Planning Unit
Adult Education Department	United Fund
Developmental Disabilities Council	Private Foundation
Vocational Rehabilitation for the Blind	Office of Criminal Justice

+May require local matching funds on all projects.

VOLUNTARY ASSOCIATIONS AND CONSUMER GROUPS (Black Badges)

Association for the Blind	P.T.A.
Association for Retarded Children	Association for Children with
Association for the Deaf	Learning Disabilities
United Cerebral Palsy League	Black Community
Epilepsy League	Neighborhood Association
Association of Vocational	Association for the Physically
Trade Schools	Handicapped

LOCAL SERVICE AGENCIES (Red Badges)

Community Mental Health Center	Goodwill Sheltered Workshop
Speech and Hearing Clinic	Schools--Special Education
Urban League	Programs
Community Action Agency	Schools--Cooperative Project
Model Cities	(Vocational Education and Industry)
Private Industrial Schools	Schools--Adult Education
U.S. Employment Services Local Board	General Hospital--Physical and Medical Rehabilitation Unit
Private Educational Performance Contractor	Hostel for Mentally Retarded
	Child Guidance Clinic
Local Vocational Rehabilitation Agency	County Welfare Department

COMMUNITY INFLUENTIALS (Blue Badges)

State Representative	Chairman of Local School Board
Mayor's Human Resource Commissioner	Juvenile Court Judge
Chairman of Council for Exceptional Children	University Consultant on Vocational Education
Industrialist	Community College President
National Association of Businessmen	Pediatrician
Union	President of Local Medical Association
Junior Chamber of Commerce	National Education Association President
Journalist	

NONPLAYING PARTICIPANTS -- PROCESS OBSERVERS (Orange Badges)

---

* This section may be duplicated as a help to players.

HELPFUL HINTS TO PLAYERS

FUNDERS

Agency administrators and other players will soon be approaching you with
requests to fund their projects. Funders should establish clear priorities
and guidelines within the first 15 minutes of playing time. Priorities
should be posted at the funders' table. Some funders prefer to keep their
priorities flexible, responding to proposals that interest them as they
come in, others are more influenced by who submits the proposal than by the
content of the proposal. Funders may go aggressively into the community to
seek the kind of proposals they are interested in. Some demand matching
funds from other state, federal, local, voluntary, or private agencies. In
evaluating proposals, check them over for consistency, for accuracy, and for
closeness of fit with your criteria or priorities. While you may not be
able to fund all the proposals that are submitted to you, there is no
reason to turn proposals down for which you have the funds. Do not keep any
money back for the next fiscal year. You must spend all your money and
credit before the end of the fiscal year.

LOCAL SERVICE AGENCIES

Agency administrators and planners are successful only if the proposals
which are funded (1) add new resources to their agencies; (2) complement or supplement the services they are able to provide to client populations. Successful administrators will consider those resources they
have and those they can concert in support of their program ideas. They
will often tailor their project designs to the priorities and interests
of funding or allocating agencies.

VOLUNTARY ASSOCIATIONS and ORGANIZED CONSUMER GROUPS

Voluntary associations and organized consumer groups advocate on behalf of
their members or some other population which is directly affected by deficiencies in the service system. They will limit their efforts to those
issues of direct concern to their members or constituencies. They succeed
only if such projects are funded. Consumers would do well to build coalitions with appropriate agency personnel and community influentials whose
interests may coincide with their own.

COMMUNITY INFLUENTIALS

Community influentials are concerned about the welfare of the community.
They are also concerned about maintaining their own influence through
successful efforts to promote or to block programs. While there is no
"final score" in this game, influentials measure their success by the
number of coalitions they joined and the number of proposals submitted by
each coalition that was approved by a funder. Unsuccessful coalitions
or unsuccessful attempts to block other projects reduce their influence.

T H E   I N T E R - A G E N C Y   C O O P E R A T I O N   G A M E

PROPOSAL FORM*

ISSUES THIS PROPOSAL IS ADDRESSED TOWARD	Issue Numbers	Issue Name
	_____	_____
	_____	_____
	_____	_____
	_____	_____

PROGRAM OBJECTIVES

1. Who is to be served (client characteristics)?

2. Describe the services to be provided.

3. Describe the anticipated outcomes of service (how many people will be served, what changes in their conditions are expected, and so on).

4. Describe your monitoring and evaluation procedures.

FUNDING SOURCES

To whom is the proposal being submitted?

1. Local source(s) of funding   (a)_____ _____%
                                      (b)_____ _____%

2. Central funding source(s)   (a)_____ _____%
                                      (b)_____ _____%
                                             Total   100 %

---

* Both sides of this form may be duplicated for player covenience.

PROPOSAL FORM, SIDE 2

AUSPICES AND SPONSORSHIP	1.	Which is to be the sponsoring agency or agencies - that is, in what organization(s) will the service be administratively lodged?

_____
_____

2. Who is to be on the project's advisory panel or Board of Directors?

_____   _____
_____   _____
_____   _____

ADDITIONAL INFORMATION

1. If inter-agency cooperation is required, describe the nature of the projected linkages.

2. If you are projecting consumer or citizen involvement, describe the nature of that involvement.

STATEMENT ON COMMUNITY SUPPORT AND OPPOSITION -- ACTUAL RESOURCES COMMITTED

		Money and Credit	Facilities	Personnel	Energy	Political Influence	Legitimacy and Legality
		green	white	blue	red	black	gray
Signatures of Players Contributing to PAC (role name only)	Number Needed for this Proposal						
	RESOURCES COMMITTED TO THIS PROJECT						

THE INTER-AGENCY COOPERATION GAME

FUNDER'S PRIORITIES FORM*

1. | Name of Funder

2. | Total amount of money and credit available_____(in chips)
   |
   | Percentage+ of local matching funds required_____%

3. | Issues which   Issue No.   Issue Name
   | receive highest   (a)_____   _____
   | priority   (b)_____   _____
   | (c)_____   _____
   | (d)_____   _____
   | Other issues
   | that will   (a)_____   _____
   | receive   (b)_____   _____
   | consideration   (c)_____   _____
   | (d)_____   _____

4. | Client populations most concerned about:

5. | Agencies that will   (a)_____   (d)_____
   | receive preference   (b)_____   (e)_____
   | (c)_____   (f)_____
   |
   |
   | Other agencies that   (a)_____   (e)_____
   | will be considered   (b)_____   (f)_____
   | (c)_____   (g)_____
   | (d)_____   (h)_____

6. | Requirements for citizen support, consumer involvement, inter-agency cooper-
   | ation (if any).

   * This form may be duplicated for funders' usage. All funders should fill in
     boxes 1 through 4. Others are optional.
   + This applies to federal and state agencies only.

b. Whose proposals were best? Why? Because of their thoroughness? Because of their objectives? Because of the support they engendered? Would such a project work in your (the participants') communities?

c. Did you feel each actor played his or her role appropriately? Focus on certain actors, perhaps a funder, a representative of a consumer group, or an agency administrator. Find principles that participants might use in trying to "make friends and influence people" in a real situation.

One way to make certain that all pertinent aspects of the round are discussed is to ask the process observers to begin the debriefing session by reporting what they observed. Of course, they should be asked to prepare for this in advance.

2. Consider redesigning the game. This can be done by you alone or by the entire group following a playing session. Have participants

a. design the issues that concern them or that reflect local realities

b. identify the local community people who might be involved in a real-life version of the Inter-Agency Cooperation Game—those who would tend to be concerned with the issues identified

c. allocate resources to those persons

d. change or modify the rules or any of the forms used to play the Inter-Agency Cooperation Game so as to articulate more closely with shared perceptions of how the game really works.

3. Use the game in another situation to accomplish one or more of the following:

a. assessment of issues and testing of alternative intervention strategies

b. as a stimulus toward the development of real and permanent coalitions of persons and organizations with interests in common.

ANY OTHER IDEAS?

Other Games Dealing With Social Planning Issues at the Community Level

The following games were designed or edited by the author and are available from Gamed Simulations Incorporated, 500 Fifth Avenue, New York, New York.

Designer: Armand Lauffer

Participants are introduced to the analytic aspects of community planning as they make decisions regarding objectives, targets, scope, resource allocation, and so on. Players assume roles as planners, agency directors, community influentials, consumers, and funders. Responding to a variety of issues—for example, the needs of retarded children, public housing corrections services, senior citizens—they must decide whether or not to develop new services or maintain existing ones.

They learn the interactional or political aspects of planning as they find that limited resources propel them into a series of action coalitions, some lasting, some ephemeral. The game is easily redesigned by participants to deal with a variety of planning and organizing problems in community mental health, the fields of aging and corrections, child welfare, urban planning, and so forth.

TURN-ON

Designers: Armand Lauffer, Thomas Morton, Roger Mills

A variation of COMPACTS that deals with the role of an area agency on aging is *T*apping *U*ntapped *R*esources (*N*ow *O*r *N*ever) is also available from Gamed Simulations Incorporated.

METROPOLIS

Designer: Richard Duke

Urban planners, citizens groups, and politicians make cumulative decisions about land use and industrial development. Decisions made one year limit a support change and control efforts in subsequent years. This simulation can accommodate from 10 to 40 players and can be conducted in one or two class sessions or over longer periods of time. This is a hand-run version of a more complex internationally known computer simulation.

MUCH ADO ABOUT MARBLES

Designer: Armand Lauffer

Alias Utopias, Welfare Politics and El Barrio, Marbles permits players to create their own roles and to design a community system composed of governmental units; health, education and welfare agencies; the criminal justice systems; land developers and industrialists. The game is intended to illustrate the complex relationships between social welfare, the economy, and political decision making. Playing time is 2½ to 8 hours and can be broken up into two or three periods. Between 12 and 50 can play.

Designers: David Williams and Stanley Blostein

The committee structure of a state legislature provides the setting for bargaining, log rolling, and coalition formations. The mystique is stripped away from the lobbying process. Planners and consumers learn how and when to intervene in the legislative process. Between 20 and 60 can participate. Playing time takes 2½ to 5 hours, depending on rounds played and extensiveness of debriefing.

Recommended Readings

DUKE, RICHARD. *Gaming, the Future Language.* Beverly Hills: Sage Publications, Inc., 1975.
According to Duke, games are a powerful new form of communication. This book attempts to explain gaming's sudden and spontaneous emergence as a communication device in a variety of fields. A theoretical base is presented which provides some insight into how gaming works. Gaming as a language form is specified in detail, pragmatic specifications for game design and, finally, some speculations about the future of gaming are offered.

LAUFFER, ARMAND. *Grantsmanship.* Beverly Hills: Sage Publications, Inc., 1977.
Following the introductory chapters in which a number of planners discuss their own approaches to grantsmanship, this book moves progressively through step-by-step instructions on how to (1) develop a grantsmanship strategy; (2) assess the grants environment; (3) get and process needed information; (4) begin formulating a proposal and (5) draft the final proposal. An extensive bibliography includes information on funding sources and how to get more information.

Suggestions for Further Reading

BELL, D. C. "Simulation Games: Three Research Paradigms." *Simulations and Games,* 1975, *6;* 271–278.
BELL, ROBERT, and JOHN COPLANS. *Decisions, Decisions: Game Theory and You.* New York: W. W. Norton Co., 1976.
CARLSON, JOHN G., & MICHAEL J. MISSHAUK. *Introduction to Gaming: Management Decision Simulations.* New York: John Wiley and Sons, 1972.
COLEMAN, JAMES S. "Game Models of Economic and Political Systems," in *The Study of Total Societies,* Samuel Z. Klausner, (Ed.). New York: Doubleday, Anchor Books, 1967.
GILLESPIE, PHILIP H. *Learning Through Simulation Games.* Paramus, N.J.: Paulist-Newman Publishing, 1974.
HORN, ROBERT E. *The Guide to Simulation Games for Education and Training,* 3rd ed. Cambridge: Information Resources Inc., 1977.
LAUFFER, ARMAND. *The Aim of the Game: A Primer on the Use and Design of Gamed Social Simulations.* New York: Gamed Simulations, Inc., 1973.

Long, Norton. "The Local Community As An Ecology of Games." *American Journal of Sociology,* No. 64, 1958.

Raser, John. *Simulations and Society.* Boston: Allyn and Bacon, 1969.

Sharan, S., and C. Colodher. "Counselor: A Simulation Game For Vocational Decision Making." *Simulations and Games,* 1976, *7,* 193–208.

Shubik, Martin (Ed). *Game Theory and Related Approaches to Social Behavior.* Huntington, Va.: Krieger Publication Co., 1975.

Index